D0946697

TAX REVOLT

TAX REVOLT

The Rebellion against an Overbearing, Bloated, Arrogant, and Abusive Government

Phil Valentine

NELSON CURRENT

A Division of Thomas Nelson, Inc.

copyright © 2005 by Phil Valentine

All rights reserved. No portion of this book may be reproduced, stored in a retrieval system, or transmitted in any form or by any means—electronic, mechanical, photocopy, recording, scanning, or other—except for brief quotations in critical reviews or articles, without the prior written permission of the publisher.

Published in Nashville, Tennessee, by Nelson Current, a division of a wholly-owned subsidiary (Nelson Communications, Inc.) of Thomas Nelson, Inc.

Nelson Current books may be purchased in bulk for educational, business, fundraising, or sales promotional use. For information, please email SpecialMarkets@ThomasNelson.com.

Library of Congress Cataloging-in-Publication Information

Valentine, Phil.
  Tax revolt : the rebellion against an overbearing, bloated, arrogant, and abusive government / Phil Valentine.
    p. cm.
ISBN 1-5955-5001-1
    1. Taxation—Tennessee—History.   2. Taxation—United States—History.
I. Title.
HJ2434.V35   2005
336.2'009768—dc22   2004028978

Printed in the United States of America
05 06 07 QKP 5 4 3 2 1

To the ever-vigilant citizens of Tennessee

CONTENTS

	Prologue	ix
Chapter 1	The Sneak Attack	1
Chapter 2	Rich Heritage of Revolt	35
Chapter 3	Storm the Bastille	51
Chapter 4	Historic Tax Fights	87
Chapter 5	Threats, Bribes, and Intimidation	115
Chapter 6	Modern-Day Tax Revolts	127
Chapter 7	"We Need Troops"	149
Chapter 8	How To Stage a Revolt	169
Chapter 9	Smearing the Opposition	187
Chapter 10	The Final Showdown	199
Chapter 11	Post Script	227
	Acknowledgments	235
	Endnotes	237
	Index	247

PROLOGUE

Politics, for some, is an acquired taste. Others develop a passion for it; political junkies, they're called. Some, like me, are simply born into it. Thrust into it is more like it. At the age of twenty-seven, my father was one of the youngest legislators ever elected to the North Carolina General Assembly, and he was very active for the next ten years or so. He became chairman of the state Democratic Party and worked as one of several regional campaign managers for Dan Moore, who won the governorship in 1964. My father served in the Moore administration as legal advisor. He would later go on to serve a twelve-year stint in Congress.

Even after the Moore administration, when he temporarily left politics to devote more time to his family, he remained very active in the party. It was a family affair. We all took part to varying degrees. I remember sitting with my mother in the campaign office of the gubernatorial candidate in our little town, Pat Taylor. I stuffed envelopes and handed out campaign buttons. I talked him up at school and attended rallies when he was in the area. At the age of twelve, I was dead into the campaign. I suppose I was supporting Taylor for the same reason my mother was: my father supported him. As strongly as I backed my candidate, I keenly felt the sting on election night when he lost—in the primary, no less. I remember that shocked feeling of incredulity that my own father had picked the loser. For the first time, there was doubt in my mind about my father's judgment. One of my best friends' father had backed the right horse, at least for the nomination. I was jealous. After all, my friend's dad had sense enough to pick the right guy. He, too, got his reality check in the general election when the Republican became governor.

As a kid, I was more interested in backing winners than worrying about issues. It took me several more years to figure out why my father had backed a losing candidate. Politics isn't—or shouldn't be—about picking winners. It's about backing a philosophy and a candidate who embodies that philosophy. It's about a commitment to a set of ideas and ideals and sticking to them. It's about supporting someone because of what they stand for and who they are, not just being on the winning team.

I was certainly not atypical in backing my father's candidates and causes. Study after study will tell you that the primary reason people vote for a particular political party is that their parents voted that way. Too many Americans mechanically go through the motions each election day, never bothering to think for themselves. I broke the familial apron strings when Reagan came to power. For the first time I was actually listening to the words instead of following the herd. I was thinking for myself, and I realized that although my father had Roosevelt and Kennedy as role models, his party was no longer the same. His party was not my party. FDR and JFK had been replaced by Walter Mondale and Jesse Jackson. Reagan offered a new hope for our country, a hope not found in the stale rhetoric of the Democratic Party. To me, it seemed a clear choice between the optimists and the pessimists. Being the eternal optimist, I knew where my heart was, and I never looked back, never regretted the move.

I would consider myself moderately conservative, although many people who listen to my radio show would peg me much further to the right. A lot of that stems from our income tax fight in Tennessee. Since I was at the epicenter of a tax revolt, one might get the impression that I am anti-tax. I want it understood up front, I am not opposed to taxes. Taxes are an essential part of our society. They pay for services we all need and desire. They afford us, for instance, a state-of-the-art military that protects our freedom. What I oppose is excessive taxation, when governments take more than they need. I also know that, in many cases, less is more. As is often the case, when you lower taxes you actually increase the flow of tax money. That was Reagan's point. His domestic message was simple: lower taxes equal a more robust economy, which equals more tax dollars in the federal coffers. Although lowering taxes to get more tax money is counterintuitive to some, it makes sense once you fully follow the logic. When you have more people working and more people making more money, you increase the amount the government takes in. This was proven during the 1980s as we saw tax revenue double during that decade, despite what the liberal revisionists tell you.[1] But this point is scarcely heard above the din of class warfare waged by those on the left.

The second part of that Reagan economic philosophy was to get control of our runaway government. Unfortunately, even with the tremendous growth in tax revenue, the Democrat-controlled Congress outstripped the prosperity with unprecedented spending. The result was bigger deficits and an ever-increasing national debt. The sad part is, if Congress had passed Reagan's budgets instead of their own, we would've seen a balanced budget by 1989.[2]

These notions of lowering taxes and at least holding the line on government spending are basic to conservative principles. Because of Reagan, I made it a point to back candidates who adhered to that philosophy, no matter how grim their prospects of winning. Since 1980, I have backed some winners, and I've backed some losers. I've voted across party lines, a few Democrats, mostly Republicans, but my reasoning was always consistent. In 1994, a year that would prove to be a watershed year for the country, and especially Tennessee, I paid particularly close attention to the candidates.

In '94, the Tennessee Republican Party was energized. The primary catalyst of that enthusiasm was not a Republican at all but a Democrat named Bill Clinton. Lincoln Day dinners across the state were overflowing with enthusiastic supporters determined to take their country back from the Clintonites. The Tennessee Republican Party chairman at the time, Randall Richardson, asked me to emcee a candidates' function for the party. That's where I first met then-Congressman Don Sundquist.

Nineteen ninety-four was an unusual year for Tennessee in that we were electing not one but two U.S. senators. Al Gore had resigned his seat to join Bill Clinton on the 1992 Democratic ticket, and it was time to fill his seat. On election day, there was a Democrat governor and two Democrat U.S. senators. By the next morning the people had chosen a Republican governor, Don Sundquist, and two Republican U.S. senators, Fred Thompson and Bill Frist. It was the dawning of a new era. Tennessee had been controlled primarily by Democrats since Reconstruction. Although they still controlled the General Assembly, there was a decidedly different mood, and the General Assembly leadership decided it was time to cozy up to the new Republican governor. As it turned out, they got a little too cozy, and thus began the transformation of Don Sundquist.

It also marked the transformation of the citizens of Tennessee, and this, in part, is their story. The same spirit that enabled them to break the one-hundred-year-old stranglehold of the Democratic Party emboldened them to take on a corrupt political system. Like a determined goal-line defense, these ordinary men, women, and children rose up on numerous occasions, against insurmountable odds, to beat back those trying to push an unconstitutional income tax into the endzone. But this is a story less about tax fights than it is about empowerment. It's a true story of how a relatively small band of active citizens inspired an entire state, mobilized thousands upon thousands of people, and defied the conventional wisdom that their cause was lost. It's also a story of similar struggles across the country and throughout our American history. Our rich history is filled with tales of civil uprising and revolt against an unresponsive government. When push comes to shove, it's usually the grassroots movements that effect change. People simply get fed up with their government and wrestle the reins of power away from it. In Tennessee, many of these same citizens would wield that same power to deny Al Gore the White House in 2000.

Since 1991 I have kept a journal. The purpose was, and remains, to be able to go back and understand events as they unfolded without the cloud of faulty memories and rewritten history. All entries have been work-related or are my observations on political events. I have intentionally refrained from including my personal life in these writings. I thought it neither relevant nor prudent to mix the two. During the three years of the Tennessee tax revolt, I kept detailed notes. Reading back over them, I found them extremely helpful and instructive in understanding the events as they unfolded; therefore, I chose to include some of them in this book. Many of these entries reveal far more than was reported by the news media at the time. Being on the inside of the revolt, I observed the inner workings of what was being reported and what was *not* being reported. This book is peppered with those entries in order to give you more of a sense of what it was actually like to be there. Time tends to dull the memory, but these entries bring those events back into sharp focus. They detail my impressions about the people around me who were the driving force in this grassroots effort to make the people's wishes known and turn back a runaway and abusive government.

But these citizens of Tennessee are not unique. They weren't the first nor will they be the last to resurrect the ideals of our founding fathers. The principle of a smaller, more responsive government is an idea that may be, on occasion, temporarily impeded but never derailed. That patriotic repulsion to heavy-handed rule still elicits anger. Gritting teeth and flaring nostrils still sometimes result in action. One does not necessarily need tea to throw a tea party, and David can still bring down Goliath.

A word of caution for the historical critics, however. This book is not intended to be a definitive book on all tax revolts. Others have attempted that with varying degrees of success. The historical accounts of past tax revolts are included merely to set a baseline for such revolts, to give you a better understanding of our nation's legacy, not to bore you with every nuance and detail of every tax uprising in the history of America. The historical revolts included in this volume are important, not only in demonstrating what they inspired, but also to amplify and contrast just how quickly and completely many Americans have moved toward total apathy. Most people never involve themselves in such movements. Every tax rebellion dating back to the Boston Tea Party was instigated and carried out by a relative few, but those few inspired the others. That was certainly the case in Tennessee where we rallied, at the most, several thousand protesters at any given event out of a state population numbering nearly six million. But each protester represented scores, if not hundreds, of angry Tennesseans who felt exactly the same way and only wished they could have been present.

I was once described in a radio interview as the General Washington behind the Tennessee tax revolt. I had to stop and correct the host. I was not the General Washington. My compatriots in talk radio and I were the Paul Reveres of this movement. We merely informed the people. The citizens took it upon themselves to act, and you shall meet some of these modern-day patriots. You will also meet the real General Washingtons of the movement, the people who worked diligently against the tax. Chances are, in no matter what state you reside, you know people exactly like them: people on the brink of rebellion against an overbearing, bloated, arrogant, and abusive government. It might be your neighbor. It might be your co-worker. It might be an elected official. After reading this book, it just might be you.

One

THE SNEAK ATTACK

S*aturday, June 10, 2000*—The streets of downtown Nashville around
the Tennessee State Capitol were desolate. No cars. No people. A
ghost town, typical for a Saturday in that part of the city. A day when
state workers, who ordinarily swarmed over the several bureaucratic
city blocks, headed for the relaxing haven of the lake or the park—
anywhere to escape the grind of government work. The hot sun beat
down on Legislative Plaza, the expansive municipal courtyard in the
shadow of the State Capitol building. With its ornamental trees
planted among concrete and marble and monuments to Tennessee
history, it serves as an oasis in the midst of a bustling downtown.
Underneath the plaza, like termites silently burrowing away inside an
otherwise apparently healthy structure, state legislators and senators
filed into the underground parking garage in preparation for a stealth
assault on the pocketbooks of the state's citizens.

Tennessee was one of but a handful of states without a state income
tax. The end result of the resistance to the state income tax was a relatively low tax burden. By most yardsticks, Tennessee ranked in the

bottom five in per capita taxes. This fact was the source of a large degree of pride for many Tennesseans. The income tax had been proposed over the years—even passed at one point before being shot down by the courts—and each time it was met with the displeasure of a populace that enjoyed its low-tax status. That's not to say that Tennesseans don't care about people less fortunate. The state ranks thirty-fourth in average adjusted gross income of all the states, yet ranks third in charitable contributions.[1] That's certainly putting your money where your mouth is. After all, Tennessee is the Volunteer State, and that certainly applies when it comes to volunteering money. That's the way the founding fathers envisioned our society. We were to rely on the government for very little aside from national defense and a stable currency. Otherwise, we were expected to take care of our own. In return, the federal government would lead a relatively austere and unintrusive existence.

While absence of an income tax was a source of pride for most, it was an irresistible target for those who wanted to expand the role of government beyond the tolerable bounds of the majority. The people enjoyed keeping more of their hard-earned money in their own pockets. The career politicians saw gold in them thar pockets, and they aimed to take it any way they could. A secret coalition of like-minded politicians had gathered to discuss how they would pull off the heist, all the while telling the public they no longer had designs on their income. If they could manage this sneak attack on the pocketbooks of unsuspecting Tennesseans, this would rival the genius of the Great Train Robbery.

The Tax Scheme

Leading the cabal was a crusty, chain-smoking state senator by the name of Bob Rochelle, the speaker pro tem of the Senate, whose penchant for wearing dark suits gave him the look of an undertaker. State Senator Marsha Blackburn, who helped lead the opposition to the income tax in the Senate, described Rochelle as "the stereotypical Southern politician."[2] Like something out of a Faulkner novel, the bespectacled, bulldog-faced senator anxiously awaited the arrival of his fellow chamber-mates that lazy Saturday morning.

It's not hard to imagine Rochelle sitting behind his desk, his nondescript necktie loosened around his thick neck. The top button of his dress shirt undone. The top of his balding head glistening with perspiration as he takes another drag from his cigarette and tugs at his suspenders.

Rochelle had set his sights on that new vault of money, the state income tax. Once he got his teeth into something, he purportedly never let go. The Associated Press described him as "a consummate dealmaker who revels in the political game and usually wins."[3] His backroom deals and arm-twisting were legendary. Lt. Governor John Wilder, the elder statesman of the Senate, was much too timid and apprehensive to carry the governor's water on the income tax. Rochelle was one of the few politicians who had shed the shroud of ambiguity and now openly supported the state income tax. He became the point man for the lobbyists and the union leaders and anyone else interested in squeezing more money out of the taxpayers. Confident his Senate seat was safe, he set about the task of propagandizing the issue in order to gain support.

His latest scheme would tax "the rich" in order to save "the children," raising an estimated $2 billion, a sizeable chunk compared to the state's $18 billion budget, especially when you consider the state portion in taxes was less than half of that $18 billion. All was going according to plan that sleepy Saturday. Another secretive, closed-door meeting the previous day had born fruit. Deals had been made. Arms had been twisted. At last he had the votes—tentative and fragile as they were—to pass his income tax plan, a plan considered dead in the water by political observers because of the overwhelming negative public backlash to it before. This was to be a stroke of political artistry and Rochelle relished the moment. He thrived on the gamesmanship of politics, and this was political chess at its best. As he anticipated his opponents' next move, it appeared to be checkmate, a mere formality. There was nowhere to go, no way the opposition could salvage the game. Having painstakingly positioned all of his pieces, he now sat back in his chair, rubbing his chin, ready for one last move.

Despite the lack of support for a state income tax, he knew it held the key to untold political fortune. Imagine the government he could grow if he could just unlock it. Never one to worry about what the people wanted, Rochelle relentlessly pursued his quarry. In his mind, he knew what was best for the state, and he would not be deterred. I'm sure he had thoroughly convinced himself that the end justified the means. He was absolutely persuaded that the government had the right—no, the obligation—to provide all these programs and services he and his colleagues had devised. The more people the government could take care of, the better. He didn't much care how he accomplished his goal. As long as he held the element of surprise, he was confident he could usher the income tax through before anyone was the wiser. What he didn't count on was an informer deep inside his political machine.

Unbeknownst to Rochelle, I had been alerted the day prior, in the waning moments of my afternoon radio talk show, that a plan had been hatched to push through a state income tax on Saturday, the following day. Johnny B, my producer and sidekick, had passed the information along to me from a well-placed source we'll just call "Hawkeye." I questioned whether my source was accurate. I was positive that either the information was faulty or Johnny had simply misunderstood what Hawkeye had told him. After all, we were sure that the tax had been killed with no chance of being resurrected this legislative session. Weren't we? The word inside the General Assembly was there just wasn't enough support for the measure. We had been fighting this tax for a year. Despite the complicit media, despite all the pleas that it was "for the children" and the predictions that the state would fall into the sea if we didn't adopt an income tax, the people were unmoved. Even the cooked polling numbers didn't convince them because, in reality, legislators could find but a few constituents who expressed a desire for a tax, and an avalanche of opposition.

Still, the leadership pressed forward only to find that, even in the face of their pleading and browbeating, few legislators were willing to risk their political lives in order to pass it. It was considered political suicide, and Rochelle had given up on ever passing it. Little did we know that numerous closed-door meetings were taking place, in direct violation of the state's sunshine laws, where pro-tax forces were hatching their plans far away from the glare of the media. In public, these same people were conceding that support for the income tax was not there, and they were looking at alternatives. We were led to believe that we had defeated attempts to pass the tax. This was disinformation, as it turned out, planted by pro-income-tax forces to keep the opposition off-guard. Behind the scenes, Rochelle on the Senate side teamed up with Speaker Jimmy Naifeh in the House. Rochelle and Naifeh, together with Governor Don Sundquist, became the "Axis of Upheaval" against the citizens of Tennessee. They had been feverishly cobbling together just enough support to pass the income tax measure. The foregone conclusion was if the Senate gave them cover, the much more skittish House would follow suit. Once the two houses passed the measure, the skids were greased for it to become law, since Governor Sundquist had made his dramatic transformation from staunch income tax opponent to rabid income tax advocate.

THE MORPHING OF A GOVERNOR

A no more unlikely turncoat ever graced the Tennessee political landscape. No betrayal has ever shocked me more than that of Don Sundquist. That needs to be understood on the front end. His dyed-in-the-wool conservative credentials were beyond reproach. An Illinois transplant, Sundquist moved into the Memphis area at age thirty-six. Having been chairman of the National Young Republicans, Sundquist quickly ingratiated himself with the local Republican establishment, so much so that they elected him Shelby County Republican chairman within three years of his move into the area. Within five years of leaving that post, he ran for Congress against native son Bob Clement, whose father had been a three-term governor of the state. Despite his famous name, Clement was defeated, and Sundquist went to Washington to help fulfill the Reagan agenda.[4] He built a reputation as one of the most conservative members of Congress. He scored high marks with the American Conservative Union each year, usually scoring in the eighties and nineties out of a possible one hundred, even reaching a hundred one year. The only anomaly was in 1984, when he scored a dismal nineteen. Perhaps it was a harbinger of things to come. With his overall conservative credentials and his congressional experience, he had the perfect résumé to be the next governor of Tennessee—or so I thought.

I remember very well the night I first met Don Sundquist. I was the master of ceremonies for a Republican candidates forum. Before I introduced all of the candidates on stage, I introduced myself to him. Looking back, he was unusually pleasant and chatty. I don't recall ever seeing him like that again, even before our falling out. Of course, he was in full campaign mode, which might explain his atypical cheerfulness. That night, I wrote in my journal:

Sundquist, in particular, went out of his way to be nice. I'll have no problem supporting him in his race for governor.

In addition to his conservative background, I genuinely liked the man. Subsequently, I campaigned for candidate Sundquist, even making speeches on his behalf. This was prior to my permanent venture into talk radio. I was still in music radio, and I did this in spite of my policy not to get publicly involved in political campaigns. Ordinarily I thought it bad business for a host of a music morning show to lay his political beliefs on the table, but I believed very strongly in the man and his message. I believed in his conservative track record and his campaign promise never to support an income tax. I knew we had something special in our state, a relatively small government with low taxes. I felt strongly about protecting that. I knew the prior administration had made a major push for the income tax, and I was relieved to, at last, find a candidate strong enough to stand up and make a no-state-income-tax pledge. Not only was it a pledge, it was the lead plank in his campaign platform. His opponent would not promise to oppose a state income tax, and Sundquist made hay with that fact. Interestingly enough, that same opponent, Phil Bredesen, would find himself in the governor's mansion eight years later, after learning his lesson from the first run and making his own promise not to support an income tax—at least in the first four years.

Steve Gill, my good friend and colleague in the tax fight, knew Sundquist from a different angle. Having run for Congress in 1994, Gill, a 6-foot-4-inch former basketball player for the University of Tennessee, saw Sundquist on the campaign trail. They were like-minded politicians with the same determination to see Republicans in charge on the state and national level. Steve came very close to winning that congressional seat in '94 and decided to try again two years later. In 1996, Governor Sundquist went so far as to hold a fundraiser for him at the governor's residence. Even then, Steve had no inkling that Sundquist would transform himself into the darling of the special interests and labor unions.[5] Nobody did.

Having campaigned for Steve, including helping him with a fundraiser, I had always found him to be an engaging speaker. In 1998, he took a position at WLAC in Nashville as their morning host. Ironically, I would return to Nashville from a stint in Philadelphia as afternoon host that very same day, April 16, 1998. It was also the same day a pair of tornadoes tore through downtown Nashville, some calling it an omen of things to come.

Sundquist started his first term as governor doing just what one would expect from a conservative. He helped lead the nation in welfare reform with his Families First program. At least the idea was right: get able-bodied people off welfare by insisting they go back to work. It would be years later that I would discover the more people we got off welfare in Tennessee the bigger and more bloated the Families First program became.

It's important to note my affection for Don Sundquist prior to his election as governor and during his first term. I must confess, however, to feeling a bit sorry for him at times. Although certainly capable, I didn't think he was the sharpest knife in the drawer, but he didn't have to be. He just had to hold his own against the Democrats who ran the General Assembly and he could count his time in office a success. As it turned out, he was much shrewder than I imagined.

In 1998, upon my return to Nashville from Philadelphia, I was invited to the media Christmas party at the governor's mansion. My wife, Susan, and I had our picture taken with Governor and Mrs. Sundquist. As we shook hands, he had that deer in the headlights look on his face. We made idle chat before the flash, and I got the distinct impression that, despite my involvement in his campaign and my years of support on the radio, this man had no idea who I was. Susan agreed but would comment some months later in the heat of the tax fight, "He sure knows who you are now." Needless to say, the invitations to the governor's mansion stopped coming.

Making Sense of the Budget

I had only been gone from Nashville for eighteen months when I started my talk show at WLAC radio in April of 1998. Although I returned to a different station than the one I left, I fell back into the rhythm of the city without missing a beat. Governor Sundquist welcomed me back and became a regular listener to the show. It was an election year. Sundquist was seeking his second and, by state constitution, final term as governor. He had token opposition from perennial political candidate John J. Hooker. With his white straw hat, tacky suits, odd behavior, and frivolous lawsuits, Hooker had become a caricature of himself. Once a political powerhouse and king maker, nobody took him seriously any longer. Much to the embarrassment of the Democrats, he won their nomination for governor. His victory in the Democrat primary merely underscored how inept the party had become. While the Democrat hierarchy covered its eyes, Hooker ran a high-profile campaign and was blistered by Sundquist in one of the worst political thumpings in the state's history.

Once again, Don Sundquist had run on a no-state-income-tax platform. He made speeches recounting his four years of governmental bliss, hawking a strong state economy and a fiscally sound government that was responsive to the people but lived within its means. Time after time he made the case of why the state did not need a state income tax to meet its obligations. Although Sundquist would later run from it, this "no new tax" stand was a large part of the Sundquist appeal. The very fact that the Democrats failed to run a serious candidate was because of Sundquist's immense popularity, largely because he had promised never to support a state income tax and kept that promise in his first term.

On February 8, 1999, Sundquist reiterated his opposition to a state income tax in his State of the State speech. "You will hear from those who say we ought to preserve special breaks for some businesses and impose an income tax on working Tennesseans," he announced. "That's not tax relief; it's not tax reform; it's not tax simplification; and it's not tax fairness. All an income tax does is raise the tax burden on Tennesseans and create a way to finance the easy and endless expansion of government. Tennessee does not need a state income tax."[6]

Even as he uttered those words, Sundquist had already devised his own tax plan. As he outlined in his speech, he planned to eliminate what he saw as "special breaks for some businesses" by enacting a special business tax. Although Sundquist didn't see it this way, his proposal was tantamount to an income tax. Under the Sundquist plan, the state would assess a 6 percent "excise tax" on profits to corporations, partnerships, limited liability companies, and sole proprietorships. In addition to this excise tax, any compensation above $72,000 per employee would be subject to the tax.[7] A tax on compensation *is* an income tax! The fact that organized labor had come out in favor of the measure was a sure sign that Sundquist had turned a corner. After all the years I had supported him, I was reluctant to throw him from the train. I thought there must be a logical explanation.

The business tax was the brainchild of Sundquist's commissioner of finance and administration, John Ferguson. He came to the governor in December of '98, prior to his leaving on a trade trip overseas, with some urgent news about Tennessee's tax structure. Beth Fortune, the governor's press secretary and a former reporter for the *Nashville Banner*, remembered the conversation. "Ferguson said, 'We've got a problem with the business taxes. They're really going south.' He was very concerned about it," Fortune recalled. "The governor had—and rightly so—great trust in John. When John made the case for tax reform the governor listened." The "Fair Business Tax," as it was called, took a pain and pleasure approach. The added tax on businesses was the pain, but the pleasure was a proposed repeal of the sales tax on grocery food. "It did not come about without a lot of discussion and, I think, a lot of soul searching for the governor," Fortune said.[8]

On March 3, 1999, we discussed the proposal on my show. Governor Sundquist called in, unsolicited, to answer any questions about his proposal. I was quite courteous and respectful. After all, this was the man for whom I still had a great deal of admiration. But even though I was eager to give him the benefit of the doubt, I was scratching my head about this new tax. Not three months prior he had been extolling the solvency of the state. Now he was projecting a deficit of $365 million and working the state up into a panic over what to do about it. Something wasn't right. If, in fact, we were facing a financial crisis, why did it take him four years in office to see it? The prospect that he was either inept or dishonest began to creep into my mind. I wondered if the fact that Tennessee governors were limited to two consecutive terms played a part in his waiting until reelection to "discover" a state financial crisis. That night I logged this in my journal:

March 3, 1999—Governor Sundquist just released his 1999–2000 budget. What has everyone in an uproar is his plan to start taxing LLCs (Limited Liability Corporations) so they can't hide from the taxes other corporations now pay. The problem is, many small businesses across the state are struc-tured as LLCs and they're raising hell about it.

He also wants to remove the tax from food. I don't quite understand why he wants to make one tax more equitable while making another inequitable. My thinking is, a tax on food is one of the few ways the poor contribute to the state. If you're really poor you can qualify for food stamps. Then you not only don't pay tax on food, you don't pay for the food itself. It seems that we have all sorts of programs in place to help the poor, which I fully support, but it's time we gave a little relief to the average worker.

During the course of our conversation that afternoon he continually pointed out the need to equalize the tax system through his business tax. I agreed that the tax system was unfair on some levels. Instead of the business tax, I cited the many exemptions to the sales tax. Those with the most powerful lobbyists or influence, like the newspapers, had managed to exclude themselves from the tax. By my estimates, we could close the exemptions and lower the overall state portion of the sales tax from six cents on the dollar to four cents. The difference was, my proposal was revenue neutral. I saw no need to continue spending at the rate we were spending. If his motivation was actually tax fairness, as he professed, why did his proposal raise over $400 million in new revenue? I asked if there weren't some fat in this budget that we could trim to stave off any tax increase. His mood darkened. "If you think you can find some waste in this budget," he bristled, "go right ahead."

For two weeks after the Sundquist call, I had been thinking long and hard about what he said. If I thought I could find waste in the budget, perhaps I should, indeed, take a look at his proposed budget. After a little asking around, I obtained a copy of the current budget proposal from our newsroom. I opened it with trepidation. It was 375 pages of enough numbers and charts and boring text to make an accountant doze. I closed the cover and stared out the window. A foreboding of drudgery enveloped me. I'd never gone through a state budget before. Where in the world would I start? How would I make heads or tails of the numbers? I let the huge volume rest on my desk for about two more weeks. Then I began to look at it differently. My reaction was exactly what Sundquist had wanted. Who in their right mind would take the time to go over all those numbers?

I hopped on the phone to State Senator Marsha Blackburn. I had known Marsha since Sundquist's first campaign for governor and had followed her career into his administration. Although I hadn't talked to her much about the issue of Sundquist's tax plan, I knew she had come out in opposition to it, despite her close friendship with the governor. Obviously, if she was willing to challenge the sitting governor of her own party who had once appointed her to head the state's film commission, she was someone of integrity . . . and guts. I wrote in my journal:

I applaud Marsha, especially since she's been such a close friend to the governor. She may have sacrificed that relationship in order to do the right thing. I think she gave a lot of other Republicans cover who otherwise might have been reluctant to speak out against him.

Marsha would go on to become one of the true leaders in the Tennessee income tax rebellion. I had always known her to be energetic and knowledgeable in everything she pursued. I knew she would have firsthand insight that would make wading into that budget document much easier. I met her at her home, and we sat at her kitchen table as she explained what the numbers meant and how to read the budget. Armed with that knowledge, I went home and set about the daunting task of sifting through the numbers to see if I could unearth any waste.

It was akin to cramming for a final exam. I wasn't sure how much time I had, so I spent every waking hour poring over the massive document in between prepping for my talk show. I read every last page, taking copious notes, then I read it again, cross-referencing budget items and following confusing spending trails. The tedious process of following chunks of money through the budget was maddening. It was like untangling a thousand garden hoses. At times I felt like throwing the whole thing in the trashcan, but I was determined to unravel the money mystery. At last, I began to make headway. (I must admit that there were plenty of confusing tables and jargon, but after several nights of studying, I got the hang of it. The most blatant waste was clearly delineated within the pages of the budget proposal. I wasn't making anything up. It was all right there in black and white. In fact, there was surely much more waste that wasn't listed in the budget.)

Meanwhile, pro-tax lawmakers cried on their respective floors that there was just nothing left to cut. Democrat State Senator Jim Kyle, another member of the "Axis" from Memphis said, "I spent four weeks trying to find ways to cut, and it just wasn't there."[9] Oh, really? As I more closely inspected the document, I was astounded by what I found. There were items that no one in the mainstream media was talking about. I found $24 million for four new golf courses, $220,000 for a golf cart crossing (it would be renamed a "safety crossing" to try to sneak it through the next budget), almost $1 million to refurbish Alex Haley's boyhood home, and $1 million for the Country Music Hall of Fame. These were just a few of the blatant examples of waste.

State Representative Mae Beavers, a staunch opponent of the income tax, had found some of the same items I had found. Mae had courageously stepped to the forefront in opposition to Sundquist, the titular head of her own party, over his newly-proposed tax. While many of her Republican colleagues in the State House of Representatives were timid about facing off with the governor, Mae was not.

Mae and I compared notes and agreed that if we were truly in a budget crisis there was no need to spend money on these items. I maintained we had no business spending money on them, period, even in good times. In addition to the outright frivolous spending, there were grossly inflated figures for work to be done at state facilities, like $510,000 to renovate a kitchen at one state facility and $450,000 to air condition a kitchen at another. I also learned that the entire state government had been growing at a rate far exceeding inflation and population growth. All told, I found approximately $1.4 billion in savings, over three times the estimated deficit. It was my first real indication that this "crisis" had been fabricated.

I learned through my budget research that the sacred cow of higher education was filled with waste. As college students roamed the halls of the General Assembly crying for more tax dollars, I was unearthing the fact that seven of our state-supported schools were showing a drop in enrollment while adding faculty and piling on more money. Meanwhile, these ingrates were whining that their tuition would have to go up if we didn't raise taxes. That led me to expand my research. I compared the tuition rates in Tennessee to the eight states that bordered Tennessee. I found that only North Carolina had a lower tuition rate. In fact, Tennessee ranked forty-first out of the fifty states in tuition costs.[10] Early the next year, more gasoline would be thrown on the phantom education problem fire when a study was released showing that University of Tennessee professors' salaries, when adjusted for cost of living, were the highest in the nation![11]

The biggest mess in the budget came in the form of a healthcare program for the poor designed to take the place of Medicaid. The TennCare program was hatched by the previous governor in cahoots with the Clinton administration after the embarrassing failure of Hillary Clinton's attempt to socialize medicine. TennCare was simply HillaryCare on a smaller scale, planted in Al Gore's home state and expected to overtake the rest of the country like kudzu.

The idea of managed care was nothing new, but TennCare attempted it on a statewide scale. Not only did it insure the poor, it took in the uninsurable and even the disinterested uninsured. Pretty soon people were rolling into the state from all over the country to take advantage of this government handout. While the national average of citizens on Medicaid—the program TennCare replaced—was one in ten, the number of citizens on TennCare was one in four! That's right! Twenty-five percent of the population was on medical assistance from the state, and the numbers continued to grow. The benefits under TennCare were so good, some employers were encouraging their employees to drop their company coverage for TennCare.

Governor Sundquist and the supporters of big government lauded the virtues of TennCare, while those of us opposed to runaway spending continued to point to the increasingly enormous costs associated with the program. The abuse within the system was staggering. Sundquist and his allies were dealt a punch to the gut when an audit of TennCare revealed widespread mismanagement. "We found long-standing problems in practically every operational area," revealed Arthur Hayes, director of the state audit. In one year alone, the auditors discovered that the state of Tennessee had paid over $6 million to insure 14,000 dead people![12] Still, the governor stood by the program as fiscally sound and refused to take the steps necessary to bring it under control. Instead, he pushed for higher taxes. There was no denying that TennCare was one of the root causes of the excessive spending, and I outlined that in my budget analysis.

It was April 15, 1999—tax day, ironically enough. Sundquist met with State Representative Tommy Head, the House budget subcommittee chairman, about the governor's business tax proposal. Head didn't like it. It didn't tax enough people to suit him. They seamlessly moved from the governor's business tax proposal to discussion of the income tax. Barely two months had passed since Sundquist had adamantly insisted that we didn't need an income tax. Now he was meeting with one of the strongest proponents of one. Rumors of under-the-table deals began to fly, but the governor's press secretary, Beth Fortune, insisted the governor had not changed his position. However, she chose her words carefully. "An income tax will not be his proposal, and he will not be leading the charge," she informed reporters. He will not be leading the charge? Would he be *supporting* the charge? When pressed, her response was a little more telling. "The governor is not ruling out the possibility of signing legislation that may or may not include other forms of taxation," she said.[13]

It was becoming obvious that Sundquist was up to something. The legislature was called into a special tax session. An income tax package surfaced, and Sundquist indicated he would support it. Anti-income-tax lawmakers, especially Republicans who had supported Sundquist, were outraged. The governor tried to steer Republicans in the Senate toward the income tax, and they would have nothing of it. On April 22, 1999, State Senator Jeff Miller, another leader in the anti-income-tax movement, spearheaded a Republican revolt in the Senate and tried to shut down the special tax session. "We're not going to impose an income tax, and we need to let them [voters] know today," the Republican from Cleveland, Tennessee, said. "We're putting them out of their misery. We don't need to let them go through another weekend to worry about this. We need to quit trying to force something down the throats of people." Bob Rochelle fired back. "If you have another solution, quit whining, put it on paper, and bring it in. Show your stuff," he said. The Senate recessed as income tax proponents from the Senate and House met with the governor. After a brief meeting,

Speaker Jimmy Naifeh returned to a waiting House of Representatives. As he entered the chamber, he looked at Lois DeBerry, the speaker pro tem, and made a slashing gesture across his throat. "Lois, it's over," Naifeh conceded.[14]

I knew if everyone else could see what I had seen in the budget, this nonsense about needing more money would be exposed. Since Sundquist had challenged me to find ways to cut the budget, I sent the results of my research over to the governor's office. There was no response. I also posted the budget analysis on our Web site at PhilValentine.com on April 25, 1999, and the result was a raging firestorm. Ordinary citizens who read the report were livid. On April 27, State Representative Beth Harwell purportedly made copies of the budget analysis and passed them out to everyone on the House floor. Most representatives didn't have time to examine the budget as I had, and they were flabbergasted by the findings.

Immediately, the power elite attacked the analysis and me. I found their self-righteousness to be particularly annoying. How dare I presume to be able to read a budget? In their minds, a lowly talk show host couldn't possibly tackle the complexities of such a document. Only the self-anointed authorities on such matters were qualified to make sense of those big numbers. What were my qualifications, they wanted to know? What degrees did I possess that qualified me to speak authoritatively on this subject? Well, I could add and subtract, and these numbers weren't adding up. They smirked condescendingly at how I had distilled the mathematical double-speak into plain English. In reality, they were frightened. The average citizen could now read for themselves how badly they had been taken to the cleaners all those years.

Sundquist was furious. He denounced the budget analysis and began to lash out at me and others who dared speak of cutting the budget instead of raising taxes. By early May, State Senator David Fowler, a Republican from Signal Mountain, had begun the tedious process of identifying fat in the budget to the Senate Finance Committee. In all, he had flagged ninety different items and begun explaining each one. He only got to number eighteen when he was stopped by Bob Rochelle. "I thought we were going to hear arguments about why [the budget] is fat," Rochelle admonished. "I'm not hearing that."[15] He wasn't hearing that because he wasn't listening. Every single one of Fowler's recommendations was rejected. By then, the Sundquist business tax had been shot down. Sundquist had underestimated the power of the business lobby and overestimated the taxpaying public's reaction to repealing the tax on groceries. In place of the business tax was a Democrat-proposed 4 percent unadulterated income tax sponsored by Rochelle in the Senate and Tommy Head in the House. Sundquist said he would sign it. From his vehement opposition to an income tax in February of 1999 to his agreeing to sign one into law in May of 1999, Sundquist had shifted a full 180 degrees, thus spawning my nickname for him, "180 Don."

Those of us in talk radio were pounding the issue on the air. Now that Steve Gill was behind the microphone, we kept the politicians busy. Steve covered the income tax issue for our morning listeners on WLAC, and I took care of afternoons, nice bookends to our syndicated programming. Our air support for the cause was complemented at our crosstown talk station rival, WTN. Darrell Ankarlo covered mornings, and financial expert Dave Ramsey spread the word in his afternoon show. In most cases, talk radio is a passive medium. Sure, we gripe and bellyache about the issues, but rarely do talk show hosts get involved. Despite what some on the other side of this issue have claimed, there was no conspiracy between the talk show hosts to fight the income tax. It just happened. That's not to say that we didn't talk once we were in the throes of the fight. Steve Gill and I, especially, coordinated our efforts. But the initial decision to make this a centerpiece issue on each show happened through what I call daily "topic triage." Each host goes over the available issues and decides what to lead with. The idea of an income tax was so detested in Tennessee that it was naturally at the top of our pile. Gill, Ankarlo, Ramsey, and I were all passionately opposed to the implementation of a new tax, but it was more than that. Whenever I tried to move on to other topics, the listeners stayed focused like a laser on the tax issue. There was no getting away from it.

The four of us never held a secret meeting to plot strategy against the tax. What happened on the air merely led to action, a natural progression for two talk stations located in the state's capital. We were in a frontline position to actually mobilize the citizens, and we took advantage of that position. However, in the beginning the battle was fought primarily on the air. We only resorted to the ground war when it appeared our on-air efforts would not be enough. The opposition to our on-air efforts was fierce. As we pushed hard against the tax, they were pushing back with equal vigor. But I'm not sure the pro-income-tax forces were prepared for this kind of backlash.

In order to garner support for any tax increase, it's necessary for those pushing the tax to pit one group against another. The pro-tax crowd tried this with the business tax. Businesses, they reckoned, were not paying their "fair share." Forget the fact that businesses create the jobs that enable the taxes to be paid in the first place. After their attempts to demonize business failed, Sundquist and the Democrats held education hostage to get what they wanted. According to them, if we didn't have an income tax, the schools would suffer greatly. By then, it was clear that "tax reform" and "tax fairness" were just buzz terms for the income tax.

The Sundquist tactics were eerily similar to tactics used by the Democrats in Congress when they shut down the government in 1995. I know. I was there, broadcasting from the Capitol during the entire ordeal. I finished my broadcast one morning and headed for the restroom. When I emerged, a swarm of reporters had cornered Congressman Sam Gibbons from Florida. Not being able to pass, I listened to his rhetoric until I could stand it no longer. He was spewing off the same class warfare garbage they'd been promulgating all week—that the Republicans were "cutting Medicare to give a tax cut to their rich contributors." I piped in and asked a question of my own. "Congressman Gibbons," I inquired, from the rear of the throng of reporters, "isn't it true that the Republicans are actually increasing spending for Medicare? Isn't what you're calling a cut actually just a reduction in the double-digit increase in spending you want?" Gibbons craned his head to see who was asking the question as the lights from the television cameras turned toward me. Obviously annoyed by the line of questioning, he insisted that the Republicans were, in fact, cutting Medicare.

I knew he was lying. *He* knew he was lying. Even the *reporters* knew he was lying. Instead of pressing the issue with the congressman, they turned on me. One reporter asked to see my press pass. I informed her that I didn't have one nor did I need one. She became indignant. She insisted that I was not allowed to ask questions unless I had press credentials. How arrogant. I firmly reminded her that I was merely a citizen walking through the halls of Congress. When I hear someone telling a lie, I told her, I have an obligation and a right to call him on it. I don't need to show her any stinkin' credentials to do that! It was a matter of not allowing someone to get away with a complete fabrication at the expense of the taxpayers. That's what I was doing with Congressman Gibbons. That's exactly what we were doing with Don Sundquist.

I certainly wasn't the only one upset with the governor over his underhanded tactics. State Senator Tim Burchett, a Republican from Knoxville, fired off an angry letter to the governor. "I believe it is unethical for you to use such scare tactics as job elimination and educational cutbacks to whip the Legislature into compliance with your proposals," Burchett wrote.[16] Sundquist was using the same plan of attack as Gibbons and the Democrats in Congress four years prior. I noted the similarities in my journal.

May 6, 1999—Sundquist is doing the same thing. I'm not proposing cutting education. I merely want to slow the growth to 3 percent per year, but, in the

*language of Sundquist and the state income tax proponents, that's a cut! This
from a governor who swore over and over that he'd never go for a state income
tax.*

Sundquist's real goal was getting at more money. But why? Why this
unprecedented change?

FOLLOW THE PLAN

Tennessee was far from the first state to fall victim to the crisis-creating
strategy. Connecticut had gone through a similar struggle less than ten
years prior. Their government's insatiable appetite for tax dollars
gobbled up all available public money. Republican-turned-
Independent governor Lowell Weicker, like our own, had opposed an
income tax. Once he took office, his opinion changed. He and like-
minded legislators began the pity tour in an effort to shame their state
into an income tax. The populace was against the levy, but lawmakers
were cajoled and battered into submission. But in Tennessee, through
the efforts of talk radio hosts and tenacious journalists like Bill Hobbs
at *In-Review*, a now-defunct Nashville weekly, the citizens were well-
versed on what was actually going on in their state government.

By August of 1999, Bob Rochelle recognized that his tax plan was
meeting more resistance than he had counted on. He decided he
needed some tips on how to achieve his goal, so he chartered a state
airplane to Connecticut to learn firsthand how they had done it.
Along for the ride was State Representative Matt Kisber, Rochelle's
point man in the House.[17] At taxpayers' expense, Rochelle studied the
Connecticut plan and learned exactly how Governor Weicker and his
cronies had passed a state income tax in the middle of the night. He
came back fully armed with all the trick plays in their playbook and
began following them to the letter. Rochelle aimed to duplicate
Connecticut's success in Tennessee.

State Senator David Fowler called in an economist to counter the Connecticut plan. J. R. Clark, professor of economics at the University of Tennessee-Chattanooga, tried to educate the senators on the dangers of enacting an income tax. He pointed out that in Connecticut, personal income was expected to be 17 percent lower by the next year than it would have been had they not passed the income tax. "If you're looking for revenue enhancement, pursuing most anything but an income tax would produce superior results," he informed them. "An income tax tends to produce an economic slow-down."[18] Even Clark's gloomy projections turned out to be "optimistic." In 2002, when the double whammy of the recession and September 11th was having tremendous effect across the country, Connecticut's revenues fell 9.5 percent, and they found themselves in an $800 million hole.[19] Tennessee's revenue, by contrast, only dropped 2.5 percent.[20] And that was before the one cent sales tax increase.

By late October of 1999, Governor Sundquist and his pro-tax allies in the General Assembly had become frustrated with the likes of Marsha Blackburn, Mae Beavers, State Representative Bill Dunn, State Senators Jeff Miller and David Fowler, and others standing in the way of the income tax. He called for a special tax session of the General Assembly to settle the issue. By then, we in talk radio had been urging people to e-mail and fax lawmakers to make their wishes known. I even linked on my Web site a system for e-mailing all of the lawmakers at once. Richard McKinney, director of information services for the legislature, proposed to block any e-mails sent to all the lawmakers simultaneously.[21] Anti-income-tax lawmakers cried "foul." On October 28, Representative Mae Beavers and Senator Marsha Blackburn held a news conference to complain about the decision.

The next day, I gave a speech at a local Rotary Club gathering on the true story behind the numbers. I argued that Sundquist and his spin machine in the press had been fabricating this notion that we had to have an income tax because the sales tax wasn't keeping up with our needs. The truth was, the sales tax wasn't keeping up with their *desires*. Before the economic downturn, it was *more* than keeping up with the needs of the state, outpacing inflation plus population growth. We were doing much better than those states with income taxes. The whole notion that our tax system was broken was a farce, and Sundquist knew it. The problem was with spending.

By law, the General Assembly is not allowed to increase spending beyond the rate of growth in personal income of Tennesseans. However, that law has no teeth. With a simple majority, they merely bust the cap and spend whatever they want to. As journalist Bill Hobbs pointed out, they've busted the spending cap a dozen times over the past twenty years. The cumulative cost to the taxpayers of Tennessee has been over $3 billion.[22] That particular trick is routinely ignored by the media.

If busting the cap weren't bad enough, the governor routinely takes surplus money and spends it as he pleases. The practice is called "sum sufficient." What that means is, when more money actually comes in than is budgeted to spend, instead of socking that money away for next year or giving it back to the taxpayers, the governor authorizes the finance commissioner to divvy that money up among the departments of his choosing as he determines "sum sufficient" to run the departments. The General Assembly does not vote on it. The people are not consulted. The bureaucrats refer to this money as "unbudgeted dollars," and they routinely rob the taxpayers of this money during the good years, then beg for more in the bad.

Representative Mae Beavers cited the exact section of the state constitution that prohibits this practice. "No public money shall be expended except pursuant to appropriations made by law," she quoted. "Nowhere does it say the executive branch has the authority to spend money outside of the legislative process. But that is exactly what has been happening. That is how new programs have been created, or existing programs expanded, without the legislature appropriating the funds," she said. Mae was part of a paper tiger committee appointed by the speaker called the *Budget Reduction Committee*. The committee was formed to give the appearance that leadership was concerned about the runaway spending. Speaker Jimmy Naifeh had no intention of considering *any* of their recommendations. When Representative Frank Buck made a recommendation to cut out the roadside wildflower program and save $300,000 in state money, he was told, "Oh, we get federal matching funds on those."[23] That was one of the major problems I had been pointing out to the lawmakers. Federal matching funds are okay if they don't require the state to spend money it doesn't have. Just because the feds will match the money doesn't automatically make it a good idea. We could begin to free ourselves from the oppression of government mandates if we would first just say no to the opium of federal dollars.

By consistently ignoring the mechanisms designed to control a runaway government, the General Assembly put the state on a collision course with the income tax. Instead of living within the means of the state, they either gobbled up any surplus we might accrue or raised taxes to bankroll their spending sprees. Once they ran out of things to tax, income became their next logical target.

APPLYING PRESSURE

Before October 1999, Sundquist had been true to his press secretary's word that he would not be "leading the charge" on the income tax. He had watched as lawmakers paraded a variety of taxing options before him, including several versions of the income tax. He went back on that word as of October 26 when he unveiled his own tax plan to the General Assembly. The proposal was a mishmash of tax adjustments here and there, but the bottom line was a 3.75 percent income tax. Steve Gill and I began focusing our efforts on the governor's office. The governor had said he wanted to hear from the people, so I, quite innocently, gave out the number to the governor's office on the air. In one of those strange coincidences, Steve gave the number out on his show, too. Critics would later accuse us of orchestrating the phone-calling campaign against the governor, but I honestly didn't know Steve was doing the same thing, and we certainly hadn't discussed it. I truly thought it would be helpful if concerned citizens let their wishes be known.

I knew that my father, while he was in Congress, took hundreds of calls in his Washington office on all sorts of issues. Surely, former-Congressman Sundquist was used to the same drill. Little did I know that our combined efforts would swamp the governor's office. Sundquist was absolutely livid. He barked, "What they're doing is jamming up phones so people who have legitimate problems with the state can't reach us."[24] Legitimate problems? What, like someone's cat was stuck up a tree? The trash man was a day late? There was no more legitimate or pressing problem than his attempt to shove an unconstitutional income tax down our throats. But Sundquist had already displayed his contempt for the taxpayer. He had said that anyone who opposed his tax reform—citizens and legislators alike—was either lying or stupid.[25]

As State Senator Mike Williams, a passionate foe of the income tax, pointed out, "If they're bringing us up here under the guise of tax reform and then they say, 'Here's an income tax bill—vote for it,' that's not really tax reform."[26] Mike was one of the first to challenge the sitting governor from his own party on the issue, and he was right. Tax reform, where I come from, means *lower* taxes, not higher taxes.

Sundquist regularly made derisive comments about those of us in the opposition, the great unwashed masses. Not only did he say we were either lying or stupid, he referred to income tax opponents as "Neanderthals." Shortly after the Neanderthal comment, anti-income-tax lawmakers began referring to themselves as the "Neanderthal Caucus." I was given a shirt that said, "Proud member of the Neanderthal Caucus." The shirt was the brainchild of State Senator Marsha Blackburn's husband, Chuck. Chuck Blackburn had sketched a cartoon of a Neanderthal man on the front. On the back, it sported a definition of Neanderthal: "hunter, gatherer; protective of family; resourceful; does without when he runs out; depends on government for nothing; against a state income tax." The Neanderthal crack was a kick in the teeth to all of us who had supported Sundquist over the years. By his own definition, he was a Neanderthal himself just a few short months before, but in less than eight months the Sundquist transformation was complete. Suddenly, John J. Hooker, Sundquist's eccentric gubernatorial opponent, was looking pretty good. One listener to my show called in with a bumper sticker sighting. It said, "DON'T BLAME ME. I VOTED FOR A HOOKER."

"It was quite an evolution," press secretary Beth Fortune admitted to me once she had stepped down as press secretary. "I was shocked at first when I realized that we were considering perhaps doing that. It was shocking, and it was scary because—to a number of us who were sitting around the table and had been with him during the campaign and during the first four years—because that was a big deal, that's a big promise you make. We weren't quite sure how we were going to make the case. That's a big position to go back on." In the second term, Fortune had the unenviable job of selling the dreaded tax to the media after claiming for years that the governor would never, ever support it. I came to refer to her on-air as "Miss Fortune." I asked her after she left state government if she ever dreamed she'd find herself in that predicament. "I don't think there were any us . . . who would've ever thought we would go from the fair business tax . . . to an income tax," said Fortune, who classifies herself as a moderate Republican.[27] Still, at the time, she did her job and made the case for an income tax with a straight face, just as one in her position had to do.

We were not, as critics like to say, opposed to the tax because we thought we might have to pay more money to the government. It was about preserving our family-friendly, business-friendly atmosphere in Tennessee. There is immeasurable benefit from being one of a handful of states without an income tax. The Sundquist administration, in fact, had touted that fact in numerous pitches to entice industries to relocate to Tennessee. A Cato Institute Study released November 1, 1999, stated: "Tennessee derives substantial economic gains from being one of nine non-income-tax states. There is substantial evidence that if Tennessee were to adopt an income tax, its growth rate would be lower than it would be without an income tax."[28] The study also confirmed what those of us against the income tax had been saying all along: Tennessee had a *spending* problem, not a *revenue* problem. From 1990–1997, Tennessee had the distinction of having the eleventh highest spending increase of the fifty states. Even when you broke that down by per capita spending for the same time period, Tennessee still ranked twelfth.[29] As you read these figures it's pretty easy to see where the problem lay. The spending point was inarguable, but argue they did. They argued that every dime spent was necessary, despite all the evidence to the contrary.

State Senator Jeff Miller tried to head the income tax proponents off at the pass. He introduced a proposal for a constitutional amendment that would clarify the already constitutional ban on the income tax. In an effort to kill the Miller amendment, Sundquist's attorney general ruled that it "fell outside the scope of the call" by the governor for the special tax session. The Miller amendment was constitutionally redundant but, unfortunately, necessary in light of the complete disregard shown by the governor and leaders in the general assembly for the state constitution. Although the Tennessee Constitution allows the taxing of stocks and bonds, the taxing of income is expressly limited to those two entities. Three Supreme Court cases from 1932, 1960, and 1964 resulted in unanimous decisions from the court that a state income tax is, undoubtedly and unambiguously, unconstitutional.[30] Still, those intent on tapping into another reservoir of money chose to ignore the constitution entirely.

I continued to drive home the fact that the governor's current budget was filled with pork. From the time back in April when Representative Harwell handed out copies of it on the House floor, my budget analysis had apparently made the rounds on Capitol Hill. State Senator Douglas Henry invited me to speak before the Senate Finance Committee. As I did with most of my speeches, I planned to ad lib my comments. That was unacceptable to the senators who sat on the committee. I was asked to submit my full remarks in writing prior to making them. That ran counter to what I felt was my right to address the committee frankly and without fear of censorship. After all, I would not be given the same benefit of advance notice of any questions they might ask of me afterwards. I was also uneasy about furnishing them with all my ammunition. The element of surprise would certainly work to my benefit. I hoped to shock a few into compliance that day. I guess they looked at it more like a court proceeding with full disclosure on both sides. I was informed that either I would submit my speech beforehand or relinquish my only chance to address them. Reluctantly, I complied.

If the governor was to succeed with his plans for an income tax, the Senate Finance Committee was where it would originate. He fiercely lobbied members and boasted of sensing a "slight momentum" building for his tax. "There's no momentum for anything but for us to go home," said Senator David Fowler. Senator Jeff Miller agreed. He declared the income tax "dead." Senator Bob Rochelle retorted, "You may think an income tax is dead, but I don't." Sundquist took his message to a group of special interests who stood to gain from an income tax. In early November, he spoke to a lunchtime rally of state employees and social advocates. The pitiful contingent of government dependants included one woman dressed as an empty plate. She professed to represent the unfair sales tax on food. Sundquist played to the hapless protesters. "Our legislators need to heed the quiet calls for help," Sundquist said. "They need not be drowned out by the rantings and ravings of talk show hosts desiring to pull up ratings, not [pull] down opportunities for Tennessee."[31] Little did they know that within a few days their position outside the State Capitol would be overrun by a mob of angry taxpayers.

On the morning of November 16, 1999, I addressed the Senate Finance Committee with senators, press, and citizens in attendance. State Senator Bob Rochelle himself sat on the committee and nervously rocked his chair back and forth as I approached the podium. I began by saying, "Some of you may see me as the bane of your existence after several weeks of nonstop telephone calls, faxes, and e-mails. The governor and some in the General Assembly have laid the blame for the outrage of the proposed income tax at the feet of talk radio. I wish I could wield such influence, but I have merely served as a conduit through which the desires and frustrations of the citizens of Tennessee have flowed."

I informed them that spending in the state had increased by 58 percent over the last six years. I then detailed some of the more famous expenditures I had unearthed in my budget analysis. Most listened attentively. Some, like State Senator John Ford, fidgeted as if he were itching to respond. Senator Rochelle got up in the middle of my speech and sat down beside the state comptroller, cupping his hand to the number-cruncher's ear. I would later learn from a gentleman seated behind them that Rochelle asked if some numbers I quoted were true. The comptroller nodded, and Rochelle, frustrated and mad, returned to his seat.

I scolded the assembled senators that the "you scratch my back, I'll scratch your back" mentality was breaking the backs of the citizens of Tennessee. It was reckless spending that was the cause of any budget problem, real or imagined. What my listeners were telling me was they wanted their government to cut the waste and abuse, then we'd talk about more money.

Senator Ford began talking almost before I finished my last sentence. He launched into a tirade about how the press had persecuted him over the years. Of course, this was a man with a sordid past. Among the more humorous allegations, a trucker had accused Ford of firing shots at his truck while the senator was making his way down the interstate back towards Memphis. Senator Ford insisted that he was merely shaking his cell phone at him through the sunroof. I warned listeners to be careful when using their cell phones because some, apparently, were prone to go off! As he rambled on, it occurred to me that we were in big trouble if we were counting on people like John Ford to grasp the concepts we were putting forth. He continued his self-pity soliloquy for what seemed like an eternity before he finally yielded the floor. I jotted down my impressions of him in my journal that night:

November 16, 1999—Just a stream of consciousness filled with mindless dribble. I stood there and listened, wondering how this guy ever got elected and who the idiots were who voted for him. This guy couldn't figure his way out of his own suit without help.

After I left the podium, the committee was adjourned until after lunch. I took that as a good sign. Maybe my speech had actually had some impact, I thought. Apparently, I was wrong. It's hard to tell exactly what happened. Either the pro-taxers knew they had to act quickly or they just completely ignored my presentation. Representative Diane Black clued me in on another little secret. According to her, many of the committee meetings in the House were, and perhaps still are, nothing more than a show. The dress rehearsal takes place the day or night before when leadership comes in and instructs members on how to vote. Obviously, that was the case in the Senate because even as I made my plea to end this crusade for the income tax, the fix was in. They came back after lunch and voted the income tax out of committee.

Senator Bob Rochelle had won a major battle. Keeping the income tax bottled up in committee was the prime objective of the income tax opponents. With it loose, anything could happen. However, the income tax making it out of committee was not the product of one man. Although Rochelle is remembered as the architect of the state income tax, he certainly didn't act alone. According to Rochelle, the order to push an income tax came from none other than Lt. Governor John Wilder, the elderly Democrat from Somerville, in May of 1999, just six months before my address to the Senate Finance Committee. Wilder came off as a harmless, grandfatherly—sometimes even bumbling—type who revered the Senate and its members. He was fond of saying, "The Senate is the Senate," whatever the heck that means. He was the longest-serving lieutenant governor in the state's history. In Tennessee, lieutenant governors are not elected by the people but selected by the senators from their number, and they first selected Wilder back in 1971—during the Nixon administration. Wilder had survived a coup from his own party some years back by cobbling together enough support among Republicans to retain his leadership position. You don't hold on to that position for that long without being a master politician.

Wilder, who claimed to be squeamish about the tax, had called Rochelle into his office in May of 1999 and tasked him with formulating an income tax plan. "He said, 'Bob, the state needs an income tax. Go out and find the best one,'" Rochelle claimed. "I don't remember specifically telling him to do that, but if he says it, I did," Wilder responded. "I may have done it. But then I had a campaign, a summer experience . . . and a lot of other people telling me I needed to sign that pledge."[32] The pledge he referred to was a "no income tax" pledge that Steve Gill had coordinated with Grover Norquist at Americans for Tax Reform. He had asked me to help him secure signatures.

Publicly, Wilder was maintaining that the income tax was unconstitutional, but privately he was telling pro-tax lawmakers in both chambers he would help them pass it. In meetings with anti-tax advocates, he would urge them to stick to their guns and not back down.[33] This, apparently, infuriated Rochelle and other tax-backers. Word started circulating that another coup was about to take place and Wilder was going to be booted from his position as head of the Senate. That's when income tax opponent State Senator Tim Burchett intervened. He informed Wilder that the income tax effort was all part of a plan to remove him from his position as lieutenant governor. "I've told him it's all about power and greed. They want a state income tax, and they want to get rid of John Wilder," Burchett said at the time. "It's all part of the same plan."[34] Burchett was trying to help Wilder by alerting him to what he thought was a scheme to oust him from power. Burchett didn't know at the time that Wilder was actually the source of the income tax!

Wilder played dumb and debunked Burchett's theory to the press. His support with the pro-tax forces was solid, but he didn't have the nerve to go through with backing the tax at that particular time. Wilder's about-face on the income tax issue, just one day after the Senate Finance Committee vote, blew a hole in the side of Rochelle's boat. Rochelle's income tax scheme, the one he had drawn up at Wilder's behest, was taking on water. If the lieutenant governor was backing the tax, it gave more vulnerable senators on the committee enough cover to support it. With Wilder's blessing now gone, they dared not support it in a full Senate vote.

At the time, we weren't privy to all the backstage theatrics. What we *did* know was that our sources inside the Senate were telling us they simply did not have the votes to pass it in the full Senate. Still, we didn't want to take any chances. Just to let them know we were watching, WLAC organized a protest downtown that included all five radio stations in our cluster. That was to be the day of the first horn-honking tax protest. All five stations participated by urging motorists to drop by the Capitol on their way to work and blow their horns to let the people inside know they were there. It was one of the most surreal experiences of my life. The cacophony of horns blaring from all makes and models of vehicles with drivers from all walks of life, all with one common goal, was . . . magical.

As the horns blared outside, the seventy-eight-year-old Wilder paced back and forth in the rear of the Senate chamber, hands in his pockets, keys jingling on his belt. "We don't need to be here," he muttered to himself. "We don't need to be here."[35] By noon, Rochelle knew his goose was cooked, and the Senate adjourned the special tax session without deciding on any new revenue. Even though the horn-honking was simply an effort to create an atmosphere downtown to remind the General Assembly we were watching, we had discovered a useful tool, and we vowed to break it back out if it became necessary. Little did we know, the horn-honking protest would become a hall-mark of the revolt.

Two

Rich Heritage of Revolt

The Tennessee tax revolt was certainly not the first of its kind. The very foundation of our great republic is built with the hand-hewn stones of rebellion. Historically, we haven't taken too kindly to tyrants, of either foreign or domestic flavor. Thomas Jefferson believed we are obligated, as children of God, to break the shackles of oppression. His motto: "Rebellion to tyrants is obedience to God."[1] He and our other founding fathers were ever mindful that government could suddenly grow out of control. I'm not melodramatic enough to believe our tax fight in Tennessee was on an equal footing with the American Revolution, but the driving spirit behind both is the same. We, as Americans, take special pride in protecting our God-given rights as outlined in the Declaration of Independence and the Constitution. Almost always, those who choose to usurp basic liberties first gain control of the purse strings. John Marshall, the fourth chief justice of the Supreme Court and a Revolutionary War veteran warned, "The power to tax involves the power to destroy." Marshall was certainly correct. In light of that knowledge, a wary public is a good thing.

CREATING A CRISIS

One important lesson American history teaches us is if you're going to raise taxes or create new ones, you'd better have a darn good reason. A case in point is the history of the direct internal taxes of 1798. The American public had to be sold on the idea. Sales, property, and income taxes are internal taxes, as opposed to import and export taxes, which are considered external taxes. In 1797, egged on by former Secretary of the Treasury Alexander Hamilton, President John Adams sought internal taxes on land, slaves, and houses. In the first ten years of the brand new United States of America's history, 92 percent of its revenue was derived from duties on imports and from tonnage levies.[2]

As Hamilton, who had long advocated internal taxes, pointed out, "the object of the war . . . would supply the want of habit, and reconcile the minds of the people to paying to the utmost of their ability."[3] In other words, create a crisis, and they will willingly pay. He was right, in theory. In practice, however, the American people didn't quite see the crisis. The "war" to which Hamilton referred was a potential war with France. As you can imagine, the agrarian South wasn't too thrilled about internal taxation since a disproportionate amount of the burden would be shouldered by the Southern states. It would sow the seeds of resentment that would blossom into a full-blown war between the states some sixty years later. Now, *that* was a crisis.

It's rather amusing to watch political scientists slug it out over what actually constitutes a crisis. They try to break these crises down into subcategories in an attempt to get a handle on why some tax increases are accepted and others are not. I've read theory after theory attempting to tie down specific causes and effects and identify correlations between crises and tax increases in order to predict the ideal conditions for a tax increase. That's like trying to predict the trajectory of a gnat. Each situation is unique and utterly unpredictable. These formulas never work, and the political scientists who devise them end

up revising them over and over again to account for every new circum-
stance. The only consistency, which these pedants seem to overlook, is
perception. As the old saying goes, perception is reality. If the public
thinks there's a crisis warranting more taxes, they'll go along, whether
that crisis is real or not. Stock markets have crashed over perception.
Wars have been started and fought over it. Politicians, few of whom are
political scientists, figured this out long ago. Either use an existing or
impending crisis as an excuse to raise taxes, or simply create one, even
if it's fake. This is what the liberals have been doing for years with
varying degrees of success.

Still, the academics who can't sleep unless their world is tied up in
a neat little package continue to chase their tails and drive themselves
nuts in pursuit of logic. Politics and logic, however, seldom mix. The
currency of politics is image. You have to sell yourself and your ideas.
Sometimes that sales pitch is based in fact, sometimes in mere rhetoric.
To try to extract logic from that mix is, well, illogical. Politics is a game
of high passion, of theatrics, of persuasion. It's about knowing which
buttons to push and which issues to avoid. It's about influence. If you
can convince enough voters you're right and the other guy is wrong,
you win. If not, you lose.

The same can be said of the *policy* of politicians. You must convince
enough people that what you want to do is right. No politician can go
it alone and accomplish much. Tax increases come about by the
building of coalitions. Disparate factions often find common ground in
new money. It's these coalitions that continually lead to the expansion
of government, even though the majority of people benefit very little,
if at all, from the new revenue. "The American Republic will endure,
until politicians realize they can bribe the people with their own
money." That's a quote widely attributed to the great nineteenth
century French student of American democracy, Alexis de
Tocqueville. What our tax structure has evolved into in this country is
one that bribes a large number of citizens with *other people's money*

(OPM, which sounds like "opium," another substance that is highly addictive and ultimately destructive). In essence, we rob the rich to give to the poor. According to the IRS, the top 5 percent of wage-earners in this country pay better than 56 percent of the income taxes.[4] That's an astonishing statistic. Had the founding fathers known we were heading for such a punitive society, they would've scrapped the whole American experiment. And the advocates of big government want even more!

The liberal rhetoric during modern elections plays on our innate sense of class envy. The "haves" are made to feel guilty by those purportedly speaking on behalf of the "have-nots." We're taught, first, that we should feel guilty for any success we achieve and, second, that the liberal, compassionate thing to do is to give away that ill-gotten booty. This mentality has caused an ideological and geographical divide in America. After George W. Bush won reelection in 2004, prominent liberals advanced the possibility of secession by the nineteen "blue states," or states that went for John Kerry. This was not some fringe lunatic movement. This was coming from renowned strategists within the party. Democratic activist Bob Beckel told *Fox & Friends* the morning after the election, "I think now that slavery is taken care of, I'm for letting the South form its own nation. Really, I think they ought to have their own confederacy."

MSNBC political analyst Lawrence O'Donnell, a one-time aide to Senator Daniel Patrick Moynihan, concurred. "The segment of the country that pays for the federal government is now being governed by the people who don't pay for the federal government," O'Donnell whined.[5] In his effort to whip up discontent among the blue states using class warfare, O'Donnell forgot something: the facts. California, a blue state, boasts the nations highest per capita millionaires yet it has the highest percentage of welfare recipients in the country. New York is right behind them. Indeed, the blue states pay roughly 20 percent more than the red states in federal income tax, but the blue states have an average of 61 *percent more* citizens on government welfare. The raw numbers paint an even uglier picture. Despite the fact that there are more people in the red states, the number of people on welfare in the Kerry states is almost *three times* the number compared to the Bush states.[6]

When I once asked actor Rob Reiner, who was lobbying for more taxes, why he and his Hollywood buddies didn't just set aside a few hundred thousand a year to live on and give the rest to the government, he went ballistic. "Hollywood is the most giving community on the planet," he cried. Not so fast, Meathead. Let's go back to our red state/blue state comparison. The liberals will have you believe they give more than conservatives to charity. Here are the facts. According to the Massachusetts-based Catalogue of Philanthropy's Generosity Index, millionaire-intensive California is not the most charitable state. Neither is New York. The most giving state in the union is—are you ready for this?—Mississippi. That's right, a red state. Their "Having Rank" according to the index is 50th out of the 50 states. Their "Giving Rank," despite their relatively meager means, is 5th. That translates into a generosity index of first place. California, by contrast, is 6th in "Having Rank" and a dismal 17th in "Giving Rank" leaving them in 29th place. New York, by the way, is in 26th place. The state the liberals love to dump on, Mississippi, gives about $1,000 more to charity per person than California where the average annual income is almost $20,000 more.

Here's another interesting tidbit. Of the top 10 most giving states, every single one is a red state. Of the top 20 giving states, every one is a red state. Of the top 25 giving states, every one is a red state. All of the blue states rank 26 or below in generosity. In other words, all of the blue states are in the bottom half when it comes to charity.[7] So much for compassionate, giving liberals, eh? The bottom line is, liberals are for higher taxes, but when it comes to helping the less fortunate, without the threat of jail time, conservatives are the ones who step up to the plate.

While liberals whine and wail that we need to raise taxes, ironically, a tax increase is rarely necessary to raise funds. In fact, just the opposite is often the remedy. As has been proven time and time again in our nation's history, a tax reduction is the way to stimulate a sluggish economy and increase cash flow into the treasury. Kennedy knew this. Jack, that is. Reagan knew it. So did George W. Bush. That just happens to be the least palatable option for the politicians who've figured out that money equals power and power equals money. That's the name of the game. Grab as much as you can for your friends and/or constituents, and you hold on to the power. I believe, historically, the War on Terrorism prosecuted by the Bush administration should be remembered more for the way it was financed than the way it was fought. It may have been the only time in our nation's history when a president, faced with war, pushed through Congress tax *reductions* instead of increases to pay for it. Unfortunately, that's the exception and not the rule.

The politicians of the late eighteenth century saw a chance to broaden the power of the federal government by raising taxes. What precipitated the internal taxes of 1798 was France's harassment of American shipping in their war with England. France's attitude and actions had begun to irritate Alexander Hamilton and politicians of his political stripe in Congress. Actually, it could be argued that Hamilton was less irritated than he was intrigued by the opportunity presented with the prospect of war. As a Federalist, Hamilton believed in a larger and more centralized government. Such governments cost money. He knew if Congress swerved into a windfall like the internal taxes, he could realize his dream. Hamilton and the "High Federalists" in Congress, a wing of President Adams's own party, pushed for war with France. To pay for such a conflict, they pushed equally hard for direct taxation. There was no widespread support for such direct taxes because there was no widespread perception that war with France was either imminent or necessary—at least until the war drums drowned out the anti-Federalists who wanted no part of any conflict with France.

Those drums reached a fevered pitch after President Adams sent a delegation to France in hopes of reestablishing diplomatic relations. The three diplomats were met by agents of French foreign minister Charles Maurice de Talleyrand and told they must apologize for Adams's derogatory remarks about France. If that wasn't enough of a slap in the face, they also demanded a $12 million loan for France and—get this—a $250,000 bribe, payable to Talleyrand! Naturally, the American diplomats told them to go jump in the Seine and broke off talks with Talleyrand's agents, known in American communications as Agents X, Y, and Z. News of the now-famous XYZ Affair spread like wildfire throughout the United States. Hamilton got his wish. Perception changed overnight, and the Americans were frothed up for war. Four months after the XYZ Affair, Congress passed the direct tax in July of 1798. That was just days after the same Congress passed the Alien and Sedition Acts, four laws designed to stifle Jeffersonian Republicans sympathetic with French Revolutionaries.

But the Jeffersonians in Congress and the Southern landowners weren't the only ones unhappy about the new taxes, despite the threat of war. Opposition to the tax began to grow in the North as well, the longer the war with France failed to materialize. Folks began to perceive that the threat of war was exaggerated. If that was the case, the government didn't really need all that new tax money. John Fries, an auctioneer from Bucks County, Pennsylvania, was one who believed just that. He led a small militia against some tax assessors in their area the following year. It seems these particular assessors were counting windows in the houses they were assessing. Around that time, the value of a dwelling was sometimes determined by the size and number of glass windows, although historians differ on whether that section of the law requiring enumeration of windows was still intact at the time of Fries' Rebellion. Suffice it to say, Fries and his men didn't take too kindly to the tax or the assessors no matter how they determined the value. They detained the assessors (kidnapped is how President Adams would've described it), confiscated their papers, then released them later in the day. Despite the relatively low-key nature of this rebellion, Adams aimed to make examples out of Fries and his men.

We'll cover Fries' Rebellion in more detail later, but I bring it up here to illustrate the sentiment in 1799 compared to the reaction to very similar taxes levied after the outbreak of the War of 1812. Hamilton's assertion that people will accept new taxes if there's a crisis was true, but the crisis has to be real—or at least perceived to be real. Thomas Jefferson and the anti-Federalists in Congress repealed the internal taxes of 1798 shortly after he took the office of president in 1801. It's not that Jefferson was necessarily opposed to internal taxes, per se. He just believed the matter of internal taxes should be left to the discretion of the individual states. Jefferson wrote in 1787, "Would it not have been better to assign the Congress exclusively the article of imposts for Federal purposes, and to have left direct taxation exclusively to the States?"[8]

By 1811, the country was once again on the verge of war, this time with England, and this time for real. British ships had attacked our merchant ships, and President James Madison appealed to Congress to ready us for war. In June of 1812, Madison asked Congress for a declaration of war against England and got it. However, Congress was quite hesitant to resurrect the unpopular direct internal taxes of 1798. It was only after the war had been raging a little more than a year and the increase in tariffs had failed to produce sufficient sums to prosecute the war that Congress resorted to direct internal taxes. These taxes were markedly different from the taxes of 1798 in two notable ways. For one, they were earmarked specifically for the war. In fact, they were officially labeled "War Taxes" by Congress. Secondly, they came with a sunset provision. Imagine that. They would be automatically repealed within one year of the conclusion of the war.[9] The public enthusiastically embraced the new taxes as the patriotic thing to do. And it was one of the few times in history that taxes actually went away.

Exploiting the Greed of the People

To Alexander Hamilton's theory that people are more receptive to taxes in the face of a crisis, I would add that taxes are also more palatable in the face of something the taxpayers want. I saw the citizens of Nashville shoot down two tax increase proposals earmarked for education, only to turn around and vote in favor of a multimillion-dollar package to bring the Houston Oilers football franchise to town. They did this knowing full well that their water rates were going up and that there was a very real prospect that their property taxes would be raised, which they were—several times. This same scenario has been replicated all across the country. It's sad but true. Don't get me wrong. I wasn't for *any* of the tax increases. On the education referenda, I thought the education bureaucracy was too bloated and they should first demonstrate some responsibility in spending our money before we gave them more. On the football referendum, I was and remain adamantly opposed to corporate welfare. I'm a strict adherent to the Valentine Doctrine. This was a doctrine I developed during the tax debate in Tennessee. It simply says, "Government is there to do only what the private sector won't, can't, or shouldn't do." I was often asked what I would fund in the budget and what I would cut. When I applied that doctrine to each item in the budget, it was easy to cull out the waste.

For example: Will the private sector build golf courses? Yes. Can it? Yes. Should it? Yes. Pretty simple, then. The government should not be in the golf course business. However, the bureaucrats in our state wanted $20 million for new golf courses in the midst of what they called a financial crisis. Let's apply that same test to, say, roads. Will the private sector build roads? Probably not. The only entity that will pay for that is the government. Private companies aren't going to cough up the cash for that. Therefore, that's an area in which the government needs to be involved. Public schools fall into that same category. Sure, there are private schools, but they have the luxury of picking and choosing their clientele. If we want to educate our entire society, public schools are a necessity.

A lady once phoned my show and called me to task on the public funding of education. She didn't understand why her tax dollars should go to educate children when she didn't have any. I asked her where she lived. She said she lived in a rural section of the area. The closest home to hers was about a mile away. "Is there a paved road in front of your house?" I asked. There was. "Why should my taxes go to pay for a road that only you and another family will use? Shouldn't you have to pay to pave and maintain that road?" She got the point. There are some things that are beneficial to society as a whole. Roads and schools are two of them. Don't get me wrong. There's nothing wrong with sending your kids to private school or home schooling. However, most families can't afford to do either. An educated populace is undeniably beneficial to society, therefore we determine public education worthy of tax dollars. I would be the first to argue, however, that those dollars could be used more wisely. Still, public education benefits society, as do paved highways and Tomahawk missiles. These are areas where the private sector alone wouldn't, couldn't, and shouldn't provide for the needs of the people. In those cases we need the government or at least a government/private sector partnership.

Although it wasn't stated exactly the same, this litmus test of limited government was the centerpiece of the founding fathers' philosophy. It's nothing new. I've just concisely worded it so it's easy to understand. They applied essentially the same criteria in deciding where government should be involved. Let me tell you, our founders would be absolutely astonished at how far afield we've gone. Even Federalists like Alexander Hamilton never intended the intrusive, bloated, unwieldy government we have today. In 1802, the entire federal establishment, including the military, consisted of 9,237 people. That worked out to one out of every 1,914 Americans working for the government in some capacity. By 1975, the federal government was employing nearly five million, or one out of every forty-three Americans.[10] By the turn of the twenty-first century, federal agencies boasted that the number of workers employed by the federal government had dropped to around two million. But don't get excited quite yet. To paraphrase Bill Clinton, "It depends upon what the meaning of the word 'employ' is."

Paul C. Light of New York University says the actual number of people working for the government is much higher than the official numbers touted by the government because of what he calls the "shadow of government." Many government agencies have claimed a reduction in employees when they've actually just outsourced the same job to the private sector. Many times it's even the same person who used to perform the same task for the government who now works for a private company. Light puts the actual number of government-paid employees at a staggering seventeen million. That works out to about one out of every fifteen Americans.[11] Some sources put the number at around twenty-one million. Whatever the true number, the primary reason our governments—federal, state, and local—have grown so large is their power to tax. Give them more power to tax, and you invite more power to spend. Conversely, if you limit the taxation you can limit the spending, but the two must be done concurrently.

What politicians who obtain more power to tax have perfected over the years is the ability to consign their guilt to the consciences of the producers. These purveyors of class envy try to make success seem somehow dirty because there are those who go without. These are the same folks who complained that the Atkins diet was discriminatory because the food was too expensive for everyone to afford! I'm not kidding. These are, no doubt, the same people who devised the "progressive" or "graduated" income tax. Jefferson warned of such people. "To take from one because it is thought that his own industry and that of his father's has acquired too much, in order to spare to others, who, or whose fathers have not exercised equal industry and skill," he once wrote, "is to violate arbitrarily the first principle of association, 'the guarantee to every one of a free exercise of his industry and the fruits acquired by it.'"[12]

Wikipedia, an online encyclopedia, describes the rationale for the progressive income tax: "The argument for a progressive tax system is that people with higher income tend to have a higher percentage of that in disposable income, and can thus afford a greater tax burden." And? Just because someone *can* pay more doesn't mean they *should*. I'm sure I can pay more for a gallon of milk than someone just starting out in the working world. Should I have to? Of course not. If we're going to have a federal income tax, it should be flat and fair. Those who make more will automatically pay more in taxes.

It may come as a shock to many reading this book, but I wasn't necessarily opposed, in principle, to a *state* income tax in Tennessee. What I was adamantly against was having both a sales tax *and* an income tax. What I was and continue to be against is more and more taxation without any regard to controlling the spending. Many of the politicians will lie to your face to get their hands on more money. They'll say it's for the children and that old folks are going to die if we don't get more money. They'll say and do anything to feed their insatiable appetite for your hard-earned cash. The founding fathers faced taxation without representation. Today we face taxation with *misrepresentation*.

Again, this notion of choosing your tax is as old as the republic. Thomas Jefferson placed taxes into three categories "with which we are familiar," as he put it: Capital, Income, and Consumption. To tax in more than one category, he reasoned, was "an aggrievance on the citizens." He offered up an example: "If the system be established on the basis of Income, and his just proportion on that scale has been already drawn from every one, to step into the field of Consumption, and tax special articles in that . . . is doubly taxing the same article."[13]

It makes sense, if you think about it. You use your paycheck to purchase goods and services. If that paycheck is taxed, you've paid your fair share. If, however, you pay again every time you purchase something, they're taxing that same paycheck over and over again. That was my primary problem with the state income tax. If you were going to eliminate the sales tax and replace it with an income tax, then we could talk. If you simply wanted to add another tax on top of the one we've got, you're in for a fight.

Initially, I thought, of all the forms of taxation, an income tax was the most stable. Once I started really researching the issue I learned I was wrong. The sales tax has been far more stable for Tennessee than the income tax has been for other states. The modern-day sales tax we know today began in 1932, during the Great Depression, in Mississippi and has spread to nearly every state in the union. The reason state governments turned to the consumption tax at the height of the Depression is that the state income tax was far less stable. It stands to reason that people are still going to buy things if they're out of work, even if they have to borrow to do it. They may not buy as much, but they will still consume and, in turn, pay taxes on those goods. If they're out of work, however, they'll produce absolutely no income. And no income tax.

I also reached the same conclusion as the Mackinac Center for Public Policy when they concluded, "Theory as well as the preponderance of empirical evidence suggest strongly that sales taxes have less adverse impact on a state's economy than do income taxes."[14] It's hard to stimulate an economy when the tax man grabs his share right out of the gate, even before the money has had a chance to circulate. Sales taxes, on the other hand, have proven to be easier to swallow for consumers because they're paid in much smaller increments. The sales tax also gives the taxpayer some power over how much they contribute. Not to mention that it catches those in our society like prostitutes and drug dealers who manage to dodge the income tax. No matter how much those people hide from the income tax, they'll eventually have to buy something.

Also, this notion that the sales tax is regressive because poor people pay a greater percentage of their income in sales tax is nonsense. That's like saying a pair of pants is regressive or a car or a movie ticket. Sure, they pay a greater percentage of their income in sales tax, but they pay a much larger percentage of their income on *everything* they buy than do the rich.

A simple way to look at it is the gas tax. A guy pulls up to the pump and fills up his Rolls Royce. The guy next to him fills up his ten-year-old Buick. They pay exactly the same tax on exactly the same amount of gas. Why? Because they use the exact same amount of road. Does the gas station attendant come out and hit the Rolls owner up for another twenty bucks? No! Since when does the rich guy have to cough up more for schools and libraries and fire and police just because he makes more money? Since the class warmongers started hitting him with a progressive income tax, that's when. But you know what? When that rich guy went to buy that Rolls, he paid a heap more in taxes on it than the Buick owner. You can also bet that he buys more expensive clothes and eats at more expensive restaurants and buys all sorts of expensive items for his expensive home. And he pays taxes on all of it! You see, those who make more generally spend more, thus they pay more in sales taxes. That's the way the founding fathers envisioned it. Never did they dream that we'd be penalizing hard-working, industrious citizens. But that's what the graduated income tax does.

This country is built on hard work and industriousness. We're driven by the promise of the American dream that says we're free to achieve what our minds can conceive. But we're a very patriotic bunch here in the U.S., too. We don't mind paying for things we think are necessary to preserve our freedoms. Prior to World War II, income taxes were paid in a lump sum at the end of the year. Because of the war, the government began withholding money from paychecks in order to have a steady stream of cash to fight the war.[15] Hardly anyone batted an eye. Of course, after the war ended, the practice continued. Although the cause was certainly worthy, there was a tremendous amount of waste in government, but winning the war was paramount in the minds of Americans.

Even in the midst of the War of 1812, Thomas Jefferson warned of extravagant taxes. With the passage of the direct tax, he saw that the politicians were gouging the taxpayers in the name of patriotism. He urged his countrymen not to blindly and obediently open their purses, saying, "If anything could revolt our citizens against the war, it would be the extravagance with which they are about to be taxed." He added, "that although the evils of resistance are great, those of submission would be greater."[16] That's been the dilemma we've faced throughout our storied history in this country. How much is enough? That's the question we have struggled with in Tennessee. Oftentimes, as in our case, the answer becomes apparent. Enough is enough.

Three

STORM THE BASTILLE

On June 9, 2000, after getting the tip about Bob Rochelle's income tax scheme, I spoke directly with Hawkeye. I had relayed the information in the waning moments of the show, but I must confess, I thought Johnny B had gotten it wrong. Once I got the story straight from Hawkeye, a chill ran down my spine. There was no mistake. They planned to run the income tax the very next day. This particular incarnation of the tax would apply to incomes over $100,000, but, of course, no income tax remains just the burden of the wealthy, never mind the fact that taxing only a certain segment of society is patently unjust and discriminatory. When our current federal income tax began, more than 90 percent of Americans were exempt from filing.[1] Try finding anyone who is exempt today! Regardless of who was being taxed, I couldn't believe what I was hearing. We had worked so hard.

More common-sense voices, like State Representative Bill Dunn, a Republican from Knoxville, advocated freezing the current budget and making minor adjustments. He proposed such a budget in the House with State Senator Marsha Blackburn as the Senate sponsor. "Since the governor has insisted on presenting a budget based on an income tax that the people don't want, I feel we should have an alternative—working with the existing budget and adding to it . . . not taking a budget that's too big and cutting from it," he said.[2] The pro-income-tax forces made sure the Dunn bill went nowhere.

I feared there was nothing we could do to stop the income tax juggernaut. Having not gotten the message until just before I left the air on Friday, I was afraid there would be no way to alert enough people in time to make a difference. That Friday night, I wrote in my journal:

They have the votes to pass it and expect to do just that shortly after they convene tomorrow at 1:00 PM. [Hawkeye] had hoped I could warn the people before I got off and put pressure on the lawmakers but feared now it was a done deal. Those sneaky bastards are trying to pass an income tax when they think no one's looking. Taxing the rich is just the foot in the door to taxing everyone, and I feel helpless to stop it.

The morning of Saturday June 10, 2000, I groggily pulled myself out of bed. After learning of Senator Rochelle's planned tax scheme the afternoon before, I spent a largely sleepless night, tossing and turning, concerned as to what should be done about this inevitable vote. What could I do? I wouldn't be back on the air until Monday afternoon. By then, we may already have a state income tax. Before I finished my first cup of coffee, the phone calls began. Complete strangers, many just concerned citizens who felt helpless in light of what was about to happen, pleaded for me to help. As I fretted over our conundrum, I resigned myself to the fact that nothing could be done. I planned to go swimming and forget about it, a promise I had made to my young sons.

But the calls continued. One caller had inside information that the vote was scheduled for a Saturday specifically because they knew talk radio opponents wouldn't be on the air. This Saturday vote, they claimed, was not merely happenstance. It was a concerted effort on the part of Rochelle, Sundquist, and their cronies. They fully expected to pull the wool over everyone's eyes. My blood boiled. We had been fighting this income tax for a solid year, and I didn't want to let them win this way. I *couldn't* let them win this way—this cowardly way of quickly passing the tax on a weekend, then slinking back to their districts, claiming they were forced to find new revenue "for the children." I could imagine Rochelle taking a deep drag from his cigarette, his twisted grin turning into a demented smile as the vote was tallied. I could see the sniveling backroom dealers divvying up the spoils of the new tax, the governor retiring to the executive mansion with the satisfaction that he had out-foxed the people.

I placed a call to State Senator Marsha Blackburn at 10:30 AM. She confirmed the ugly truth, that the General Assembly was preparing to ramrod a state income tax through that very day. They were scheduled to convene at 1:00 PM with a vote shortly thereafter. This proposal, it was thought, would be more palatable to the citizens of the state because of the higher threshold. This was a tax on the rich, so they said—people making over $100,000 per year. Who would possibly be against that (except for the very wealthy, and they didn't have the numbers to launch a massive protest)? But Marsha and I both knew this was the proverbial camel's nose under the tent. Once Rochelle was given the key to the vault there would be no question but that he would want everything in it. Marsha urged me to help them fight it. "I don't know that there's anything I can do," I informed her, helplessly.

"Just tell the people the truth," she said.

I sat there for a moment holding the phone in my hand. "Just tell the people the truth." Those words echoed in my mind. In a mere moment I considered everything, explored every angle. I weighed my chances of being effective against my desire to rest and relax and not have to deal with the problem. I thought about the consequences if I didn't act. Then, suddenly, I made up my mind. I guess I knew all along what must be done. I knew I couldn't live with myself if I didn't at least put up a fight. Talk radio had led the charge against this unconstitutional tax by informing the citizens about what was really going on with the state budget. Talk radio would be there for the showdown of a vote, even if we met defeat.

I quickly pressed the hang-up button on the phone, released it for a dial tone, then punched in the number of our program director, Billy Shears. Heretofore, the war against the tax had been relatively conventional. They proposed new ways to generate revenue, and those of us opposed to new or higher taxes pointed out the waste in government and encouraged living within our means. We talk show hosts then invited our listeners to call their representatives and voice their concerns. With the knowledge of Rochelle's surreptitious plan, the rules had changed. It was time to take the fight to the next level. It was time to unleash our secret weapon.

I informed our program director that I wanted to stage a special broadcast of *The Phil Valentine Show* at high noon on Legislative Plaza, directly in front of the State Capitol for the hour leading up to the vote. He resisted at first, arguing that it would be difficult to get the proper permits on such short notice and urging me to broadcast from the studio with live reports from our news team. I insisted that the only way we stood a chance of defeating this tax was with a massive show of force. He wondered just how many people would be actually listening on a Saturday, a problem that had also crossed my mind. Still, I painted a picture of cars encircling the Capitol blowing their horns in protest, and he agreed it would have more impact than a studio broadcast. The question was, could we put it all together in ninety minutes? He asked if I minded if Steve Gill joined me. Of course not. I welcomed the help. He and I had been a relentless team against the income tax. It was only appropriate that we fight this latest attempt side-by-side.

We had seen a remarkable turnout at the first horn-blowing protest with our cluster of stations back in November, two days after I testified before the Senate Finance Committee and the income tax was headed for the Senate floor. I was mesmerized by its effectiveness. I had witnessed everything from Cadillacs to beat-up trucks to city buses participating. It was a genuinely moving and patriotic experience. We hoped to duplicate it before the big vote, but this time our task would be much more difficult. Unlike the first horn-honking, which was staged as merely a way to get their attention as they deliberated over the tax options, this was a red alert. Back then, they didn't have the votes. Now they did, and we weren't sure we could alert the people in time.

Also, instead of five or six stations teaming together, there would be just one, on a Saturday, no less, when our listenership was at its lowest level. While the last demonstration had more of a party atmosphere, this one was deadly serious. We needed as many bodies and horns down there as we could muster, but under the circumstances, that would be a long shot. Still, we hoped to capture at least part of that excitement and enthusiasm of the first protest. We would need that kind of passion to defeat this latest attempt.

Steve Gill was certainly no stranger to politics. He knew the inner workings of how deals like this were struck. He also knew there was no way to beat them at their own game. As effective as we had been disseminating information, informing the listeners of swing votes, and giving out telephone numbers, they had obviously found a way around all that pressure. Now it was time to combine our efforts in a little guerrilla warfare down at the State Capitol.

After I hung up with Shears, I called Patrick Hennessy, Steve's producer. Patrick always had his ear to the ground, and I wanted to compare notes. His sources were telling him the same thing: the state income tax was in the bag. He had been in touch with Steve, but like me, Steve was hesitant to broadcast on Saturday. I knew exactly how he felt. The last thing I wanted to do was spend the whole day in the scorching sun, talking until I was hoarse, on the outside chance it would make a difference. But we both knew that we were the last line of defense. Once Patrick informed Steve of our plans, he was ready to roll and agreed to meet me there. I offered my apologies to Susan and the boys and headed out the door.

STAKING OUT OUR POSITION

I arrived at Legislative Plaza just before noon to find our two promotions guys, Keith Kaufman and Jeremy Bennefield, feverishly setting up the remote equipment. As the sun beat down on our heads, I laid out my notes on the broadcast table. It was a very humid eighty-eight degrees. The pavement made it even hotter. I glanced up and down the street in front of us, devoid of any cars or pedestrians. It was eerily quiet, like the calm before a storm. There was nobody in sight. I fully expected a tumbleweed to blow across the street. The Capitol building loomed directly in front of us, more like a solemn monument of sandstone and marble than a beehive of hidden activity. We were all alone on Legislative Plaza, save the occasional legislator or aide who chose the broad daylight access to the Capitol across the plaza instead of the private tunnel underneath the street. Like birds in anticipation of a torrential downpour, legislative aides scurried about below street level, stuffing their boss's hands full of the latest tax proposal information and whispering the anticipated vote count.

Keith and Jeremy lit the fuse on the broadcast, and the newscast boomed from our speakers, the tell-tale sign that we had a connection with the studio. Steve Gill crossed the street and joined me at the table just as the news was ending. We shook hands, both nervously excited about what might transpire. He shared my trepidation about the crowd. These were unchartered waters. We really didn't know what to expect.

As we prepared for the broadcast, a young legislative staffer skipped across the street separating Legislative Plaza from the State Capitol. As he neared the middle of the street, he turned, walking backwards, and stared back at us. "Ooooh, nice crowd," he sniffed, then turned and bounded up the steps to the Senate chambers. I feared he might get the last laugh. Yet what this sniveling little staffer didn't realize was that we had not yet begun our broadcast. We were still in the top-of-the-hour news. We were still moments away from cracking open the microphone and letting Rochelle's cat out of the bag.

At six minutes after noon, the familiar strains of my theme song bounced off the walls of the Capitol building. The fight was on. The sound of our voices booming through large speakers against the still of a Saturday afternoon must've sounded strange to those inside. Curious eyes peeked out from behind velvet curtains in the Capitol.

I came on the air, not with alarm in my voice, but shock, really. "For those of you just joining us," I began, "it looks like we're going to have an income tax." The only sound in the background was the steady hum of our generator. It was *that* quiet.

Senator Marsha Blackburn was at the microphone with us. "This is something they've been trying to cook up in backroom, deal-making, smoke-filled-room meetings," she said, solemnly. She added that the deal was put together so quickly that there was nothing yet available on paper for her to review. "I called this morning at 9:37 over to the department of finance and administration to see if I could get a copy of the plan," she said. "I said, 'If I'm going to vote no on something, I at least want to know what I'm voting no on.'" According to the Senate agenda, senators would have just thirty minutes to look over the bill before a vote was taken.

Representative Bill Dunn was listening from his legislative office and called the show six minutes into our broadcast. "The people in the Nashville area have the unique opportunity," he said, "to come down here and participate, physically, in the process. It's time for those who want to hang on to their money and spend it the way *they* see fit to meet their family needs, they need to get up out of the chair or stop wherever they're going in their car and turn around and come downtown and let people know what they think."

"Indeed," I added, "we need to have people come down here and honk their horns and let these people *hear* your outrage." No sooner had I made the plea when a lone honker sounded his horn. The game was on.

After my interviews with Marsha Blackburn and Bill Dunn, Steve Gill warned the listeners, "Hey folks, you're going to wake up Monday morning with a little surprise. This legislature doesn't have the guts to make public policy in the public policy arena. That is the worst thing about the whole process."

At that early point in the broadcast, we had maybe a dozen or so cars driving by and blowing their horns. A handful of protestors began to trickle onto the sidewalk to either side of our broadcast table. It was small, but it was a start. I looked up at the Capitol and could see different individuals now pulling back curtains to get a better look at the commotion below, curious but totally undisturbed. Some punched colleagues and pointed down at the skimpy crowd, chuckling to one another.

Representative Mae Beavers joined us on the air. As she began to speak, we had to pause to allow a large truck horn to pass. She was furious at the scant amount of time they were being given to see the tax plan. "We can ask questions," she said "but when you haven't had time to look at it to see what's in it, how can you ask many questions?"

Slowly and steadily the crowd began to swell. My confidence began to build with each additional protestor, but I was far from confident that we could attract more than twenty or thirty people. The horns began to overpower our microphones fifteen minutes into the broadcast. Steve and I began to ratchet up the urgency. Representative David Davis, an income tax opponent, called in from his office inside the Capitol and was completely drowned out by the horns. I apologized for not being able to hear him above the noise.

"That's okay," Davis replied. "That's what I like to hear. The only way these people are going to get the message that we don't need an income tax is for people to be down here honking their horns and being seen outside."

Raymond Baker, a political consultant who opposed the income tax, called in. Listening to the horns in the background, he said, "It sounds like with what y'all are doing, that folks aren't quite as asleep as they were hoping we'd be."

If they were asleep they were certainly waking up now. When we came back from the commercial break at 12:35 PM, the horns were constant. No longer was there just the sporadic burst, it was wall-to-wall horn-honking. Angry callers lined up on our phone lines to express their rage. We had a full bank of callers, and I had yet to give out the number. The people were not pleased, and they couldn't wait to blow off some steam on the radio.

I reiterated the point that the whole sneak attack was happening because the tax-pushers thought talk radio would not be able to respond. "We may doze," I said, "but we never close. We're here to make sure that you know what's going on, even if they don't want you to know."

Robert, an outraged listener, called in on his way out of town. "If we have Republicans—and I am one—that vote for this, they better find another dadgum state to live in because they're not going to survive here!"

We got news reports from inside the Capitol from our news director, Ted Werbin. At around 12:40 PM, he said, "I can tell you that the people up here are hearing the horns. Whether it's going to have any impact or not, I don't know." He added, "I was just in the Senate chamber where they're posting additional security in the balcony. All I can tell you at this point is, the building is starting to fill up a little bit. There are people milling about now, and I think people listening to the horns are, perhaps, getting a little bit antsy."

By 12:45 PM, the handful of motorists joining our protest had suddenly turned into hundreds of automobiles encircling the Capitol in both directions with horns blaring. It was deafening. I could hardly hear myself talking in my own headphones, let alone hear Steve. Protestors now lined both sides of the street holding homemade signs ranging from "No Income Tax" to "Sundquist & Rochelle—Enemies of the State."

People brought their spouses, their kids, their dogs. The crowd more resembled what you'd see at a church picnic, except they were protesting, and they were loud. I was in total disbelief and amazement that so many people had turned out on such short notice. I remember my nervous excitement turning to downright giddiness. Steve and I were inspired by the response, which only made us bark louder into the microphone to build the crowd even larger. We were counting down the minutes until they went back into session at 1:00 PM.

In the meantime, those who had hatched the income tax plan in a Conference Committee meeting had been burrowed away, deep down inside the belly of the Capitol, comparing notes and taking a head count. They were totally oblivious to the noise outside until they emerged. State Senator Marsha Blackburn gleefully recalled "when they came up the escalator and they were turning around and they were going 'What is happening?'"

A few Nashville police officers slipped into the crowd just in case they were needed. They mostly stood there and observed, many with smiles on their faces. Had they not been in uniform, they would have been protesting, too. Passing motorists dropped off water and food for Steve and me. Being novices to this whole protest idea, we didn't erect a broadcast tent as we would on all future protests. Instead, we baked in the June sun as the temperature flirted with ninety and urged the crowd to grow stronger and louder. It was extremely hot, but we weren't about to give up. If these folks were willing to stand out on that blazing sidewalk, then we were willing to stand our ground as long as it took. How many different motorists participated in the protest is hard to pin down. There had to have been hundreds. They just kept coming and coming and coming. Those on foot numbered in the hundreds, as well.

The large crowd captured the attention of the TV news cameras. They waded into the multitude as the once-amused faces behind the curtains in the Capitol melted into concern, then sheer panic. Lydia Lenker, a reporter for WTVF-TV in Nashville, passed our table and shouted, "Why are you against this tax?" never stopping for a response. Once set up across the street with the Capitol as the backdrop, she labeled the horn-honkers the "Lexus Brigade." By my count, there was one Lexus in the whole crowd, a guy who became a regular but left his Lexus at home after that first day. The rest were ordinary cars driven by ordinary people who knew that taxing the rich was just the beginning. Eventually they would be targeted as well.

Paul Shanklin, a good friend of mine and the guy who produced and voiced all those wonderful song parodies for Rush Limbaugh's radio show, just happened to be in town from Memphis recording his latest CD. He heard the commotion and dropped by just before we ended the first hour's broadcast. "People that are away, they're at the boat, they're at the lake, or whatever, come Monday they're going to go, 'What!?!'" he said. "I just couldn't believe it. Driving up here I'm thinking, how deaf *are* these guys."

Delay Tactics

We ended the first hour. Having originally planned just a one-hour broadcast, there was no way we were going anywhere, not with this kind of response. I announced that we would stay until there was a vote or they went home, no matter how long that took. The top-of-the-hour break gave me a chance to stretch my legs during the news. I walked over and thanked the protesters on the sidewalk and began to really drink in the history of the moment. The feeling I had is almost indescribable. It was easily the most patriotic feeling I had ever experienced. It was far more exciting and exhilarating than I could've ever imagined, and I was engulfed in emotions.

I never really had a sense of what it meant to be truly involved in the American process until that day. Most of us live our lives, taking our freedom for granted. Now I was at the epicenter of a citizens' movement fighting to beat back an unconstitutional tax. This was exactly what made our country great; the ideals of our founding fathers and the freedom to express those ideals in such a public demonstration.

I scanned the faces in the crowd. It was almost as if I inspected each face in slow motion. I took special notice of their facial expressions, noting the shapes of their mouths as they shouted, the emotion in their eyes, the passion in their voices. These people were feeling the same thing I was feeling. There was a certain confidence in our numbers. There was a definitive, tangible feeling that we were on the right side of history, that we were standing up for the principles that created this country. You could actually feel the excitement swelling up inside of you. The spirit of our founding fathers was all around us, and we knew it. We could taste it. We were battling a disconnected and unresponsive government. The people were there to take back their government from those who had abused the privilege of running it. I was not just happy to be there, I was immensely proud.

PUSHING THEM BACK

The House and Senate both convened at 1:00 PM, held their normal prayers, then recessed to give the income tax advocates more time to wrangle up the votes. Steve and I continued our frantic plea into the second hour for all able-bodied citizens to make their way to the Capitol. We hit them with facts about the budget and details of how the whole dirty deal came down behind closed doors. "If this is such good public policy," Steve shouted into the microphone, "why are they afraid to do it in public?"

At one point the noise was so deafening I stopped to let our listeners soak it in. "You hear that?" I asked, directing my question not only to those who hadn't made it down yet but to the General Assembly members holed up in their offices tuned in to our show while awaiting word on when to vote. "That's the sound of freedom!" The incessant sound of automobile horns continued.

Inside the Capitol, terror had been struck in the hearts of those fence-sitters who had agreed to the Rochelle plan. They imagined a quiet Saturday, a difficult vote, and time to deal with their guilty consciences on the drive home. Nobody expected a civil revolt. Even separated by thick blocks of sandstone, concrete, and marble, the noise outside penetrated, ever so slightly, both chambers. Each time the large doors opened to allow a senator to enter or exit, the sound grew louder until the door slowly swung shut. Senators eyed each other nervously. This was much more than they had bargained for when they agreed to Rochelle's plan. His support was starting to unravel. The original vote, scheduled for 1:00 PM was pushed back until 3:30 PM.

Steve and I continued with the pressure. We pleaded for more and more people to come join us, and come they did. The crowd now covered not only the sidewalks in front of the Capitol but also a good bit of Legislative Plaza behind where we were broadcasting, as well as the granite steps leading up to the Capitol doors. Protesters chanted "Ax the tax!" and "No new taxes!" There was a small group of pro-income-tax protesters, primarily state employees, that seemed out of place and overwhelmed by the anti-tax throng. One circled the Capitol with her thirteen-year-old daughter who hung out the window waving a homemade "Yes taxes" sign. "Rich people got to pay!" the little girl shouted, obviously indoctrinated in class warfare by her mother.[3] The mother/daughter team were, by far, the exception and not the rule. The mass of humanity visible from the Capitol offices was decidedly anti-income-tax and unquestionably angry. When the leadership looked out and saw we had no intention of leaving, the vote was then rescheduled for 4:00 PM, then again for 5:30 PM. We had not only held our ground, we had begun to push them back.

Speaker Naifeh wearily approached the podium and announced to nervous House members, "We are still working on a solution to the budget. We get close and then we get apart. If you'll let us have a little more time, we're working, and we're trying to get you out of here. . . . I'm tired, and I know you are." Members who had waited all day for some kind of vote on something, anything, grumbled to one another.

"Fellas, we might as well just be stumps in the forest," said Representative Phillip Pinion, in disgust.[4]

As the sun beat down on the multitude of anti-tax protesters, both on the sidewalks and in their cars, honking their horns, a small contingent of pro-income-tax protesters came marching across Legislative Plaza toward the Capitol. About twenty-five of them, primarily union folks and state employees, waded into the anti-tax crowd. One carried a sign reading, "Tax You & The Lexus You Rode In On!!" obviously a reference to reporter Lydia Lenker's Lexus Brigade comment. One pro-tax protester made our case for us. "People hear the word 'tax' and it immediately turns them off. But if people were truly aware of the additional state services, I think quite a few of them would have a change of heart."[5] That was the point. We didn't *want* any new state services!

Although the teachers' union people were there, they certainly were not representing the actual teachers. One Tennessee teacher said, "I don't need a tax to make me a good teacher."[6] Amen. I would venture to say that nobody at our rally was against paying teachers a decent salary. However, the union insists on raises for all teachers, the bad as well as the good. That's not the way the real world works. I'm more than thrilled to pay good teachers more, but to just keep throwing more money at the teachers' union is lunacy. There needs to be accountability. Not only with teachers but in all facets of government spending. That's the salient point that brought all of these protesters together. They were sick and tired of seeing state spending increase at outrageous levels with absolutely no one being held accountable.

As the day wore on, more and more people continued to show up. Several were bringing stacks of cut-up cardboard boxes to use as makeshift signs. Depending on what was going on inside, they would grab their Magic Markers and a piece of cardboard and scribble their sentiments down in big, bold letters.

Five-thirty came and went, and the protesters were still there. The income tax leaders called the House/Senate conferees back together at 6:30 PM to try to salvage the tax. Witnessing the pandemonium outside all afternoon weakened the resolve of those fence-sitters who had been convinced to go along the day before. Support for the tax began to unravel, and the meeting deteriorated into a sea of confusion. State Representative Ulysses Jones, a pro-income-tax Democrat from Memphis, was exasperated with the whole affair. He turned to a colleague who was watching the spectacle unfold in front of them. "You know when you're at the circus and the little car comes out with all the clowns that don't know where they're going?" he said, gesturing to a group of lawmakers gathered at the front of the Conference Committee hearing room who all seemed to talk at once.[7]

Tax pushers finally reached the conclusion they were getting nowhere. At around 8:30 PM, the General Assembly was sent home, and another vote was scheduled for 1:00 PM on Monday. Protesters cheered and hugged one another and high-fived each other as horn-honkers laid on their horns as hard as ever, shrieking for joy out the windows. The people were elated with the power they had wielded.

State Senator Douglas Henry, a twenty-nine-year veteran of the Senate, said he had never seen a more chaotic and pressurized end to a session.[8] We had won the day, but we were far from winning the war. Rochelle and Sundquist were doggedly determined to pass the tax. With enough arm-twisting and sweet-talking they could conceivably pull enough lawmakers over to their camp for one vote, and one vote is all it would take. As State Senator Marsha Blackburn so aptly put it, "They only have to win once. We have to win every time."

Rochelle and Sundquist must've thought that surely this throng that showed up en masse on a Saturday would not be able to return in the middle of a work day. The pro-income-tax pushers were addled, but they were not, by any means, swayed from their mission. If anything, they were more determined than ever to shut us down. The next battle was to be at the very same location in less than forty-eight hours.

Although Steve and I were pleased with the results of our efforts, we also questioned whether we could draw a crowd at 1 PM on a Monday. One thing was for certain. We were now confident enough to try.

LET THE SPIN BEGIN

Even though there were thousands of people down at the Capitol, this issue would be decided by the hundreds of thousands, if not millions, who would not be able to attend. That's where the media spin came in handy. As much media bias as I've seen in my day, I was stunned by the blatant attempt that was made to completely misrepresent what happened that Saturday. Lydia Lenker from WTVF-TV reported that "the most expensive cars money can buy" turned out for the protest. She repeated her depiction of the horn-honking protest as "The Lexus Brigade."

Paula Wade, a pro-tax reporter for the *Memphis Commercial Appeal*, picked up on Lydia's cue. She described the parade of vehicles around the Capitol as "high-dollar automobiles from Mercedes-Benz, Lexus, Range Rover, and BMW. Nashville multimillionaire car dealership owner Lee Beaman was among the protesters, as was former state TennCare director Rusty Seibert, who is independently wealthy."[9] Nowhere in her article was there any mention of the pickup trucks, the Buicks, the Hondas, and the service vehicles driven by ordinary citizens who were wise to what was happening behind their backs. Sure, Lee Beaman and Rusty Seibert were there. They were just as alarmed as anyone that an income tax was about to pass. However, there were thousands of other citizens who weren't rich, but who knew they would not remain exempt.

Lydia ended her piece by having her cameraman zoom in on a father and his little girl who remained on the sidewalk long after the protest was over. As the camera panned back over to Lydia, she remarked, "These protesters don't even have jobs. They've just come out to join the excitement." Now, wait a minute. I thought this was the

Lexus Brigade. I thought this was a protest of the well-heeled. It was obvious, or at least it should have been, that Lydia was propagandizing. She would later claim she got threats on her life and would try to blame it on me. I never once urged anyone to harm her, but I certainly did point out her biased reporting. When you blatantly lie about an issue as emotional as the income tax, you have to expect some folks are going to get angry. The responsibility lies entirely with her.

The *Tennessean* newspaper barely made mention of the protest in their lead, front-page story on Sunday morning. The delay in the tax vote was entirely due to the citizens outside, but they only got one line near the end of the article: "Outside, income tax opponents urged on by radio talk show hosts Phil Valentine and Steve Gill circled Legislative Plaza in front of the Capitol building, honking their horns and waving signs," they reported.[10] Another article focused on the protest but noted that the *pro*-tax protesters "*bravely* carried signs with slogans like 'Tennessee taxes help the poor/God loves the poor'"[12] (emphasis added). The article also characterized it as a rich man's protest, then proceeded to point out that some of the homemade signs contained bad grammar and were misspelled. Bad grammar and typos don't tend to be hallmarks of the rich. Another article dealt exclusively with the eight other states without an income tax and how their situations were completely different from ours. In other words, they could sustain an adequate tax base without an income tax, but we couldn't.

The point that was lost in all of these reports—print and television—was the diversity represented at the protest. We had rich, middle class, and poor. We had black and white, male and female, young and old. This was an issue that touched everyone, and they responded. The news media were confounded. At first some television reporters tried to completely ignore talk radio's role in the protests, but as time wore on it became harder and harder to explain to TV viewers that people just materialized in front of the Capitol with no prompting.

THEY'RE BA-A-ACK

Monday, June 12, 2000—Just two days after we thwarted their initial sneak attack, Rochelle and his henchmen were back in action. Steve Gill and his morning show partner, Terry Hopkins, broadcast from our spot in front of the Capitol. Since the vote wasn't scheduled until 1:30 PM, the urgency was not there. A decent-sized crowd showed up for the horn-honking but nothing like we'd seen on Saturday. I wondered if we'd be able to draw an adequate crowd to scare them off when the vote came down.

I grabbed a paper that morning to see what kind of propaganda was coming from the other side, and the Tennessean was at it again with this front-page headline: "Middle-Class Retirees Gain Most under the Proposed Income Tax." In their attempt to paint the anti-income-taxers as the "evil rich," they included lines like, "Allied against the tax are wealthy Tennesseans and business interests that see the tax as hurting their bottom lines."[11] They didn't mention that the alliance also included truck drivers, salespeople, and little old ladies on fixed incomes who all saw the proposed income tax as the beginning of a bad dream.

In one of the more bizarre twists to the story, I began receiving calls at home from the wife of one of the pro-tax lawmakers. I don't dare reveal her name here. I will simply refer to her as "Hot Lips." This partic-ular lawmaker had no idea his wife was calling me. As far as I know, he doesn't know to this day. Although Hot Lips never let on to him, she was vehemently against the income tax. She would call and feed me inside information about when they were meeting and what they were up to. She would clue me in on strategy and what they were saying about me behind my back. No one lawmaker was in control of the events as they unfolded, but her insight was extremely helpful. It allowed us to stay a step ahead of them, and she confided that they were frustrated and enraged that we seemed to know what they would do next. That wasn't entirely because of the information I gleaned from Hot Lips, but I was able to put enough of the pieces of the puzzle together, with her help, to get a pretty good picture of what was going on.

As promised, the General Assembly was back and ready for action Monday, and so were we. This time our competitor, WTN radio, also showed up but set up on the other end of Legislative Plaza, away from all the action. We had already staked out the prime real estate directly in front of the Capitol, and this time we had a broadcast tent which made the sunshine much more bearable.

I would be less than honest if I said there wasn't competition between certain stations to "own" certain events. Steve Gill and I felt a certain ownership of the tax revolt since we had been at the forefront of the issue. That's not to say that other stations weren't within their rights to take a stand, too. But we had originated the horn-honking protest and were perfecting it. It's only natural that we would be a little protective over it. However, in the long run, Steve and I understood that the common cause was bigger than any petty rivalries.

Darrell Ankarlo, WTN's morning man, had been railing against the tax on his morning show. He had brought his show down to Legislative Plaza the prior November, the day before we started the horn-honking. He had also returned the day of the honking for our massive five-station protest. In the latest round, WTN had been conspicuously absent. They had chosen, for whatever reason, not to come down on Saturday when the vote was scheduled to take place. When Ankarlo showed back up on Monday, some from WLAC were not happy. Of course, we had no right to keep him from the event, but some saw it as an encroachment on our territory since we had worked long and hard that previous Saturday as the only station involved.

I must admit, though, Darrell won me over. I became convinced his intentions were honorable when he brought his microphone over to cover a spontaneous rally Steve and I were holding. He carried our speeches live on his station. That was an indication on his part that partisan radio rivalry could be set aside for a common goal. From that point on, Ankarlo and WTN attended many of the protests, and we peacefully co-existed.

Dave Ramsey's motives were never really suspect. Dave, WTN's financial guru, and I had worked together when I was doing the WTN morning show several years prior. He was never a "radio guy" and never wanted to be. His approach to his own show and his success in syndication have always been a direct result of the fact that he didn't think like a radio guy. Not only did Dave join in the protest from a fiscally conservative point of view, he even went so far as to talk about my efforts in the tax fight and give my Web address out during his show. Had he been a direct employee of WTN he might have found himself in hot water, but Dave enjoyed the autonomy of a syndicated show. We were facing a crisis, and he wanted his listeners to respond. If they could gather valuable information at my Web site, so be it.

As it would play out, we would need all the help Dave and Darrell were willing to give. The forces pushing the state income tax were much stronger than we had bargained for. People were folding under their pressure. It was up to us to remind them of who was boss—the citizens who put them in office. Several were in dire need of a spine transplant, and we would need more steady hands than showed up on that first Saturday to assist in that operation.

Many people who could not attend the protests were formulating their opinions based on what they read in the newspapers, and what they were reading was decidedly pro-income-tax. One of the few exceptions to the agenda writing at the *Tennessean* was a young reporter named Kate Miller. That Monday, after the initial Saturday sneak attack by Rochelle and his forces, she came by our broadcast table for a short interview.

Over the years, I've developed a sense about reporters. I can usually tell by their questions, their mannerisms, their eye contact—or lack thereof—where they're coming from and whether or not they have an agenda. Kate struck me as fair. She'd only been on the job at the paper less than a week, she informed me. Hopefully, she hadn't been there long enough to develop an opinion about me through other reporters or to be corrupted by the liberal-leaners in the newsroom, which were plentiful. I told her about the Lydia Lenker report and the "Lexus Brigade" accusation and urged her to observe the horn-honkers for herself. She assured me she would, asked a few more questions, then left. A little later, she stopped back by merely to let me know what was going on inside the Capitol building. A nice gesture, I thought. Was I wrong to trust her? Was she playing me? If she was, it was working.

We preempted our regular syndicated programming, and Johnny B and I took over at 9:00 AM. The crowd slowly began to build. By noon we were back to the fevered pitch of Saturday. Many of the originals were there, but there were many new faces as well. Protesters once again lined the sidewalks. A small, pitiful contingent of pro-income-tax protesters huddled together in a group of about six or seven, holding their signs touting the income tax as "for the children." Of course, these were a small number of union state employees who wanted an across-the-board pay raise instead of having to earn a raise on their own merits. I suspect an income tax was the only way these particular employees would ever see more money. The prospect of actually earning it was completely foreign to them. The regular rank-and-file state employees were on the job, many supporting our efforts. What added insult to injury was the fact that these pro-income-tax protesters were on the clock!

As I learned later, Randy Rinks, a Democrat from Savannah, Tennessee, had proposed the House version of the income tax in a secret meeting the prior Thursday, one day before Hawkeye tipped me off. Rinks had once commented that a constituent told him if he voted for Governor Don Sundquist's business tax proposal, he "wouldn't need but one fish for [his] fish fry."[13] Although Rinks may have been afraid to tax businesses, he obviously had no compunction when it came to taxing individuals. The Rinks scheme was agreed upon in one of many secret meetings held by legislators and senators behind closed doors that clearly violated the state's Open Meetings Law. While I updated the listeners with the latest information we had, Jimmy Naifeh, the speaker of the House, was marshaling his troops to pass the tax in his chamber.

Naifeh was the quintessential Southern lawmaker. He slightly resembled Humphrey Bogart as a heavy in one of his darker movies, but he was more a caricature of a backwoods wheeler-dealer. His penchant for wearing those white "ice cream suits" only added to the clown-like atmosphere that surrounded him. I only saw him show his face outside during a protest once. He and a few of his cronies ventured a mere step or two outside the massive iron doors just across the street from our position from a doorway that led into the belly of the Capitol. He waved at me with a big, exaggerated grin, then tugged on the lapels of his white suit while bouncing on the balls of his feet. I thought, perhaps, he wanted to strike up a dialogue, so I called out and invited him over. The smile suddenly drained from his face. He waved me off, shoulders shaking with a sarcastic chuckle, as he turned and disappeared behind the large doors. It was only later that his incongruous behavior made sense. A caller to Steve Gill's show had called Speaker Naifeh an "A-rab Boss Hogg," referring to his Lebanese ancestry. Apparently Naifeh thought I made the comment. It wasn't the first time, nor would it be the last, that I would be erroneously accused of saying or doing something. It came with the territory.

Like any big-spending liberal, Speaker Naifeh was frothing at the mouth over the billion-plus dollars in extra revenue the income tax would bring in. Unbeknownst to many outside the House, he had been corralling votes for some time and was ready to act if the Senate came through—even before, if necessary.

Orchestrating all of this like some maniacal puppeteer was Governor Sundquist. He pulled every string available to him to apply pressure. I wrote in my journal that night:

[Sundquist's] unnatural fixation with this income tax is baffling, especially in light of the fact that he campaigned twice with this as his centerpiece. He repeatedly vowed to never allow an income tax. I so wish I knew the true story behind his conversion. I can't imagine that it would be pleasant.

Just before noon, Darrell Ankarlo from WTN approached me with a great idea that would put an exclamation point on the whole horn-honking affair. At 12:30 PM, both stations urged listeners to blow their horns for a solid minute. You don't think of sixty seconds as being that long until you hear hundreds of horns blowing simultaneously. It was absolutely deafening. I later got word that we made our point with those inside. Even the thick walls couldn't muffle all those horns blasting at once.

One-thirty came and went. No vote from the Senate. The anxious crowd gathered around our tent to hear what was going to happen. Speaker Naifeh, apparently impatient with the Senate's inaction, called the House into session. He was mad at being thwarted on Saturday, and he was determined to pass that tax. He whipped his soldiers into line and headed for a roll-call vote. The angry crowd outside was louder than ever. The hallowed halls of the Capitol softly echoed with chants and the distant blaring of a thousand horns. Lawmakers wiped the sweat from their brows. The noise from outside was probably more effective in the hushed tones caused by the marble and concrete. Almost like a gnat, it was a constant subtle distraction.

Democrat House members sat anxiously at their desks as Republican members pow-wowed downstairs. All there was to do while they waited was listen to the horns blaring outside and be alone with their consciences. The tension was as thick as the smoke in one of Bob Rochelle's backroom meetings. Members patted their brows with their handkerchiefs, checked their watches, gazed up at the empty podium, then over to the large doors at the rear of the chamber. They knew that any moment the Republicans would walk through those doors and the vote would be on, the vote of their life. Still the incessant horns continued outside, an endless drone that seemed to know no end. The sound began to echo in their ears, like some form of sadistic torture. Why don't they stop? Please, make them stop!

Suddenly, one lawmaker dropped to the floor: Kathryn Bowers, a pro-tax Democrat. Doctors were called in. She was taken to a room off the House floor and attended to. Her blood pressure had spiked. She would need hospital attention. She was loaded on a stretcher and carried away, her face covered to hide her identity from the waiting television cameras. This only added to the immense pressure within the House chamber.

Then another: Republican Raymond Walker, another pro-tax legislator. He managed to compose himself enough to struggle out the door and make it to the hospital on his own, where he was admitted.[14] According to State Representative Diane Black, many more legislators sought the attention of the House nurse, a fact that was not reported by the media. Over on the Senate side, State Senator Curtis Person had been admitted to the hospital earlier in the day for elevated blood pressure and was resting in his hotel room. State Representative Mae Beavers would later comment that she had never seen people under such immense pressure. Representatives with years of experience were buckling under the weight Speaker Naifeh was placing on them.

With these lawmakers gone, that meant Naifeh was going to come up two votes short of passage. The vote was delayed. The Senate quickly got word of the events in the House, and they delayed their vote as well. Courageous bunch, weren't they? Naifeh waited to hear word from the hospital. Representative Black, a registered nurse, attended to one of her fallen colleagues. Speaker Naifeh entered the room and ordered her to leave. The attending physician, another legislator, overruled Naifeh and insisted that she remain, since his specialty was pediatrics and she had worked as an ER nurse.[15]

Outside we awaited word of what was going on. Rumors of the legislators being hospitalized trickled out to us, but we couldn't confirm the report. To be honest, it sounded too preposterous to be true. Some called it divine intervention. Fortunately, the illnesses were not life-threatening, just stress-related.

I got word that both chambers were adjourning for the day. I let out a sigh of relief. We had won another day. This would be the only way to win this war, one day at a time. God only knew how long it would be before they tired of our vigilance outside the Capitol. However long it took, we were resolved to be there. I turned to the crowd and announced the news of the adjournment. The crowd erupted into a loud cheer. I drank in the enthusiasm from their faces. I would reflect on those small victories in the moments of discouragement that would color the months ahead.

They're Ba-a-ack . . . Again

Tuesday, June 13, 2000—Rebuffed by overwhelming opposition to the income tax the day before, legislators tried a different slant. Just one day after two pro-tax legislators had to be hospitalized, the proponents of the income tax offered up the idea of a constitutional amendment promising never to raise the rate nor lower the exemption. Since a constitutional amendment takes two different General Assembly sessions, it didn't seem like a viable plan. However, what the plan *did* do was expose the fact that the so-called "crisis" obviously wasn't immediate, as they had been whining. Here we were just two and one-half weeks from the end of the fiscal year and there was no budget and no sign an agreement would be reached. If they were grasping at the straw of a constitutional amendment that would take years, simply to pass an income tax, how real could the "crisis" be?

By this point, lawmakers like State Senator Mike Williams were seeing red. Mike smelled a rat and didn't mind expressing it. "I don't like to talk in terms of conspiracy theories," he said, "but with the

Conference Committee (assigned to resolve House-Senate differ-ences) tilted toward an income tax, it makes me tend to believe that the squeeze is being put upon us . . . so the only door we can go through is toward an income tax."[16]

I checked the paper to see what kind of treatment I got from the reporter I met the day before, Kate Miller from the *Tennessean*. My instincts were correct. Her piece was very fair and quite accurate. With the exception of one quote made by Steve Gill that was attributed to me, the article was dead-on and even-handed. She confirmed my contention that Lydia Lenker's "Lexus Brigade" handle was completely wrong. She noted that I described the crowd as a grassroots protest made up of people from all walks of life. "The steady line of honking pickup trucks and eighteen-wheelers, as well as Cadillacs," she wrote, "seemed to support his view."[17] I checked back to earlier in the week and found another article co-written by her headlined, "Creeping Income Tax Worries Taxpayers." Could it be we'd found a sympathetic writer at the *Tennessean?* I wasn't going to go that far; all I could ask for was an unbiased writer. Kate, refreshingly, appeared to be just that.

Just three days after the initial sneak attack, we left nothing to chance. We were back in full force in front of the Capitol. Once again, the horns began to honk, and the protesters filled the sidewalks. I pounded home the truth between 9:00 AM and noon. By noon, the vote on the income tax was delayed until 1:00 PM. The vote on the tax was scheduled in just under a half hour. Steve and I thought the folks inside should get a little better taste of the mood outside. We turned up our loudspeakers and addressed the crowd. We informed them of exactly what was going on and where we were with the income tax. They were determined to push forward with the income tax despite the will of the people. Apparently, our protests outside weren't enough. We needed to get the citizens closer to the action. At the end of our speeches, we urged all those assembled to walk peacefully up the Capitol steps and into the building and let the lawmakers know their feelings. The crowd turned en masse and headed across the street, up the steps, and into the front doors of the Capitol. I noted in my journal:

It was like a Frankenstein movie. The angry crowd ascended the steps and piled into the House gallery. The overflow spilled into the hallway and screamed angrily at tax supporters as they filed by.

All we were missing were the pitchforks and the torches. Many of these protesters had been out in the hot, relentless sun since Saturday. They crammed into the hallways and began chanting. One protester clutched an early-American version of the U.S. flag. A state trooper approached the man and demanded the flag. "You're not taking my flag," the man said, calmly. The trooper persisted. "I'm telling you— you're not taking my flag," the man repeated. Then a young girl took hold of the other end and the two raised it. The crowd began singing "God Bless America." The trooper, frustrated, turned and walked away as the singing continued.[18]

Lawmakers began filing through the hallway on the way to their respective chambers. Angry citizens called out at them and chanted slogans like "Ax the tax." Legislators were visibly taken aback. As long as the crowd was outside, they could, perhaps, deal with the pressure. Now the crowd was inside and right in their faces. When the last of the lawmakers had disappeared into the chambers, the protesters piled into the gallery to watch the proceedings. The lawmakers got an up-close taste of their constituents that afternoon, and it was not pretty. Once those lawmakers looked over their shoulders to see the packed gallery glaring down at them, the reality of the situation was driven home.

The way I knew what was going on inside was by seeing reports on television. I had chosen not to join the crowd. A befuddled listener asked me the next day why he had seen us get everyone stoked up only to see me walk away as everyone climbed the steps. It was a good question, and I thought it important for people to understand. To me, there's a fine line between being an activist and a publicity hound. I am ever cognizant of that. This issue was too important to simply use as a stunt. The face those lawmakers and the citizens of the state needed to see was the angry face of a jilted public, not the face of some radio guy trying to get his mug on TV. I felt my presence would only detract from the moment, not add to it. In retrospect, I did the right thing.

Speaker Naifeh took to the podium. He gazed solemnly around the room as everyone stopped their conversations and listened to what he had to say. "The Conference Committee plan does not have, or does not appear to have, any consensus at this time." That was it. The massive assault hatched by the pro-income-taxers behind closed doors in secret meetings had been repelled by the citizens of Tennessee. The protesters were jubilant. Against all odds, they had done the unthinkable. They had actually taken it upon themselves to get involved and change the course of history. I thought back to my mood just a few days prior when Steve Gill and I sat alone on that desolate street. We had no idea if even two people would show up that day. We had felt dejected and unsure when that legislative aide skipped across the street and arrogantly mocked our efforts. How I wished I could see him again.

It Ain't Over 'Til It's Over

The income tax died that day, but just for that fiscal year. Darrell Ankarlo, Dave Ramsey, Steve Gill, and I were all named "Heroes of the Taxpayer" for the month of June 2000 by Americans for Tax Reform, a Washington D.C.-based taxpayer advocacy group headed up by tax reformer Grover Norquist.[19] But the real heroes were the people who came out in droves to fight the tax. They had put the fear of God in members of the General Assembly.

However, the pro-income-tax forces were not through yet. Seeing his chance at passing the income tax slipping away, Governor Sundquist sent in his chief lieutenant in the pro-income-tax ranks, Attorney General Paul Summers. Summers had issued an opinion that the income tax was constitutional, despite two prior rulings to the contrary by two separate state Supreme Courts. He spoke to the General Assembly and offered his gloomy prediction. If they passed any budget that didn't include an income tax, Sundquist would veto it. If they didn't pass Sundquist's budget, which called for the income tax, state services would be shut down. "If state employees don't have to report to work, who guards the prisons?" he asked. "Who patrols the highways? Who treats the mentally ill? The potential answer is nobody."[20]

Despite the threats, the lawmakers were more frightened of the people's wrath. A week later, on June 23, 2000, the General Assembly met again and passed a budget without an income tax. Sundquist, derisively calling it the "Fudge-It Budget," vetoed it four days later, the first time a governor had done so in the history of the state.[21] The House wasted no time in answering the governor's veto. Needing just a simple majority to override, they voted two hours later to override the veto by an embarrassing vote of seventy-eight to nineteen. On June 28, the State Senate met to vote on the governor's veto. We organized another horn-honking protest down at the Capitol to urge lawmakers to vote for the override. They did. The Senate override was also overwhelming with a margin of twenty to nine. The General Assembly had foiled the governor's plans to shut down the government and create a crisis.

What Happened to Sundquist?

After the Summer of 2000 tax fight, I began to yearn for the answer to the question that Pat Buchanan would ask me a couple of years later: "What the hell happened to Sundquist?"[22] Former Wisconsin Governor Tommy Thompson asked the very same thing at the 2000 Republican Convention in Philadelphia. I had no idea. His transformation wasn't just troublesome, it was bizarre.

What was additionally irritating was how the Sundquists treated those of us who continued to hold his no-income-tax position even after he had abandoned it. Not only was Governor Sundquist getting nasty in the press, but his wife was taking it personally, too. Martha Sundquist approached Lee Beaman, a Nashville businessman and Republican contributor, and scolded him for participating in the tax protests, telling him he should be ashamed of himself. I, too, had a little encounter with Mrs. Sundquist at the 2000 GOP Convention in Philadelphia. At a party for the Tennessee delegation, I walked up to a group of friends who were enjoying the party. Among them was Martha Sundquist. When she saw me, she gave me a disapproving head-to-toe look, threw her nose in the air, then turned on her heels and walked off. I found this sort of behavior bizarre in light of the fact that Governor Sundquist had been a rabid anti-income-taxer. He had campaigned vigorously on the issue—twice! He had stated in no uncertain terms that an income tax was bad news. What could have changed his mind?

In puzzling over this, I remembered the old adage, "Follow the money." I researched Sundquist's campaign fundraising records and discovered something unusual. Faced with only token opposition, Sundquist's war chest for the 1998 campaign cycle brimmed with over $5.4 million. His Democrat opposition, by contrast, boasted a paltry $10,475 since his campaign was self-financed.[23] Sundquist had John Jay Hooker beat in the money department 516-to-1!

It's not like Hooker ever had a chance of beating Sundquist. A Sundquist victory was a foregone conclusion even before the Democrat primary. Certainly after the primary, when Hooker won the nomination, it was obvious he was the sacrificial lamb. Besides, Hooker had filed a lawsuit alleging that giving or receiving campaign contributions violated state law. The chances he was going to fatten his wallet with contributions was nil. Sundquist was limited to just one more term as governor and had announced he would not seek any other office after that. What was he going to do with the money? I want to make it clear that I don't have any hard evidence that Sundquist's war chest and his flip-flop on the income tax issue are related. I will say that in the quest to determine "what the hell happened to Sundquist," the overkill in his fundraising was certainly suspicious.

The income tax showdown of 2000 marked a dramatic change in Tennessee politics. The era of hiding behind the veiled curtain of citizen apathy was over. As Marsha Blackburn pointed out to me years later, the income tax in and of itself was not so much what infuriated the public. It was the sneaky way they were going about it. "To try to use legislative trickery to move an issue that they wanted to see happen, not through the normal process but through a shortened process, a hastened process, they [the citizens] found that to be particularly distasteful," she said.[24] The taxpayers were now armed with the truth, and they had asserted their will like no other time in the state's history.

But we had no delusions that the income tax was dead forever. Like a thief in the night, it would be back. We just didn't know when.

GORED IN TENNESSEE

I think it's important to point out a seldom-noticed residual effect of the tax protests in Tennessee. Remember, the year 2000 was an election year. Not only were state positions in the General Assembly contested, but we were in the midst of a huge presidential campaign. Al Gore was seeking the office against George W. Bush. It was a foregone conclusion that Gore would take his home state.

However, many of the same people who came to despise abusive, bloated government in the state during the tax debate also came to see Al Gore as big government incarnate on the federal level. I took every opportunity to point out that Gore was cut from the same cloth as the politicians who tried to ram a state income tax down their throats.

With the exception of Don Sundquist, who had become a RINO, Republican In Name Only, the major players in the pro-tax movement like Speaker of the House Jimmy Naifeh and Speaker Pro Tem Bob Rochelle in the Senate were in lock-step with Gore. The same went for the forces outside the chambers who beat the drum for the endless expansion of government like the unions and the ultra-liberals at the newspapers. Gore, who spent little time in the state, was totally oblivious to the anti-income-tax mood of its citizens. On top of that, he made it a regular practice on those rare occasions he came back to visit to tie up the interstate system around Nashville during rush hour instead of scheduling his motorcade after hours. The citizens began to see the same arrogance in Gore they had witnessed in their own unresponsive, dictatorial state leaders.

I was also lucky enough to have a couple of stories fall in my lap that shed Gore in a not-so-presidential light. One in particular connected Gore with a group of men in the area who had come to be known as "The Hillbilly Mafia." These were men who used strong-arm tactics to rule their counties with an iron fist. They were perceived as the same "good old boy network" that ran things on the state level, the same bunch that wanted to heap more taxes on the citizens. These stories were completely ignored by the mainstream press but were picked up by Internet news services, like NewsMax.com and WorldNetDaily.com, through which many of these citizens had grown accustomed to getting the real news. Since the major newspapers weren't carrying these stories, Gore's people totally ignored them—a gross miscalculation.

That's not to say that the vast majority of Tennesseans were paying attention to these reports. Many people were not even aware of them. But enough very angry, very active citizens were paying attention, and these people were energized enough to get out and vote. The cumulative effect of these minor stories, along with the growing unflattering perception of Gore as arrogant and disconnected from the state, as well as his connection to the same forces that wanted to foist an income tax on the citizens, chipped away at his support base. While most of history will forever focus on the Florida recount, Florida would have been a moot point had Gore merely won his home state. Not since McGovern in 1972 had a major party candidate lost his own state, and the stunning difference in 2000 was that, unlike McGovern who got shellacked, Gore won the popular vote nationwide.

Again, the active few defied the conventional wisdom and, once again, changed the course of history. I think this is very important when it comes to combating voter apathy. Most people believe they can't make a difference—but they can and they do. The people of Tennessee not only made a difference in the tax struggle, they changed the course of history in the closest presidential election ever held in this country. Suffice it to say, if those Tennesseans who voted against Gore had stayed home, Al Gore would've been the forty-third president of the United States.

A TAX ANTHEM

Being Music City, the tax revolt spawned a song that we used throughout the duration of the fight. On June 28, 2000, during one of our protests, I had been asked by a passerby who had no idea what was going on, "What's that noise?" I looked at her for a moment and said, "It's freedom ringing." Those words stuck in my head, and I couldn't get them out. I was doing a split shift that day. I had covered the mid-morning shift, and we decided to run Rush Limbaugh at his regular time while we waited to see if the governor would sign the budget. I went home to catch a quick nap but found myself lying awake with those words echoing in my head. They were now accompanied by a tune. Unable to sleep, I got up and went to my home studio and began plunking out the tune on the piano. The words began to flow, and I recorded a rough version of the song that afternoon and finished it that night.

A few days later, I played the song for a couple of friends of mine who were music veterans. Bill Cuomo co-wrote songs like "Oh, Sherrie" for Steve Perry, created the signature sound for Kim Carnes's "Bette Davis Eyes," and produced music for a Bond movie, Barbra Streisand, and many others. The guy knew his stuff, and I wanted his opinion from a technical standpoint to see if I needed to re-cut the song in a real recording studio or just leave it like it was.

His partner, Beeb Birtles, also a good friend of mine, looked at the song from a different angle. Being one of the original members of the Little River Band and having co-written some of their hits like "Happy Anniversary," Beeb instantly started picking out background vocal parts. His distinctive harmonies gave LRB their unique sound. He put that same talent to work on my song, arranging the background vocals. Bill went to work immediately in his studio. When I came back the next day, he had arranged a new intro and had begun putting the song together. He handled all the keyboard parts. Beeb added acoustic guitar and background vocals. I sang the song and played lead guitar. We hired a session musician with quite a musical pedigree of his own to play drums. Ron Krasinski has played and/or recorded with countless big-name performers, including Olivia Newton-John, Seals & Crofts, Barry Manilow, Melissa Manchester, and Sheena Easton. Bill mixed it all together, and we packaged it as a CD single with sound bites from that June 2000 protest mixed in on one cut and the song by itself on the other track.

"What's That Noise" was released on August 1, 2000. By the end of the month, it was number one on the Tower Records Local Artists chart in Nashville. We continued to use the song as an unofficial theme song for the next two years. The lyrics spoke to what we were doing.

> *Did you hear what the man said?*
> *There's a storm a-brewing.*
> *The people are watching,*

And they know what you're doing.
The passive days of old are through,
They've found the strength,
They're standing up to you.
What's That Noise?
It's freedom ringing.
What's That Noise?
It's liberty singing.
At the top of her voice,
A God-given choice,
To take control of destiny.

Four

HISTORIC TAX FIGHTS

The struggle over taxes has not only shaped our country, it's how we got started in the first place. Had there not been a tax revolt, there would have been no revolution. Without the American Revolution we would not be enjoying the quality of life we enjoy today. Rebellions are good for this country. I liken them to market corrections in the stock market. Every now and then we need a reality check. We need to get back to the basics of what it is we're trying to accomplish as a nation. To date, there have only been relatively minor corrections. To get back to what the founders envisioned it's going to take quite a bit more than just the Tennessee revolt. But that day is coming. We're closing in on what will be a major correction in our tax system. The simple fact that the vast *minority* now shoulder the vast *majority* of the tax burden makes the whole system unsustainable as it is. Government is trying to be all things to all people, and eventually those most burdened by the taxes raised to feed such a monster will revolt.

It's surprising that it hasn't happened yet. As you'll see in this chapter, the people of America have been known to revolt over far less of a tax burden than we bear today. (They're especially cranky when you tax their booze.) As this chapter takes events in chronological order, it's interesting to watch the progression of just how much abuse Americans will take from their government. At the beginning, it was very little. Over time, government got gradually more intrusive, and Americans grew more tolerant of taxes. It took those few who were paying attention to sound the alarm when government tried to grow too big too fast.

THE SUGAR AND STAMP ACTS

Following the French and Indian War, which ended in 1763, the British sought the financial means to defray the costs associated with the war and protect the colonies from further attack. Parliament passed a number of resolutions in 1764, including a tax on sugar, molasses (for making rum), coffee, and other items—thus the duties became known collectively as the Sugar Act. It also regulated the export of lumber and iron. Interestingly enough, the tax on molasses actually was decreased from the amount levied by the Molasses Act of 1733 from six pence per gallon to three. However, the Sugar Act was passed with more teeth, with the intention of cracking down on those who chose to ignore the Molasses Act. The result was a stiffer British navy presence and enforcement of the duties and a noticeable dent in the rum trade with the West Indies. In fact, all trade with the West Indies and other nearby destinations was sharply curtailed. The colonists were not too thrilled.

It was not just the tax but the heavy-handed way the British went about collecting it. The Sugar Act also called for suspected smugglers and tax evaders to stand trial in a vice-admiralty court in Halifax, Nova Scotia. Before the act, suspects were tried in local colonial courts where the defendants were more likely to be acquitted.[1]

What sprung from the Sugar Act was a growing sentiment that

England had no right to tax the colonies at all because the colonists enjoyed no representation in Parliament. This idea caught on throughout the colonies, which had heretofore agreed on very little. When the Sugar Act failed to produce the expected revenue, Parliament conceived a new tax: the Stamp Tax.

The year 1765 was a huge year in the shaping of the coming revolution. The Stamp Act of 1765 required the inclusion of a stamp on virtually anything printed, including legal documents, licenses, newspapers, and pamphlets. This sort of taxation was already common in England, but again, the colonists felt it unfair to them given their lack of representation. It was also the first direct tax levied against America. Direct taxation, at the time, was thought to be especially insulting. The Stamp Act is cited by most historians as the force that bound the colonies together, the wind that fanned the flames of fury that led to the Revolutionary War.

Exacerbating the situation, the Quartering Act was passed in March of 1765, requiring colonists to house and feed British troops. This was seen as another tax on the people since they had to bear the expense of taking care of the troops. In May, Patrick Henry presented seven resolutions to the Virginia House of Burgesses, declaring that only the Virginia legislature had the right to tax Virginians. He boldly stated, "If this be treason, make the most of it."[2] Also in 1765, a group of shopkeepers and artisans in Boston formed a secretive group called The Loyal Nine. They plotted means of protest and agitation against the Stamp Act. Soon their numbers grew far beyond the original nine and they became known as the Sons of Liberty.

Their first famous act of defiance took place on August 14, 1765, when they hanged in effigy the "Distributer of Stamps" for Massachusetts. The British ordered the local authorities to remove the figure, but they refused out of fear of their own lives. By then, a large crowd had gathered around the effigy. Before nightfall, the crowd burned the tax collector's property, moving on to his house. There, they beheaded the effigy, then pelted the distributor's house with rocks as the horrified occupants helplessly peered out from within. After the occupants fled the property, angry protesters ransacked the house as the frightened British militia and town officials turned a blind eye.[3]

Later that year, in October, the Stamp Act Congress was convened in America to discuss just what to do about it. It was decided that a boycott of British goods was in order, and trade with England suffered substantially. Furthermore, many colonists refused to use the stamps on their documents, and courts would not enforce their use in legal documents.

The Sons of Liberty soon spread to every colony. Their prime objective was to frighten Stamp distributors throughout the colonies into resigning. A large number of the Sons were printers and publishers who fomented insurrection in their publications. Nearly every newspaper chronicled on a daily basis the activities of the Sons. Looking back, it's absolutely amazing that such a movement could become so widespread in such a short period of time given their relatively primitive means of communication. Keep in mind that this was all taking place *before* the Stamp Act was even in force, which wasn't until November of 1765. It gives you an idea of just how hated these taxes were.

After the tax went into effect, another group in New York turned to violence, burning the royal governor in effigy, then looting houses and harassing British troops. British General Thomas Gage, commander of all English military forces in America, demanded that the New York assembly force the colonists to comply with the Quartering Act. They refused.

By early 1766, many of the royal governors had gone into hiding. They couldn't very well count on the sheriffs and British militia because many of their members had joined the Sons of Liberty. The various Sons chapters in each colony communicated and coordinated with one another, and it was assumed that the British army would soon arrive in full force to put down the rebellion. The first efforts to unite the colonies were not made by the legislatures but by these disparate groups of rebels. Instead of sending more troops, King George III repealed the Stamp Act in March of 1766 after an appearance in the British Parliament by Ben Franklin. The king's motivation for the repeal was not so much the unrest in America but the outrage in England over the boycotts. The Stamp Act was killing business at home and doing more harm than good.

Things settled down a bit back in America, save the occasional outbreak of violence over the still-in-force Quartering Act. Sensing that full revolution had been averted, Parliament turned its attention back to the problem at hand. They needed revenue, and they needed it now. Testing the waters for another type of tax on America, Parliament turned to Ben Franklin, who remained in England as a representative of several colonies that sent him to do their bidding. "Did you ever hear the authority of Parliament to make laws for America questioned till lately?" they asked of Franklin on the floor of the House of Commons. "The authority of Parliament was allowed to be valid in all laws except as should lay internal taxes," he answered.[4]

Stamp taxes were *internal* taxes. Duties on imports were not. They were *external* taxes. Perhaps by his use of the term "internal taxes," ol' Ben had unwittingly left the door wide open for the British. Or perhaps he knew exactly what he was saying and was merely echoing the sentiments of his employers back in America. Either way, he would quickly change his mind once back in Philadelphia when he learned that his good name had been tarnished by the incident. Regardless of the reason for the blunder, Parliament felt bold enough to give the tax thing another try. They quickly learned how wrong they—and Franklin—had been.

THE TOWNSHEND ACTS

In June of 1767, the Brits were at it again. King George named Charles Townshend, known as "Champagne Charlie" to his friends, the new

Chancellor of the Exchequer.[5] Duties under the Townshend Act were levied on a few items like paper, dye, glass, and tea. The beef this time was not so much in the taxes themselves but how they were collected. Along with this new act came something called a writ of assistance. This was a non-specific court order that allowed customs officers to search anyone's property, anywhere, anytime, for contraband. This violated the age-old British notion that a man's home was his castle. Champagne Charlie had just given the British officials the keys to the castle. Not surprisingly, corruption among the tax agents was common. These unsavory tax collectors, three in Boston in particular, helped Americans define exactly what they disliked about British taxation. *Everything.*

Although Charles Townshend died shortly after the passage of his act, the resentment lived on. The Americans were growing more and more agitated with each collection of the tax. The petitions, boycotts, and some violence cranked up again. Tax collectors were tarred and feathered. In 1768, John Hancock, who would go on to possess the most famous signature in American history, was at the center of one altercation involving one of his ships, the *Liberty*. Customs agents seized the ship for possessing banned Madeira wine. The Sons of Liberty arrived on the wharf en masse and roughed up the Customs House. They also took a pleasure craft belonging to one of the collectors and used it as the centerpiece for a bonfire. Efforts to prosecute Hancock failed, and he went on to be elected to the legislature the following year. Incidentally, Hancock had been a guest at King George's coronation in 1760.[6] Those happy days were long gone.

In March of 1769, Philadelphia joined Massachusetts in the boycott of British goods. Virginia followed suit in May after the royal governor of Virginia dissolved the Virginia House of Burgesses. By October, the boycott had spread to New Jersey, Rhode Island, and North Carolina.[7]

Pockets of violence continued to erupt, such as the Battle of

Golden Hill in New York City, which was not so much a battle as a clash with British troops. The Sons of Liberty had erected a "liberty pole" in what is today City Hall Park. This was a rallying point for speeches and protests and the like. On January 19, 1770, the British got fed up with the taunting and got the bright idea to cut down the liberty pole. The crowd was furious and they detained the British soldiers. Other troops ran to their rescue. They chased the crowd to a nearby field called Golden Hill where the crowd continued to taunt the soldiers. The troops charged the crowd with fixed bayonets and several people were seriously injured, though no one died.

THE BOSTON MASSACRE

The incident at Golden Hill must have been on the minds of rein-forcement troops when they marched into Boston on March 5, 1770. British troops had occupied Boston since October of 1768, and these fresh troops were sent to help keep the peace. Since there was about one troop for every four Bostonians, things were a little cramped. The commanding officer demanded his soldiers be quartered in the homes of Bostonians. The Boston council refused. The British backed down and found lodging in abandoned factories and in tents set up on the outskirts of town. The same day, a young barber's apprentice hurled an insult at a sentry on duty in front of the Customs House. The soldier gave the young boy the butt of his rifle up-side of his head.

The boy cried out and returned with some friends, many young boys like himself. Someone rang a church bell and practically the whole town poured out. By this time, the sentry was getting nervous and called for backup. Six men came to his aid. The crowd began to taunt the soldiers and throw snowballs and ice at them. The soldiers had unloaded guns with bayonets. The crowd knew this and slowly crept forward, shouting at them and goading them to fight. When the crowd had surged to just inches from the bayonets, the soldiers loaded their guns and prepared to defend themselves. This only served to anger the crowd further. They dared the soldiers to shoot, then began bashing them with clubs. At that point, the soldiers fired into the crowd, killing three instantly and mortally wounding two others. The crowd scattered. The soldiers were quickly arrested and thrown in jail, and all British troops were withdrawn from town.[8]

News of the "Boston Massacre" quickly spread throughout the colonies. As you might imagine, it was embellished with each telling, and groups like the Sons of Liberty used it to their advantage. The Massachusetts Superior Court delayed the trial until fall, allowing time for tempers to cool. As an interesting side note, the lead counsel for the defense was none other than John Adams. The captain in charge of the troops and four other soldiers were acquitted. Two other soldiers were found guilty of manslaughter, had their hands branded, then were drummed out of the army. The overwhelming evidence presented by Adams that the soldiers were attacked first quelled any violence that might have otherwise taken place after the trial. No matter, the Boston Massacre was thrown on the pile of the myriad grievances against the British and helped stoke the colonists' ever-growing hatred of them.

A frustrated Parliament, confounded by the continued American boycott of their goods, tried something different. On April 12, 1770, Parliament gutted the Townshend Acts and removed the taxes on everything but tea. They retained the tax on tea for two reasons: it was the most lucrative of all the taxes, and they wanted to let the colonists know they were still boss. That little slip would be their undoing.

THE BOSTON TEA PARTY

America and the mother country enjoyed an unusually harmonious period for three years after the repeal of the Townshend Acts in 1770. Except for the Gaspee Affair, when an overzealous revenue cutter's captain caused his ship to be burned to the waterline in Rhode Island, things were relatively calm. It was, as it turned out, the calm before the storm. Never knowing when to leave well enough alone, the Brits once again found a way to annoy the colonists. They still didn't get the message: no taxation without representation! Heck, by then, the colonists didn't even want representation. They knew they would be vastly outnumbered in Parliament. They just wanted to be left alone. But that wasn't going to happen.

There are a few misconceptions about the Boston Tea Party that need to be addressed. The popular notion that the rebellion was over taxes is only partially accurate. It's true that the dreaded Townshend Acts were repealed except for the tax on tea. However, the Tea Act of May 10, 1773, actually lowered that tax considerably. What the Tea Act also did, which really upset the colonists, was prop up the British-owned East India Company by giving them a monopoly on the tea market in America. The colonists still didn't like the tax on tea, no matter how low it was. They had come to the conclusion that England had no authority to tax them at all. And they liked a British monopoly on tea even less.

The real epicenter for resistance to the tea tax and monopoly was in Philadelphia. In October of 1773, Philadelphians managed to force the resignation of British tea agents in their town. A month later, a Boston committee was formed and endorsed the actions in Philadelphia. They tried to get their own tea agents to resign but failed. Like Philadelphia, the Bostonians were upset at not only the tax but also the monopoly on tea by the East India Company. Remember, the colonists had been boycotting British products for years and had, in turn, been buying smuggled Dutch tea. The British aimed to put a stop to this, so the ships that sailed into Boston Harbor were loaded with surplus tea from England that was to be sold to pro-British merchants in America at rock-bottom prices.

Selling the tea at prices below the Dutch tea would, the British figured, drive the Dutch tea off the market. Boston wasn't the only port-of-call for the tea. Tons of tea were also heading for New York,

Philadelphia, Charleston, and other ports.[9] News of the scheme leaked, and the importers of the tea to the other ports were so overcome by fear that the tea intended for New York and Philadelphia was returned to England. The Charleston tea was stored, according to some historical accounts, in government warehouses.[10] The Boston ships stayed in port. The merchants of Boston knew that if the British succeeded in dumping under-priced tea on the market, they might be emboldened to try it with other products. The merchants were determined to put a stop to it.

They first tried to reason with Royal Governor Tom Hutchinson. Over five thousand townspeople, led by Samuel Adams, gathered to petition the governor. They requested that the tea not be unloaded and the three ships carrying it be sent back to England.[11] The governor refused their request, or, by at least one eyewitness account, simply avoided it by heading to his "country seat at Milton."[12] The new law said duties on the tea must be collected within twenty days of the ship's arrival. That made the deadline December 16, 1773.

That night, members of the Sons of Liberty gathered to plot their next move. Once they got word that one of the ships had been refused the right to leave the harbor that night to return the tea to England, they headed to Griffin's wharf where the ships lay, surrounded by armed British ships. Some sixty participants, led by Samuel Adams, Paul Revere, and others, donned Indian costumes and boarded the three ships without incident.[13] The ship captains handed over the keys to the holds, and, over a three-hour period, the patriots proceeded to remove three hundred forty-two chests of tea, crack open the chests with their tomahawks, and dump the chests into the water.

Townspeople began to gather to watch the spectacle. Several tried to stuff tea into their pockets and coats. Upon seeing this, the patriots would pull the tea from their pockets, sometimes ripping the coats from their backs, then push them back into the crowd. As they ran from the scene, citizens would give them a punch or a kick for good measure. It's not exactly clear why the British stood idly by. Perhaps they didn't want another Boston Massacre on their hands. The next morning, there was a fair amount of tea still floating in chests in the harbor. To prevent townspeople from absconding with the tea, men rowed out to the chests and pounded them with their oars until they sank.

The British government was furious. Part of the reason they needed to kill the Dutch tea trade in America was that the East India Company was in serious financial trouble. Now those pesky colonists had just destroyed £9,000 worth of tea. The British reacted with predictable heavy-handedness. They weren't the only ones who thought the Sons of Liberty had crossed the line. Even Ben Franklin was outraged and demanded the British government be paid restitution. The British responded with the Coercive Acts of 1774. They would come to be known in America as The Intolerable Acts.

The first Intolerable Act closed Boston Harbor until the tea was paid for, which it never was. The second took away Massachusetts's Charter of 1691 and their rights to self-government. The third allowed the British government to remove the culprits to England for trial. The fourth reinforced the Quartering Act. The fifth, the Quebec Act, had little to do with the Tea Party but extended the boundaries of the province of Quebec.[14]

Ironically, the Boston Tea Party would spur the colonies to convene the First Continental Congress on September 5, 1774, a pet project of Ben Franklin's. Franklin, who vigorously denounced the Tea Party, might never have brought the colonies together had it not been for the Tea Party and the subsequent Intolerable Acts. The colonies were on their way to revolution, and it all started with a tax.

SHAYS' REBELLION

Winning the American Revolution would not immediately make the Americans more agreeable to taxes. They understood the new government needed money, but they fell back to the general consensus of the people that preexisted the Townshend Acts. External taxes—tariffs, duties, etc.—were acceptable, but internal taxes levied directly on items they purchased were not. The problem after the Revolution was that the federal government was virtually powerless. Before the Constitution was official in 1789, the federal government's power was derived from the Articles of Confederation. Adopted in 1777 and ratified in 1781, the Articles gave very few powers to the federal government. One of the especially weak areas was the power to tax. War debt was tremendous and was being borne by the individual states.

Massachusetts was especially hard-hit. The problem was, Massachusetts, like much of the rest of the country, was in the midst of an economic downturn. New England merchants were, once again, importing large quantities of British goods. This sucked a lot of hard currency out of the economy. Wholesalers sold to retailers on credit who, in turn, sold to back-country farmers on credit. This chain of debt worsened when England closed their Caribbean Islands to American shipping. Wholesalers began calling in their debts. The merchants couldn't pay, so they sued the farmers. The farmers couldn't pay, so they were hauled off to debtor's prison.

To make matters worse, Massachusetts Governor James Bowdoin had embarked on an ambitious mission to retire the state debt by the end of the 1780s. The state initially attempted to raise the necessary funds through duties and imposts, but the depression in trade meant there wasn't enough money there to do the trick. Bowdoin turned to the hated direct taxes on property and a poll tax, which taxed people to vote. (That same tax would be used after the Civil War to keep blacks from voting.)

Like the British attempts at direct taxation, Bowdoin's taxes would trigger another revolt that came to be known as Shays' Rebellion. Contrary to popular belief, Shays' Rebellion was not made up wholly of dirt-poor farmers. In fact, most were not poor at all, but well-to-do gentlemen, many of whom had been officers in the Continental Army. Very few were ever hauled before a court for indebtedness, let alone imprisoned. These men were motivated by the same principles that founded the government. They detested the newly-formed state government they viewed as anti-republic and tyrannical in the tradition of the British. The 1780 Massachusetts state constitution included an aristocratic, unrepresentative Senate that most benefited the rich Bostonian businessmen of the day. The courts set up by the constitution closely resembled the British colonial courts of old.[15]

Daniel Shays, a former captain in the Revolutionary War and distinguished veteran, was but one of several who organized a group of men to voice their grievances to the new governor. Men were being hauled off to jail when they were unable to pay the land tax, and Shays and his like-minded compatriots wanted it stopped. Governor Bowdoin turned a deaf ear. In addition to the burden of being hauled off to Boston to face trial, farmers were met with unscrupulous lawyers who jacked up their fees. The farmers labeled these particular attorneys "pests of society." Thomas Grover, a Shays ally, noted his reason for the revolt as the "large swarm of lawyers . . . who have been more damage to the people at large, especially the common farmers, than the savage beasts of prey."[16]

Initially, the rebels concentrated on freeing farmers who had been imprisoned by the courts for debt or failure to make tax payments. In August of 1786, Shays and his followers began to forcibly prevent county courts from passing judgments on debtors. In September, they forced the Massachusetts State Supreme Court to adjourn. Shays drew up a battle plan to take the federal arsenal in Springfield. Once armed, he planned to march to Boston and "destroy that nest of devils who, by their influence, make the Court enact what they please."[17]

They attacked the federal arsenal at Springfield in early 1787 but were repelled by federal troops. Shays' men scattered back into the woods as three rebels were killed by canon fire. Meanwhile, the governor appointed General Benjamin Lincoln to command forty-four hundred men to fight against the rebels. General Lincoln and his men arrived on the scene in Springfield. They chased the rebels to Petersham, Massachusetts, where, in February 1787, Shays and his men were defeated. Roughly a hundred fifty rebels were rounded up and tried for treason. A handful were convicted and hanged. The others were eventually pardoned. Shays escaped to Vermont and was tried in absentia and sentenced to death. In April 1787, Bowdoin lost reelection to John Hancock who had served as governor immediately preceding Bowdoin. Shays petitioned for amnesty and it was granted by Governor Hancock in June of 1788.[18]

It should be noted that although farmers took up arms in similar rebellions over the same issues from New Hampshire to South Carolina, the most serious fighting was in Massachusetts. Shays' Rebellion was, by far, the most famous of its kind of the day. The perhaps unintended consequence of Shays' Rebellion was the urgency it created to adopt a more comprehensive federal document that gave more power to the federal government. With the idea of merely strengthening the Articles of Confederation, representatives from the states scrapped the Articles and adopted the Constitution instead. Shays' Rebellion was the centerpiece in many arguments in the debates that formed and shaped the U.S. Constitution.

THE WHISKEY REBELLION

To understand the Whiskey Rebellion of 1794, you must first understand the mindset of those behind it. Historians paint a picture of a brave President George Washington donning his Revolutionary War uniform and leading thirteen thousand troops into Western Pennsylvania to put down a cadre of outlaws who refused to pay their taxes. However, the true story is much more complex, with good guys and bad guys on both sides.

The epicenter of the rebellion was located, ironically, in and around what's known today as Washington County, Pennsylvania, near modern-day Pittsburgh. Settlers of western Pennsylvania had to contend with a lot of hardship. Not only did they fight the British during the Revolutionary War, they also had to contend with Indian raids, many instigated by the British. These British-led Indian attacks continued even after the war, as English forces from Canada hoped to peel off the western frontier from the United States. Although they had fought for independence, many a western Pennsylvanian's idea of independence was being independent of any central authority, including the newly-formed United States.

As early as 1775, the Transylvanians, as they called themselves, petitioned the Continental Congress to be recognized as a separate colony. Their relatively long distance from Philadelphia, about five hundred miles, and the rugged terrain across almost impassable mountains, gave them a feeling of detachment from the rest of the country. To complicate things, both Pennsylvania and Virginia claimed the area. In 1776, they declared themselves the independent state of Westsylvania. As you might imagine, with no clear-cut authority it was rather difficult to enforce state laws. Which state actually had authority? People pretty much ruled themselves until Pennsylvania was given formal authority over the territory in 1781.

Even after the Constitutional Convention of 1787, the debate over western Pennsylvania continued. In 1788, the British, looking down upon the situation from Canada, saw an opportunity to exploit the discontent. They planted the seeds of secession, communicating their idea to several influential members of the community, among them General John Neville. Neville would become a central figure in the Whiskey Rebellion.[19]

So, you had a fiercely independent people hundreds of miles from eastern civilization trying to sort out their problems, repel Indian attacks, make it through the harsh winters, and scrape out an existence on their farms. This gives you a good idea as to why they were none too happy when Alexander Hamilton, a snotty aristocrat from New York

City, pushed through an excise tax on their whiskey, America's very first "sin tax." He called it a "pernicious luxury" and figured the national government could not only make money from it but could, in tandem, regulate a morally destructive habit.[20]

Whiskey may have been a "pernicious luxury" to easterners, but in many backwoods sections of the country it was much more. Many farmers ran their own stills, and whiskey passed for the currency of the day in those parts. When the newly formed United States slapped a 28 percent tax on their product, to be collected at the source, they were understandably disgruntled. One of the reasons given was to defray the cost of defending the settlers against Indian attacks. The United States had lost two major expeditions against the Indians in 1790 and 1791. Had they actually won, the settlers might have had more loyalty toward the U.S., but since they were getting their fannies whipped, they weren't doing them a whole lot of good. So much for gratitude.

Other historians point to the deal Hamilton devised to absorb the debt of the states to bring them under the federal umbrella and the plan to construct the capital city of Washington D.C. and its related costs as the reasons for the tax. Whatever the case, Transylvanians, or Westsylvanians, had no intention of being singled out. To add insult to injury, rich easterners were buying land in western Pennsylvania, land that already belonged to the farmers. The move was sanctioned by the state of Pennsylvania. The farmers either had to buy their land back or move.

The whiskey tax passed Congress in 1791 with the South in opposition to it and with Pennsylvania and Virginia evenly split over the measure.[21] In retrospect, this stood to underscore the growing schism between the North and the South. Under the excise tax, the first internal revenue service was established to collect the tax. Farmers were required to register their stills once a year at a single office in each county. Washington County had no such office, which meant traveling great distances to comply with the law. Most didn't. When they were busted, trials were not permitted to be held in their home county. They had to travel all the way to Philadelphia. The cost involved in travel, lawyers, and transporting witnesses only served to infuriate the farmers.

A meeting of citizens from four counties took place at Redstone Fort on July 27, 1791. This was not your ordinary assemblage of rabble-rousers. The attendees included two associate justices, a registrar, and David Bradford, deputy attorney general for the state of Pennsylvania. It was decided that those in attendance should meet in their respective counties, then send a delegation to Pittsburgh on September 7, 1791. One day before the Pittsburgh meeting, a group of men kidnapped a revenue collector, stripped him naked, shaved his head, then tarred and feathered him. They also stole his horse. After he published his account of the incident in the *Pittsburgh Gazette*, the Whiskey Rebellion was on.[22]

Congress was not unsympathetic to the farmers' plight. They passed a bill that allowed the settlers to be tried closer to home. Alexander Hamilton ignored the law. Before they could pass a second, Hamilton had a federal court issue more arrest warrants, this time against dozens of farmers.[23] General John Neville, who had so vehemently opposed the whiskey tax, was summoned to Hamilton's side. When he left the appointment, he was the new excise supervisor in charge of collecting the tax![24] Rebels twice took over his house and marched through Pittsburgh.

The situation escalated when John Neville, accompanied by U.S. Marshall David Lennox, set out to issue summonses for tax-evaders to appear in court in Philadelphia. On July 15, 1794, they arrived at the doorstep of William Miller, who refused to obey the summons. A confrontation ensued between thirty or forty of Miller's friends and Lennox and Neville. After some tense moments, the crowd parted, and the two men were allowed to leave. After they had traveled some fifty yards, a shot rang out. No one was hit. Alexander Hamilton would later contend that one of the rebels aimed but missed; however, that's doubtful. Lennox returned to the crowd for a good dressing down, then left.

The Mingo Militia, organized under George Washington to fight the Indians but now ardent whiskey tax opponents, heard about the confrontation and headed to Neville's house hoping to find Lennox and Neville together. Lennox was not there. Neville answered the door. Upon seeing the crowd, he drew his gun and shot and killed Oliver Miller, William Miller's son. He then sounded a horn alerting his slaves who opened fire from behind the crowd, wounding several of the militia. The militia retreated, regrouped, then headed back to Neville's house the next day. The group, led by James McFarlane, was five hundred strong. When they reached the Neville home, General Neville was gone, but his home was being protected by approximately ten men from nearby Fort Pitt. McFarlane's men opened fire on the house. After about an hour of fighting they heard a plea from inside the house for a truce and, according to legend, saw someone waving a white flag. McFarlane ordered his men to cease fire and stepped out from behind a tree to accept the offer. A single gunshot from inside the house dropped McFarlane in his tracks, and he died on the scene. The rest of the rebels seized the men inside and set fire to the house.

A day or so after McFarlane was killed, David Bradford, the state's deputy attorney general, assumed leadership of the rebels. After a series of meetings, Bradford led the rebels through the streets of Pittsburgh without incident. They then marched off and torched the barn of the man presumed to have killed Oliver Miller.

George Washington, searching for a peaceful solution, offered amnesty to those involved in the rebellion, but the required number of signatures was not obtained. Egged on by Hamilton, Washington saddled up and led around thirteen thousand troops to put a stop to it. They arrived in September of 1794 and the sight of such a formidable force sent Whiskey Rebels scattering. Those who didn't escape were rounded up and hauled off to Philadelphia for trial. David Bradford fled to what is now Louisiana and later sent for his family to join him. Several of the rebels were acquitted due to lack of evidence. Those convicted were later pardoned by President Washington.

Thomas Jefferson, who detested the whiskey tax, had resigned his post as secretary of state in 1793, in part because of the whole incident and Alexander Hamilton's undue influence over Washington. He later wrote in a letter to James Monroe in 1795 that the crisis was orchestrated by Hamilton to achieve his goals of strengthening the federal government. He scoffed at the notion that the Whiskey Rebellion was an insurrection, "unless that term be entirely confounded with occasional riots. But it answered the favorite purposes of strengthening government and increasing public debt; and therefore an insurrection was announced and proclaimed and armed against, and marched against, but could never be found."[25]

The lessons learned from the Whiskey Rebellion echo down through the ages. Here are a few. Targeted taxes will almost always invite a backlash. When people are backed into a corner they will lash out. Oh, and here's a good one: don't pick a fight with the guy who just kicked the butt of the largest superpower of the day. It can be said, though, that despite the obvious defeat of the Whiskey Rebels, they won in the end. The backlash in Pennsylvania helped usher in the Jeffersonian revolution of 1800. President Jefferson repealed all excise taxes, including the whiskey tax. And western Pennsylvania was not alone in its opposition to the tax—not by a long shot. Back-country distillers from Kentucky to Georgia routinely ignored the tax, and Hamilton could find no one in those areas willing to collect it.[26] Pennsylvania was made an example to scare the rest of the country into compliance.

There are also lessons learned that work to the advantage of those who wish to tax more and grow the size of government. As I discussed in an earlier chapter, Alexander Hamilton was a master of creating, or at least exacerbating, a crisis. Most of us have never really given Alexander Hamilton much thought before, but this guy was a piece of work. He had become George Washington's trusted advisor during the Revolutionary War, and he used that influence to its full advantage. Although he's historically credited with setting our nation on a sound financial footing, he was also the first poster boy for big government.

THE FRIES REBELLION

John Fries (pronounced "freeze"), the son of a German immigrant, was a cooper by trade. Born in eastern Pennsylvania, he had served as a captain in the Continental Army and, after the war, had been sent to western Pennsylvania to help put down the Whiskey Rebellion. After the rebellion, he bought thirteen acres and settled in a little town in Bucks County, Pennsylvania, about thirty-five miles northwest of Philadelphia. There, he became a "crier of public sales," known today as an auctioneer.

Congress, to the disbelief of many of the citizens, passed a direct tax in 1798 on houses, land, and slaves, with the intention of raising two million dollars in anticipation of a war with France.[27] Alexander Hamilton had pushed this tax through with the backing of the John Adams administration as part of his grand scheme to centralize more power within the federal government. Although Hamilton was no longer secretary of the treasury, he wielded tremendous influence and was quite successful in scaring up support for a war. That support became more widespread after the XYZ Affair, in which French Foreign Minister Charles Maurice de Talleyrand demanded an apology from President Adams for his comments about the French, a twelve-million-dollar loan for France, and a $250,000 bribe payable to Talleyrand.

In addition to the direct taxes, Congress passed the Alien and Sedition Acts. These were four laws intended to quash any opposition to the war from the anti-Federalists who had no quarrel with the French. Thomas Jefferson's anti-Federalists were fueled by new immigrants who were also sympathetic to the French revolutionaries. The

Naturalization Act, part of the Alien and Sedition Acts, postponed citizenship and voting rights from five years to fourteen. The Alien Act and the Alien Enemies Act both gave broad powers to the president to imprison or deport aliens he felt posed a threat to national security. This didn't sit well with the largely German immigrants of Fries' part of the world. The Sedition Act, designed to silence those who subscribed to Jefferson's anti-Federalist philosophy, was detested the most. It banned spoken or written criticism of the government, the Congress, or the president and virtually took a meat cleaver to the First Amendment. Prominent Jeffersonians of the day were tried, and some were convicted, of sedition.

John Fries, despite his role on the pro-tax side of the Whiskey Rebellion, decided to act against the taxers. He cobbled together a band of around sixty armed men and traveled the countryside harassing tax assessors with much success. The antics of Fries and his men proved an embarrassment to Governor Thomas Mifflin. On March 5, 1798, the governor sent a militia from Reading to round up Fries and his men and arrest anyone who refused to pay the tax. On that same day, Fries was busy harassing another assessor and threatened to have seven hundred men at his disposal by morning if the assessor didn't hightail it out of town. The next day, Fries and his band marched through Pennsylvania from Milford to Quakertown where they found three more assessors. They took the assessors to a tavern, gave them a tongue-lashing, and took their papers, then set them free later in the day.

They left Quakertown and returned to Milford, where they learned of the arrest of some tax resisters in Millerstown. They immediately set out for Millerstown but were informed along the way that the prisoners had been moved to Bethlehem (about ten miles north of Quakertown). They turned for Bethlehem, intent on freeing the prisoners. The marshal in Bethlehem was forewarned of the advancement of Fries and his men, but he was grossly outnumbered and planned to release the prisoners on bail and order them to report to Philadelphia for trial. He sent a delegation with this information to meet Fries at the Bethlehem toll bridge in hopes this would persuade him to turn around and go home. It didn't. Fries and his men pressed on and arrived at the Sun Inn in Bethlehem where the prisoners were being held.

Fries showed tremendous restraint at that point. Sensing a bloody showdown, he instructed his men not to attack unless he was killed. Unarmed, he walked inside the inn to discuss the matter with the marshal. Seeing the folly of fighting what was, by then, a party of hundreds of angry men, he reluctantly released the prisoners and immediately filed a report with President Adams in Philadelphia.

Adams was hot. He ordered that a militia of twelve hundred men be organized out of the Lancaster area to track down the rebels. The troops marched on Bucks County and, with the aid of sympathetic citizens, began rounding up Fries' men. Fries fled to Bunker Hill where he hid in the bushes. Ironically, he was given away by the barking of his little dog, Whiskey, a pet he acquired and named during his participation in the Whiskey Rebellion. He was taken to Philadelphia to stand trial.[28]

President Adams, over the protestation of Alexander Hamilton, who thought Washington had been too easy on the Whiskey Rebels, pardoned Fries and his men. Fries was further vindicated when the supposed threat of war with France never materialized. As previously mentioned, the Federalists dropped out of favor, and Thomas Jefferson was swept into office in 1800. One of his first orders of business was to repeal the direct taxes levied in 1798. However, the anti-Federalists would have to resort to a direct tax of their own to finance the war of 1812.

THE CIVIL WAR

I must admit, I was hesitant to open up the can of worms known as the Civil War in this book, because the reasons for the Civil War were so varied and complicated. The bull-headed insistence on hanging on to that "peculiar institution" known as slavery was certainly a piece of the puzzle. How large a piece is still being debated today. I've reached the conclusion that the North and South were fighting the war for very different reasons. It appears the South was extremely upset over the election of Abraham Lincoln because they felt he was hostile toward the South. Whether it was ever his intention to erase slavery from the republic during his administration without war will never be known. The South sure thought he would. But Lincoln's goal was less about freeing the slaves, certainly at the beginning, than it was about preserving the Union. After much deliberation, I decided to include a brief explanation from the tax perspective because it was, in no small part, a contributor to the conflict.

The federal government drew its wealth primarily from tariffs. These tariffs served two purposes. First, they raised money for the government. Second, they helped protect the fledgling manufacturing industry in America so that more seasoned producers from other countries would not kill American manufacturing in the cradle.

At first, everything was fine. The South went along with the tariffs, even though they produced very little in the way of manufacturing. Over time, they came to realize they were buying goods at inflated prices, either buying higher-priced goods from the North or bearing the brunt of the tariffs passed along from foreign goods, and most of the money, either way, was being enjoyed by the North. The balance between agriculture and manufacturing began to teeter dangerously toward the North. The South began to see the tariffs as unjust and even unconstitutional.

In 1828, Congress passed even higher tariffs, which Southerners referred to as the "Tariffs of Abomination." The North realized it had the South in a sticky predicament where they could charge pretty much what they wanted. This forced the South either to buy the Northern goods at inflated prices or buy imported goods that were ridiculously taxed with the money going back, primarily, to the North.

The situation was remedied somewhat in 1832 when the tariffs were lowered, but not enough for the Southern states, especially South Carolina.

South Carolina nullified the tariffs of 1828 and 1832 claiming they were unconstitutional. The North cried foul, even though Northern states had, themselves, nullified federal laws, most notably the Fugitive Slave Act. President Andrew Jackson, a Southern slave owner himself, responded to the nullification by threatening military action and treason charges against the culprits. A compromise was reached and the tariffs were lowered, but they still remained too high for many in the South.

One of the planks of the Republican Convention of 1860 was a higher protective tariff on manufactured goods. It would place tariffs above 50 percent on iron products.[29] This scared the South to death. It must be noted that the Northern view of slavery was not just a moral objection but an economic one as well. They saw the use of free labor as giving the Southerners a leg up, some believing they shouldn't complain about choosing between the North's inflated prices or higher-taxed imported products.

Once Lincoln had won the election, the South began its move out of the Union. They perceived him as wanting to honor the higher tariff plank of the Republican Convention or abolish slavery, or both. Lincoln maintained that he never intended to abolish slavery all at once but was in favor of ending the expansion of slavery into new states and territories.[30] This pronouncement, in and of itself, was enough to make the Southern states feel threatened. By disallowing slavery in the new states, it would further tip the balance of power in Congress in favor of the North. The South seceded from the Union over both the tax issue and the perception that the institution of slavery was in jeopardy. Lincoln's paramount concern was the preservation of the Union. Slavery took a backseat to that.

In order to support the war, Congress passed the first income tax in 1862. It taxed incomes between $600 a year and $10,000 a year at 3 percent. Those pulling in over $10,000 per year were taxed at a higher rate. The tax was eliminated in 1872 but reared its ugly head again in 1894–95. The Supreme Court subsequently ruled it unconstitutional because it was not uniformly apportioned among the states, but it was destined to return in 1913.[31] Ironically, the South, which claimed to detest taxes, got slapped with its own income tax by the Confederacy in 1863, along with an 8 percent tax on certain goods held for sale, excise, and license duties, and a 10 percent profits tax on wholesalers. The Confederacy also levied a 10 percent tax-in-kind on agricultural products.[32]

If you're puzzled as to why we're still debating the cause of the Civil War, don't feel bad. People were debating the cause of the Civil War even while it was being fought. One of the more famous debates of the day was between two notable British writers, John Stuart Mill and Charles Dickens. Yes, *the* Charles Dickens. Mill argued that slavery was the cause of the war while Dickens insisted it was over economics. Dickens wrote, "The love of money is the root of this as of many, many other evils." Mill maintained the South "separated on slavery, and proclaimed slavery as the one cause of the separation." The two had been carrying on a war of words on other issues long before the Civil War, and both relished going at one another via their public writings.[33]

Upon examination of their arguments, one must conclude that they're both right. The cause of the Civil War was complicated and multifaceted. The invention of the cotton gin has even been thrown in the mix as a cause. Slavery clearly played a pivotal role in the war. Southerners were hell-bent on preserving their way of life. But the importance of taxes cannot be denied.

It's doubtful that either issue, on its own, would've driven the South from the Union. The two combined, along with long-simmering resentment between the two camps, proved lethal. The South felt like a jilted lover. The North wanted to keep the marriage together at all costs. The result was the bloodiest domestic dispute this country has ever seen.

TAX REVOLT

SUMMARY

The tax rebellions that shaped the early years of our republic, viewed together, are a lesson in incrementalism. Two distinct forces were at work in those early years. The advocates of a bigger, more centralized government, championed by people like Alexander Hamilton, locked horns with the forces of smaller centralized government and states' rights, heralded by Thomas Jefferson and his disciples. But it would, ironically, be the advocates of states' rights that would tilt the balance of power toward the big-government Federalists.

Through their bastardization of the term "states' rights" in defending slavery, the states' rights advocates would tarnish the term well into the next century. A hundred years after the Civil War, protectors of Jim Crow laws and institutionalized racism in the South would tout states' rights as their fundamental reason for resisting much-needed change. The slavery issue was a prickly one, even at the founding of our nation, and slave-holders such as Jefferson and Washington constantly wrestled with the obvious contradiction between calling for basic human rights of freedom while, simultaneously, denying those same rights to blacks in this country.

The slavery issue notwithstanding, the term "states' rights," in its purest form, means the right of the states to control their own destiny within the confines of the agreed-upon federal Constitution. The Constitution was never designed to totally usurp those powers of the states nor were the states ever intended to usurp the basic rights of the citizens of the United States. In contract law, attorneys will tell you what is not specifically included is known to be excluded. In other words, those rights not specifically delineated in the Constitution to be under the purview of the federal government belong to the states. The Tenth Amendment says exactly that. This notion was fresh on the minds of the early citizens of our country, and they fought back with the passion and fervor of the Revolution in order to protect those rights.

The Civil War, for all the good it did in freeing slaves and holding the Union together, forever changed that balance of power between the federal government and the states. The temporary wartime income tax would become a permanent way of life in America less than fifty years later. Citizens who cried "states' rights" in opposition to such an intrusive tax would be scolded for digging up memories of that dark chapter in our history. The federal income tax became an unstoppable juggernaut, partly because of the ugly legacy of that term but mostly because of our increasing dependence on a centralized government. No doubt, the world has changed drastically since the inception of our nation, and the costs of simply rebuffing or dissuading outside aggression are massive. Advocates of bigger government and, dare I say, socialism, have exploited this insecurity among our citizens to provide services to our people far beyond the scope of what's necessary for the "general welfare" of our nation. That general welfare notion has evolved to include countless unneeded programs and the most sinister of all—corporate welfare.

States have now taken their cue from the federal government and grown to Frankensteinian proportions. The battle against abusive and intrusive taxes has been taken to the states where opposition is more manageable and victory more likely. No longer do citizens set their sites on rebellion against the federal government, like the Shays' and Whiskey Rebellions, although I believe that day is coming. The modern-day tax rebels have targeted the states where, although the odds are still strongly against them, they can fight the good fight without the obstacles of massive populations and huge expanses of real estate. With a few exceptions, these sporadic and isolated revolts have gone largely unnoticed by the American population at large but, combined, define a trend that is beginning to permeate society. With each successful revolt, the people are coming to realize that they can, in fact, make a difference and turn the tide of higher and higher taxes.

Death and taxes may be two absolutes, but higher taxes are not, as previously believed, inevitable. In a later chapter, we'll explore some of those grassroots efforts to stop ever-expanding taxes. These inspirational stories demonstrate the awesome power of the people when they finally reach the breaking point and draw that line in the sand.

Five

THREATS, BRIBES, AND INTIMIDATION

She sat nervously on the sofa in the anteroom of the governor's office, glancing up periodically at the secretary. Another staffer sat quietly across the room, as did a member of the governor's security detail. Diane Black, a freshman Tennessee legislator of the governor's own party, looked back down at the piece of paper on her lap. Although she didn't know exactly why she had been summoned to the governor's office for a hastily-called meeting, she had a good idea. A colleague had relayed the story of his own visit to the governor's office. With that in mind, she felt it necessary to come prepared. The paper in her lap contained her argument, her documentation. She was inexperienced in politics but savvy enough to know not to show up empty-handed. Prepare for everything. Her experience as an emergency room nurse had taught her that much. Being grilled on the campaign trail by political opponents and a hostile press had brought that point into clear focus.

The door to the governor's office opened, and through it stepped Brian Ferrell, one of four lobbyists on the governor's staff.[1] He greeted

Representative Black with a handshake and invited her into the inner sanctum. As a floor leader for the Republicans, she had met in the governor's conference room many times during her first session in the legislature. She had not, however, been invited into his office. She knew it to be the equivalent of being called to the principal's office. Governor Sundquist stepped from behind his desk and cordially greeted his guest, motioning for her to take a seat in one of the chairs away from his desk reserved for one-on-one chats. He took the seat opposite her as Ferrell took his seat in a rocker off to one side.

"How are things going this first session," the governor began, pleasantly.

She indicated there was quite a learning curve, but she was managing quite nicely. They chatted for a few more moments—small talk, mainly. Black knew he was warming her up for the real reason for the get-together. His tone turned more serious as he broached the subject of the state income tax. Representative Black sat there silently. She knew where he was headed, and she dreaded his next words.

"I'm going to need your help with this," he informed her.

She stared back at him for a moment. This is exactly what she had suspected when she got the phone call to meet him just a few short hours before.

"You know," she finally answered, "I had a feeling we might be talking about this, so I brought my survey with me so you could see." She patted the piece of paper in her lap. "There are a lot of things I'd like to help you with, but this is one of those things I just don't really feel that I can. I've already surveyed my constituency, and I know what they want. Eighty-three percent of my constituents do not want this to happen."

The governor glanced at his aide in frustration. "Well, Diane, you know, roads are very important in your district."

She looked back at him suspiciously. Her head cocked slightly to one side. "Yeah, I know they are."

The governor looked down sternly at the freshman legislator. "You know if you don't support me in this effort, you'll get no more roads in your district."

She sat there in stunned silence. She couldn't believe what she was hearing. She had heard horror stories of legislators being arm-twisted. Legend had it that powerful governors would place a picture of a bulldozer in front of stubborn lawmakers and follow it with the admonition that if they ever wanted to see "another one of these" in their district, they'd go along. She never dreamed it was actually true.

"Governor, that really makes me uncomfortable," she replied, curtly. "This sounds like a threat."

Black had been around the governor long enough to read his body language. She knew when he was infuriated. He righted himself in his chair by stiffening his arms to the point of locking his elbows. Then, just above his necktie, his skin began to turn crimson and, like a wave, engulfed his entire face up to his hairline.

"This is not a threat," he answered through clinched teeth in the hackneyed cliché. "This is a promise."

Black stared back at him as his nostrils flared. "I'm going to give you the opportunity to take that back," she announced, hoping he had merely experienced a temporary lapse in sanity.

Sundquist was unmoved. "This is the way it's going to be," he replied, indignantly.

Black pursed her lips and thought carefully about her next words. She didn't take too kindly to being threatened. "I think I need to go back and let the people in my district know that this is the deal."

The governor stared back at her. Black hoped he would change his mind. She hoped he would realize what a mistake he was making, apologize, and begin the conversation anew. As she sat there looking at him, she realized that wasn't going to happen. Still, she gave him one more chance to undo what had just been done.

"I want you to know," she said, "before I walk out of this room, I'm going to tell you right now looking at you, I am going to take this back, and I'm going to let my people know."

"Well, this is the deal," he answered, with finality.

She was startled by how brazen he had become. "Fine," she said, rising from her seat. Ferrell showed her to the door. As she pulled the door closed behind her, she couldn't believe what had just taken place. She also knew she was not alone. If he was browbeating her, a friend and supporter, he most assuredly was bullying legislators with less resolve. She couldn't keep this to herself. The people had to know what was going on, and she was determined to tell them.[2]

Once back at her office, she contacted her press liaison and had her prepare a press release with exactly the deal the governor had promised. The media outlets ran the story. I remember having Diane Black on my show to talk about the incident. Naturally, the governor denied it all. Such conduct by a governor would be, well, illegal. That was just the point when the FBI decided to investigate.[3] They contacted Black a short time later. They informed her they were investigating the governor and asked to speak to her at her home. She retold her story for them and was left with a contact number if anything else out of the ordinary arose. Black remembers contacting them one more time about another incident of improper conduct but has no idea whatever became of the investigation.[4]

Diane Black's experience, apparently, was not isolated. Other lawmakers, speaking on condition of anonymity, told similar stories. The governor held the purse strings to the road money and, they said, used it fully to his advantage. "He was the governor, and he made decisions and tried to persuade people to see his side," former press secretary, Beth Fortune, said with a slight chuckle, in a tone indicating such tactics were routine with all governors. "I think he used whatever tools, legitimately, were available to him."[5] In Black's case, he followed through with the threat. A thirty-million-dollar bypass project, for which the money had already been appropriated, was jerked by the governor.

Motivation through Intimidation

Although State Senator Marsha Blackburn was not threatened directly, she was aware that others were. "I heard that from some of the other members in the Senate *and* the House," she revealed. She also found her alarm had been set off at her home on "more than one occasion."[6] Tommy Hopper, who headed up the Republican Party in the early nineties and was a vocal and active opponent of the income tax, had a similar experience. He was forced to beef up security at his Jackson, Tennessee, home after a break-in attempt using sophisticated means not available to "a common burglar."[7]

Intimidation was part of the organized plan of the pro-income-tax forces. At several of our horn-honking protests downtown, state employees would stand on the street corner, jotting down license numbers and business insignia of company vehicles from those vehicles participating. One poor fellow who worked for a home improvement company in town was listening to our broadcast as he was making a delivery. On his way back across town to the home center, he decided to ride by once, blow his horn, then head on his way. By the time he got back to work, someone had contacted his boss. He was fired upon his return.

He called my show and recounted the story for our listeners. Within an hour or so, he had a half-dozen offers for a new job and went to work for a competing home improvement company. His was the only high-profile case. I have no way of knowing how many other people were intimidated or lost their jobs by these vicious acts of retribution.

Lobbyists and Bribery

Backroom deals involving lobbyists who sometimes even craft legislation are unfortunately commonplace in American politics. Although I think lobbyists certainly have their place in the shaping of our laws, they've become way too cozy with certain lawmakers. Occasionally, the line is crossed into bald-faced bribery. I learned of one deal in which a particular legislator was being offered a high-paying job as a lobbyist in exchange for his vote for the income tax. With the lure of big bucks and knowing he wouldn't have to face defeat at the ballot box for his actions, my sources told me he had taken the bait. He had been a fence-sitter in the income tax debate, but, in reality, there was no such thing. After years of debate, there was nobody who could possibly have been undecided. Everyone had an opinion about the income tax. Those who claimed to be undecided, in my opinion, were simply waiting for the political cover to vote for it. I knew this particular lawmaker, and I liked him, but I was not about to allow this bribery to take place without letting the people know exactly what was going on. I strongly considered contacting him personally but, in the end, thought that might only serve to inflame the situation. He would, quite naturally, deny the deal. I decided on a different course of action.

I wanted to give him a chance to do the right thing. I wanted to expose the deal without ruining his life in the process. I took to the air the afternoon after learning about the deal and laid the scheme out for my listeners without identifying the lawmaker in question. I was very angry. Usually, I tried to control my rage, but on this particular day I could not hide my disgust. I told my listeners of the entire plan, withholding only the names of the lobbying firm and the legislator. Knowing he listened to my show each afternoon, I then turned my comments directly to him. I told him I knew exactly who he was. I knew every nuance of the deal. I knew, to the dollar, how much they were offering him, and I was giving him fair warning that if an income tax vote came down and he voted for it, I would expose his name without hesitation.

I got a call from my source the next day. This person had run into the legislator in question in the hallway and told me he looked like he had seen a ghost. There were actually tears in his eyes. He was shaking, nervously fidgeting, eyes darting up and down the hallway. He confided in my source that he had heard me talking about his deal just moments before on the radio. He said he was only trying to provide a better life for his family. He had never even dreamed of the amount of money he was being offered and was extremely upset that I would destroy him and his family when all he was doing was trying to do right by his wife and children. Call me cold-hearted, but I didn't feel even a tinge of sorrow for him. There are plenty of honest ways to provide a better life for your family. Perhaps he was too close to the situation to even realize that he was not being courted by this lobbying firm on the merits of his skills. He was being bought.

It reminded me of Mr. Potter in the movie *It's a Wonderful Life*, when he calls Jimmy Stewart's character, George Bailey, into his office, offers him a high-paying job, and tells him his "ship has just come in." George is flattered by the offer and temporarily blinded by what the money can do for his life and his family until he shakes Potter's hand to seal the deal. All at once, he realizes exactly what's going on and rises with indignation, furious with Potter for trying to lure him in and even more furious with himself for flirting with the idea of selling out. I hoped this legislator would have such an epiphany. Fortunately for him, he never got a chance to vote on the income tax. But, to this day, I have lost all respect for the man because I'll never know, and perhaps *he'll* never know, if he would've done the right thing in the end.

That was one legislator and one lobbying firm. I have no idea how many more deals like that were offered or, worse, consummated. It brought into clear focus, though, how corrupt the system had become and how badly in need of reform we were.

CONFLICT OF INTERESTS

Speaking of lobbyists, one of the most outrageous relationships in this whole affair was the relationship between Speaker of the House Jimmy

Naifeh and a lobbyist by the name of Betty Anderson. Betty was regarded as the most powerful lobbyist in Nashville, representing local governments, pharmaceutical companies, telecommunications firms, insurance companies, education unions, and healthcare providers, among others. Before becoming a lobbyist, she edited the teachers' union's newsletter, later becoming their chief lobbyist. The teachers' union was one of the strongest proponents of the state income tax. She had an unusually "cozy" relationship with the speaker. He may deny that he was ever influenced by her, but that's just not plausible. You see, Betty Anderson was sleeping with Speaker Naifeh. How do I know that? Because Betty Anderson is Jimmy Naifeh's wife! Yet, the mainstream media, particularly the *Tennessean*, saw no problem with that.

TRYING TO REFORM THE LOBBY RULES

We had a crisis in Tennessee, all right, but it had nothing to do with the tax system. It was the systemic corruption and conflict of interest. Lobbyists had free rein in the halls of the General Assembly. Their access was virtually limitless, while ordinary citizens were locked out of their own House. It was, and is, a disgrace, yet only a few have seen fit to try to correct the problem. According to the Center for Public Integrity, a nonprofit watchdog group on ethics and accountability in politics, Tennessee ranks near the bottom in lobbying disclosure laws.[8]

Democrat Representative Frank Buck from Dowelltown tried to clamp down on some of the loose lobbying rules, only to see his measures go down in flames. "It's very obvious that the (lobbyists') influence in the General Assembly is much greater than it should be," Buck said, "and any effort to change it is met with stiff resistance." One bill introduced by Buck would require lawmakers and their families to reveal how much money they receive in consulting fees from government vendors. The fact that they're even *allowed* to receive consulting fees from government vendors in the first place is unbelievable!

Instead of concentrating on correcting these egregious problems within their own body, the governor and General Assembly chose to pursue a state income tax to keep the whole gravy train rolling. And they wondered why the citizens were upset.

POWER TO THE PEOPLE

Some of the pro-income-taxers proved to be rather comical. The government parasites that claimed to take over our spot in front of the Capitol were one example. They bragged that they had overrun our position and had scared us away. What they didn't know was that, at the time they set up, there was nothing going on to protest. We chose to stay away until there was actually a tax to protest. They camped out on the location for something like nine days in a little tent city they called "Camp Tax Reform." They received some very favorable press that claimed the group had driven us away. Nothing could've been further from the truth. Once the action heated up again, we rallied the troops downtown, and the hundreds of anti-income-tax protesters who showed up dwarfed their pitiful showing. Many of the opposition's number were out-of-town college students from Vanderbilt. One even slipped up and told a reporter she was there because her college professor had told her to come down and protest![9]

The group sported a front man who looked like a guy who'd gotten into the brown acid at Woodstock. This guy wore tattered blue jean shorts and a ratty t-shirt. He would stand for hours on the concrete barricade that was erected on Legislative Plaza after 9/11 with a yellow "Vote 'Yes' for the Income Tax" umbrella and dance to the head-banging music being spewed from the speakers of two radio wannabes who called their "radio station" WDUM, which I thought was quite appropriate. In a move that was emblematic of the whole income tax fight, these "DUM" guys powered their entire operation with a power line that was plugged directly into the state building! While we brought our own generator and would have to power down on occasion during newsbreaks to refuel, these clowns were sucking power at taxpayer expense. One enterprising protester followed their power cord all the way into the building and unplugged it.

HOMELESS JIM

A ragtag fixture of the downtown panhandler scene, who went by the name "Homeless Jim," was a regular caller to my show. "Homey," as we came to call him, was the ultimate liberal who expected the government to dole out money to anyone too lazy to work. He was certainly capable of working, himself. He just chose to sit around and complain instead. He even claimed once that the reason he was homeless and jobless was because I wouldn't allow him to have a job at our station as a talk show host. Claiming to be a spokesman for the homeless, Homey would call up with arguments that made absolutely no sense. I would allow him on just for the comic effect—that is, until he went too far.

On those days when we were broadcasting from a remote location, our seven-second delay had to be disengaged in order for us to get a real-time feed from the station. Homey exploited that on his final call to the show when he finished his diatribe with "F— you!" I immediately cut him off, then announced that he had been banned from the show. The caller who followed Homeless Jim directed his comments to Naifeh and Rochelle and Sundquist and all those pushing the state income tax. "To all of you people pushing this tax," he said, "I say to you, 'What Homey said.'" Johnny B and I roared with laughter. After that, "What Homey said" became a catchphrase of sorts.

Homey didn't take too kindly to being banned from the air. In the past, he had held one-man protests in front of the radio station. He resumed his singular crusade by pacing back and forth in front of our door while I was on the air, with a sign reading, "Phil Valentine has violated my First Amendment right."

Obviously frustrated by his lifetime ban from the show, Homey showed up at a victory rally Steve Gill staged after one of our tax battles. Unfortunately, I was out of the country and couldn't make it. At the end of the rally, the sixty-six-year-old Homeless Jim approached Steve as he came off the stage, mumbled a few incoherent words, then punched Steve in the stomach and kicked him in the shin. As soon as I arrived back in town, Homey called our switchboard and vowed to do even worse to me than he'd done to Steve. I've gotten threats in the past that I've taken very seriously. That was not one of them.

Since my move back to WTN, we've lifted our ban against Homeless Jim being on the air. It's just too much fun to pass up. As long as I have one finger on the dump button, we're ready for him.

CUTTING-EDGE PROTEST

Another very strange incident happened on the public square in Lebanon, Tennessee, close to Bob Rochelle's office. Protesters staged a mini horn-honking protest and stood on the sidewalk with signs urging motorists to blow their horns. The suggestion apparently didn't sit well with one driver. He parked his car and came after an anti-tax protester with a twelve-inch hunting knife. "He said he was going to kill me and cut my guts out," the protester told police. The driver was arrested and charged with aggravated assault.

The driver claimed self-defense, saying he felt threatened by the sign the protester was waving at his truck. "If he hadn't come at me with that sign with a stick on it, I wouldn't have done anything," the culprit said.[10]

Despite the cumulative episodes of bad behavior on the other side, we were the ones labeled as troublemakers. All of this would pale in comparison to the big showdown at the Capitol in 2001. This time, the income tax proponents would go to extremes to defame the anti-tax movement.

Six

MODERN-DAY TAX REVOLTS

The early tax revolts in our republic were largely directed against the federal government. From the rebellions against the tyrannical tax policies of the British Empire to the growing pains of the new nation, the focus was on defining the powers of a centralized government.

After the Civil War, the balance of power between the states and the federal government shifted dramatically to a more centralized government in Washington D.C. Federal powers had been staked out in no uncertain terms. Although there was opposition to those newly-claimed powers, the cost of waging physical rebellion against them became almost unthinkable. Instead of boldly pronouncing their distaste of these new powers, states began emulating the power structure in Washington. State budgets began to grow beyond what was once believed their role. Federal money was sent to the states with strings attached. These strings required more and more spending from the states in order to keep the federal dollars flowing. Programs were devised on the national level and quickly became the responsibility of the states to administer. Like an overbearing parent, the federal government played the "children" against each other. If you didn't accept the responsibility of the new programs, you didn't get the money, and it went to the other states instead.

Resistance to these federal mandates has varied from state to state. Thus, the average tax burden of each state still differs. The latest data show the combined state and local taxes as a percentage of income are highest in New York at 12.9 percent and the lowest in Alaska at 6.3 percent. In other words, the state and local tax burden is over twice the rate in New York as it is in Alaska. In real money terms, that puts Alaska's per capita state and local tax burden at $2,237 and New York's at $5,320. That means New Yorkers must work an average of forty-six days per year *just to pay state and local taxes*. Alaskans work twenty-three days to accomplish the same. Keep in mind, that's not counting the federal tax burden. Connecticut, which lost its fight against the income tax in 1991, ranked fortieth in state and local taxes just two years before the tax was passed. A decade later, they ranked ninth. Tennessee, a historically low-tax state (relatively speaking) ranked forty-ninth at the beginning of the 1990s. By the close of the century, it still ranked a respectable forty-seventh, thanks to the vigilance of its citizens.[1]

What this demonstrates is that tax revolts have a much better chance of succeeding on a state and local level, where the representatives are much closer to the people, than they do at the national level. That's why we've seen pockets of resistance to higher taxes erupt in various states. Sure, there are numerous organizations diligently at work to lower the federal tax burden, but the success stories are few and far between. The real struggles have taken place at the grassroots level where ordinary citizens organize and fight state legislatures determined to take more of their money. In this chapter, we chronicle some of those inspiring struggles and explore their impact on the rest of the nation.

PROPOSITION 13

No movement happens in a vacuum. There are usually precedents set, arrows taken, hardships endured, and lessons learned that make it just a little bit easier for the next group. No doubt, we all benefit from the sacrifices of our founding fathers. Each successive battle against those who would abuse the power entrusted to them is waged on the backs of those who learned the hard way. It's still not easy to wrest the reins of power away from the power-hungry, but at least they know in the backs of their minds that, historically, scoundrels like themselves have been brought down by the unlikeliest of heroes.

Howard Jarvis was just one such unlikely hero, in the sense that he wasn't a politician. He wasn't charismatic. He wasn't charming nor particularly handsome. In fact, he was rather gruff, lacking a great deal of tact, a bit rough around the edges. A former boxer with a scrappy, never-quit attitude, he was headstrong and assiduous. Heroes are oftentimes just ordinary people like Howard Jarvis who rise to the occasion to accomplish extraordinary things. Jarvis's story is really an incredible example of grassroots activism and how it mushroomed into a national movement. Once he achieved success, the press dubbed him an overnight sensation, but that success was sixteen years in the making—sixteen years of tireless work, innumerable defeats, and dogged determination.

He was born in Mercur, Utah, on September 22, 1903. His father was a carpenter who studied law in his spare time, later becoming a lawyer and a judge. The elder Jarvis was the epitome of rugged individualism, pulling himself up by his own proverbial bootstraps. Howard was the eldest of J.R. Jarvis's five children, and they lived modestly in their little mining town about fifty miles west of Salt Lake City. J.R. instilled in Howard and his siblings a strong work ethic. Howard became the first from his high school to graduate from college and planned to study law like his father. However, life took him in a different direction. Shortly after graduating from college, he decided to buy a local weekly newspaper, the *Magna Times*, in Magna, Utah. Within a few short years, he ended up owning a chain of Utah newspapers while still in his early twenties.

Howard Jarvis became heavily involved in Republican politics. At the age of twenty-nine, he had been named press secretary for President Herbert Hoover's western campaign swing in his failed reelection effort against FDR in '32. In 1934, Jarvis attended the Republican National Executive Committee in Chicago. There he met a young district attorney from California who convinced him his future lay in California. That young DA was Earl Warren, who would one day become chief justice of the Supreme Court. The following year Howard Jarvis took Warren's advice, liquidating his newspaper assets and heading for Southern California.

He settled in Los Angeles in 1935 and ran a succession of businesses, making and losing a great deal of money. He was at the epicenter of some of the most bizarre patent fights in American history, including the garbage disposal, which he claimed he invented, and push-buttons on radios. The push-button radio battle was taken up on behalf of a friend and business partner who invented it, and it was waged against some of the largest radio manufacturers in the country who, Jarvis claimed, had stolen the idea. After a decades-long fight, the courts ultimately decided the radio companies had come up with the idea independent of Jarvis's colleague. He went to his grave believing they were robbed. Those early fights against the big boys prepared him well for the biggest fight of his life, one for which he achieved national acclaim.

In addition to Jarvis's many business ventures, he also became very involved in California politics. He was with the party through the good times and the bad. He recounts one particular ebb during his time in the hierarchy of the Republican Party when the Republicans were having a difficult time even fielding candidates, much less winning. This was 1946, right after the war, in the wake of the Roosevelt/Truman political machine. Jarvis and his Republican colleagues resorted to running an ad in the local papers trying to recruit candidates to run for Congress. Five men answered an ad in the Whittier, California, paper, and Jarvis and his associates interviewed them all, as if interviewing them for a job.

One young man came dressed in his sailor's uniform. The thirty-three-year-old had left his law practice to join the Navy in 1942. Jarvis and the other Republican leadership were impressed with him and decided a military man might make a good patriotic angle in light of the anti-communism sentiment in the country. The candidate confessed that he didn't have any money to help with the campaign, but Jarvis assured him that all he needed to do was campaign. He proved to be a great campaigner and an even better debater. The Republicans were merely hoping for a respectable showing, but much to their surprise and delight, this young sailor actually beat the heavily-favored incumbent. That young sailor was Richard Nixon. Six short years later he would find himself on the presidential ticket with Ike Eisenhower.

For forty years in California politics, Howard Jarvis was a king-maker but never a king. He ran for a U.S. Senate seat once, coming in third in the Republican primary. His strength was behind the scenes, making things happen for other candidates. In 1962 he began directing that strength toward a growing problem in California: property taxes. Property taxes were beginning to skyrocket, and more and more people were being forced out of their homes simply because they couldn't pay. Jarvis didn't think that was right, and he set out to do something about it. Having run quite a few businesses in his day, he knew a thing or two about taxes. He helped organize a grassroots group aimed at fixing the problem at the ballot box. His effort was aided by the fact that California is one of several states that allows its citizens to amend the state constitution through propositions or initiatives. Jarvis would assert later that the right of initiative is more important than the right to vote.

The group's first meeting began informally in 1962 with about twenty citizens concerned about rising property taxes. These were mostly people in their late fifties and early sixties concerned about their friends and neighbors on fixed incomes who couldn't make the property tax payments on their homes. The problem, as Jarvis and his friends saw it, was that their property taxes were being used to pay for more than simply the services used by property owners. They felt their property taxes should go to pay for police, fire and rescue, trash disposal, sewers, and other services used by homeowners and property owners. They did not feel that property tax money should be used for schools, libraries, food stamps, welfare, and other expenses not associated with property ownership.

That may sound odd to many people today, but property taxes were originally designed to pay for the expenses incurred by property owners. Today, across America, like so many other taxes, property taxes are dumped into the general funds and used to pay for everything under the sun. The concept that taxes are put in place for a specific reason is one way to keep a handle on them. Otherwise, they become part of the ever-expanding black hole of government spending, whether that government be local, state, or federal. Today, California is one of a number of states that have a statewide property tax. States like Tennessee have property taxes, but they're collected by counties and municipalities and earmarked for local expenditures.

By 1965, Jarvis's group had legally incorporated as the United Organizations of Taxpayers and served as an umbrella group for various tax-reform organizations across the state. Although they included members interested in all sorts of tax-reform issues, they remained primarily focused on reducing the property tax burden. Proposition 13, as the final incarnation of the initiative would be known, was a long time coming and many setbacks and defeats away from that original meeting in 1962. They failed on several occasions to obtain the requisite number of signatures to place the initiative on the ballot. They also supported similar measures that made it to proposition form, but those failed, too. However, they managed to build steam and make some headway, getting closer each time.

In the meantime, state spending and property taxes began to increase at alarming rates. It was simply a matter of time, Jarvis believed, before the taxpayers became incensed enough to fight back. It was a slow boil, but Jarvis made sure they stayed in the game long enough to capitalize on that inevitable eruption.

In retrospect, the California property tax revolt was the textbook example of the perfect political storm. Jarvis noted years later that California's state budget had increased from $5 billion in fiscal year 1967-68 to $15 billion in 1977–78, essentially tripling in just eleven years.[2] Between 1957 and 1977, gross personal income for Californians rose 334 percent while tax collections had increased by 874 percent.[3] From 1968 to 1977, the cost to run city governments in California rose 163 percent while the state's population only increased 14.5 percent. In Los Angeles, the population had actually dropped by 2 percent. Still, L.A. city government expenses rose by 159 percent. Starting to get the picture? Government in California was out of control, and the citizens were furious, especially when they opened their ever-increasing property tax bills.

In 1977, Howard Jarvis teamed up with another tax-reform activist in Northern California, Paul Gann. Together, they canvassed the state trying to get enough signatures to force a vote on the property tax issue. They needed five hundred thousand to qualify. They ended up with 1.5 million signatures, three times as many as they needed and twice the number anyone had ever collected before. They accomplished this feat with volunteers and only $28,500 for expenses like printing, advertising, postage, telephones, and office space.

Proposition 13 was placed on the ballot for the June 6, 1978, election. Once the signatures were certified, politicians, labor unions, and corporations came out of the woodwork blasting it. Ironically, the only major flaw, in retrospect, of Proposition 13 was the advantage it gave corporations. Reassessment of property values in California only takes place when a property is sold, and corporations have found loopholes to mask a sale when transferring ownership of the company, thus avoiding the major increase in property taxes. Since that loophole was discovered, the corporations have been hell-bent on keeping Proposition 13 just like it is. That's right. These same folks who were so adamantly against Prop 13 are now pulling out all the stops to keep it unchanged.

The concept of Proposition 13 was pretty simple. The plan would limit property taxes to 1 percent of the full market value of the property. It also capped annual property tax increases at 2 percent and delayed reassessment until a property was sold in order to protect the elderly, who simply wanted to live out their days in their own homes without being forced to leave them due to high property taxes. It would also roll back the base values for tax purposes to 1975–76 levels. That alone meant a reduction in property taxes of around 53 percent the first year it was enacted.

As you might imagine, the defenders of the status quo were in full panic mode. They employed some age-old tactics, like using children to scare the voters. Some educators told their students that classes would be eliminated and even recess would be cut out if Proposition 13 passed. (How much could recess cost?) One teacher forced her sixth-grade class to sign a note opposing the measure and then go out and shove copies underneath the windshield wipers of parked cars.[4]

The politicians preached that doom and gloom would follow in the wake of its passage. They predicted fire stations being shut down, schools closing, trash pickup eliminated, library and museum doors closing forever. From Governor Jerry Brown on down, they predicted utter destruction of the state, typical of politicians—both Democrats and Republicans—who had become addicted to the opium of power and money. But former governor Pat Brown, who was defeated a decade earlier by Ronald Reagan after telling a group of school children, "Remember that it was an actor who shot Lincoln," reached a new high in low. He wrote a letter to Republicans stating, "If I were a Communist and wanted to destroy this country, I would support the Jarvis Amendment."[5]

As is typical with most labor unions, the leadership doesn't represent the interest of its members, rather they exist to perpetuate their own useless existence. That was nowhere more dramatized than the split over Proposition 13. The leadership went all out to defeat Proposition 13, while polls showed the rank-and-file members were overwhelmingly for it. Ditto for the California Chamber of Commerce whose state board took a stand against the measure while the majority of its eight thousand members came out in favor of it.[6]

Despite all the disinformation; despite all the scare tactics, threats, and lies; despite its sponsors being grossly outspent by its opponents, Proposition 13 passed by a two-to-one margin. The people had finally had enough. They had decided to take back control of at least a portion of their tax dollars and slam the door on the greedy politicians. In the process, they made a folk hero out of Howard Jarvis. The crotchety, old curmudgeon of the California tax revolt, who had been dismissed as a crazy old coot just months before, was celebrated as an American icon. He graced the covers of magazines across the country and was a runner-up for *Time* magazine's Man of the Year award. Democrats and Republicans alike flitted around him like moths around a light bulb. Everyone wanted to be seen with Howard Jarvis. Washington politicians invited him to town to impart some of his wisdom. Even California politicians who had openly opposed Proposition 13 were clamoring for his attention.

Nothing, as they say, succeeds like success. I remember catching

Jarvis on *The Tonight Show* with Johnny Carson—proof, in my eyes at least, that his fame was genuine. He even got a bit part in the hit movie *Airplane*. Jarvis was on a roll, and he took his message and crusade to every state. His was a message that resonated. It was all about the idea that if you force the government to do more with less, they will do it. They have no choice if the people make up their minds.

Jarvis died in 1986 at the age of eighty-three. His life's mission was fulfilled, yet much work was, and is, left to be done. Almost immediately after Proposition 13 passed, and since then, its detractors have spent enormous amounts of time and energy trying to prove it was a disaster. But let's look at the facts. Aside from the aforementioned loophole for corporations, the result has been overwhelmingly positive. That's despite the hysterical rants of left-wingers who blame Proposition 13 for everything from the Polly Klass abduction and murder to the acquittal of O. J. Simpson.[7] You think I'm kidding, but I'm not.

The Cato Institute issued a study of Proposition 13 on the twenty-fifth anniversary of its passage in 2003. Michael J. New, the study's author, pointed out a timeless problem that we grappled with in the Tennessee tax rebellion. "Although Proposition 13 limited property taxes," the study said, "it failed to impose long-term discipline on state and local budgets in California."[8] It's one thing to limit taxes, but, counter to Howard Jarvis's contention that if you limit its money, government will spend less, government always finds other sources of revenue, unless you simultaneously reform the spending monster.

According to that Cato study, there are many lessons to be learned from Proposition 13. One of those lessons is the fact that Proposition 13's focus on just the property tax issue was simply too narrow. It's like the Whack-a-Mole game at the arcade. You pound one tax problem, and another one pops up. You have to deal with all of the moles simultaneously. The Cato study refers to this as *tax and expenditure limitations or TELs.*

In Howard Jarvis's defense, however, Proposition 13 was a bit hamstrung by the single subject rule of the California state constitution, which says that propositions must deal with one issue at a time. In fact, one of the points of the first legal challenge to Prop 13 was that it violated the state constitution because it was too *broad*. That lawsuit, like subsequent other challenges, was thrown out. Proposition 13 has been quite successful in protecting the homeowner from exorbitant property taxes, but other taxes have suffered. The state has raised the general sales tax and tax rates on beer, wine, gas, and cigarettes, just to name a few.

Proposition 4, pushed by Howard Jarvis's friend and ally in Proposition 13, Paul Gann, limited increases in state and local appropriations from tax revenue to population growth plus inflation.[9] Interestingly enough, Howard Jarvis didn't endorse the Gann Amendment until the eleventh hour, since he and Gann had had a falling out over who should get what credit for Proposition 13. That petty squabbling almost derailed Prop 4, but it managed to pass. The Cato study points out that the benefit of the one-two punch of Propositions 13 and 4, however, was watered down in 1990 when Proposition 111 came along.

Proposition 111 mandated increases in education spending. California's per capita spending, which had fallen from seventh highest in 1980 to sixteenth highest in 1991, jumped back up to twelfth by 2000.[10] The study points out that if spending had been held to the constraints of Proposition 4, spending would have been $25 billion lower in 2003, thus avoiding altogether the fiscal crisis that brought down Gray Davis.

Prior to Proposition 13, California ranked fifth in the nation in state and local taxes compared to average income. The year after Prop 13, that ranking dropped to twenty-fifth. Their state and local tax burden remained relatively low for the next several years until Proposition 111 mandated more education spending. By 2000, they were back up to the tenth highest taxed state in the Union.[11]

Although Proposition 13 wasn't perfect, it was certainly more palatable than the status quo of 1978, which was to constantly milk more and more money out of people's homes until you ran them out of them. Clearly, forcing an elderly couple out of their home of forty years just because their fixed income wasn't keeping up with the ever-increasing property tax was not right. Something had to be done. The politicians, drunk with the power bought with new tax dollars, were not about to fix the problem. Howard Jarvis was willing to step forward and lead the attack, and for that, he deserves a lot of credit. Perhaps not quite as much as ol' Howard was willing to heap on himself (humility not being one of his strong points), but he deserves our adoration, nonetheless. In retrospect, Jarvis's old-friend-turned-nemesis, Paul Gann, probably did more to solve the real fiscal woes of the state with Proposition 4, but Jarvis stoked up California and the country like few have ever done. No doubt he spawned a spirit in this country that still lives today, and many of the tax fights that followed owed at least a portion of their success to him.

TABOR

One tax struggle that barely made a blip on the national radar screen has turned out to be as influential with grassroots tax organizations as Proposition 13. TABOR, or Taxpayers Bill of Rights, was passed by the voters of Colorado in November of 1992. Like so many move-ments to reduce taxes—or at least limit their growth—TABOR came under fierce fire from those who desperately clung to the status quo. Colorado Governor Roy Romer pleaded with the voters to defeat the measure, calling his fight against it the "moral equivalent of defeating the Nazis at the Battle of the Bulge" and labeling its author, Douglas Bruce, "a terrorist who would lob a hand grenade into a schoolyard full of children."[12]

TABOR was simple enough for the taxpayers to get their minds around. Unlike Proposition 13, which merely limited property tax increases, TABOR limited per capita state expenditures to population growth plus the rate of inflation. It also mandated that any surplus be returned to the taxpayers each year in the form of a rebate. But that's not all. The law required that any tax increase, be it state or local, must be approved by the voters of the affected government.

In the years since its passage, it has resulted in rebates totaling in the billions of dollars. While most states, gorging themselves on the spoils of the nineties, developed financial indigestion in 2002, Colorado was one of only five states that did not run a deficit that year.[13] Much to the chagrin of Romer and his disciples, TABOR has been a qualified success. I say "qualified success" because Amendment 23, passed in 2000, poked a hole in the hull of TABOR's boat. This amendment required education spending to increase beyond the limits of TABOR. (Remember: it's for the children.) Education spending was walled off and required to grow at the rate of increase in student enrollment plus 1 percent above inflation.

Naturally, Amendment 23 and TABOR are incompatible, and spending, which was under control, began to creep back up. This led staunch TABOR supporters in 2004, like Republican Governor Bill Owens, to call for suspending TABOR until state revenues could catch up with the additional education spending.[14] This is what got California in such hot water after passage of Proposition 13 and the Gann Amendment.

Why education spending has to increase at a rate above anything else is beyond me. Education spending consumes an ever-increasing slice of almost every state's financial pie. I once referred to Tennessee's Basic Education Program as the flesh-eating virus for that very reason. (Imagine the flak I took on that one.) It stands to reason that if education spending continues to increase its share of the state budget, eventually it *will* be the state budget. Don't get me wrong. I'm a big supporter of public education. That's not just rhetoric. All of my children are in public schools. However, as Colorado learned in 2004, you simply must have limits on budgets, no matter how sacred the cow.

Colorado's path to TABOR was much less raucous than the Tennessee tax revolt. Douglas Bruce, the measure's author, said there were absolutely no public demonstrations against runaway government. Bruce, an attorney, moved to Colorado from California in 1986 and immediately became active in the movement to limit taxes. They managed to get two initiatives on the ballot in 1988 and 1990 that were similar to TABOR. The major difference in those two forerunners was they lacked a local spending limit. The first initiative in 1988 got 42 percent of the vote. The 1990 amendment came closer with 49.7 percent. By 1992, Bruce had tweaked his TABOR, adding the local spending limit that many said was necessary to prevent a massive tax shift to the local level. With the new TABOR on the ballot, it brought in 53.7 percent of the vote and became the law of the land.[15]

Much has been said and written about TABOR since it passed. A lot of the criticism is directed at Douglas Bruce, personally. As one newspaper put it, he has trouble with his "prickly personality."[16] (It's called "rude" where I come from.) Grating personality aside, Bruce has been on the right side of this argument. Even as the Republican governor was caving in to pressure to bypass the restrictions imposed by TABOR, Bruce was pointing out that the state's budget continued to grow. In fact, Colorado's budget went from just over $10 billion in 1999 to $13.4 billion in 2004.[17] That's better than 5 percent growth per year. Those who say TABOR cuts state government are the same ones who use "cuts" to describe *any* reduction in growth below what they want.

There have been no overall cuts to state government in Colorado since TABOR. They may have shifted some money from one program to another, but they've always had more money each year to spend than they had the prior year, and that certainly hasn't changed under TABOR. What TABOR has done is slow the growth of government and taxes. Colorado's per capita tax burden ranking the year before TABOR was passed was twenty-fifth in the nation. By 1998, they had dropped to fortieth. That meant only ten other states in the Union had lower taxes per person than Colorado. They remained in the bottom eleven even after the education initiative that mandated more education spending passed in 2000.

What states that pass TABOR-like amendments will discover is that they must prioritize. Government will no longer be able to satisfy the most whimsical of whims. State governments will have to begin slowing the growth of their tentacles into the private sector, and that's a good thing. It's also just a start. Once the public begins to understand how far afield government has grown, hopefully the process will begin to untangle those tentacles. The newspapers and special interests of the state have long decried TABOR and are not likely to ease up any time soon. The ultimate decision belongs to the voters. There are several states looking for ways to cap government growth in a manner making it difficult to bypass. Constitutional amendments like TABOR are the way to go.

INITIATIVE 695

Even less famous than Colorado's TABOR is Washington State's effort to control runaway government spending and high taxes. Initiative 695 went after two bugaboos in the state. The first was the motor vehicle excise tax, or MVET. The MVET was set at 2.2 percent of the value of the car. In addition, annual license plate fees were set at $23.75. Proponents of I-695 wanted to replace the MVET and up the annual license fee to thirty dollars. If that weren't radical enough, they sought a second solution to escalating taxes. They also wanted to require voter approval of all tax and fee increases. You'd have thought they'd shot Santa Claus. The special interest groups, government unions—the usual bloodsucking rabble that raises a stink when somebody monkeys with their money—came out in droves.

The Municipal Research and Services Center (MRSC) issued a "nonpartisan" study of the proposed initiative before voters went to the polls in November of 1999. They predicted all sorts of catastrophes for the cities and counties, warning that "passage of this initiative would have significant budget implications for all cities." They warned, "Cities would lose all their public safety distribution," insinuating that policemen would no longer be on the job. Further down in the report, they had to admit that the MRSC received 84 percent of its funding from the motor vehicle excise tax![18] In other words, they might very well find themselves out of business, and *that* was what really bothered them.

Despite the doom and gloom, despite the forecast of financial ruin for the state, the voters approved the measure on November 2, 1999, with 56 percent voting in favor. Immediately, the opposition filed a lawsuit to stop it. Almost a year later, on October 26, 2000, the Washington State Supreme Court ruled Initiative 695 was unconstitutional. Not that ridding the citizens of the hated MVET violated the constitution, but rather the fact that the initiative addressed two separate tax issues.

Like California, initiatives in Washington State are limited to one issue. In a rare conciliatory move, the governor and legislature saw the ruling coming and deferred to the wishes of the people by adopting the lower fees by law the previous spring. Therefore, the court ruling had no bearing whatsoever on the taxpayers. In 1999, the year Initiative 695 passed, Washington had the nation's fifteenth largest per capita state and local tax burden. They dropped to eighteenth the following year, and by 2004 they were ranked twenty-first.[19] Still in the top half, but certainly making headway.

Tim Eyman, one of the backers of I-695, offered up four more initiatives over the next few years. Four out of the five passed, including I-695. However, he shot himself in the foot and damaged the reputation of his initiatives when it was revealed in 2002 that he had diverted campaign donations to his own personal use. He was fined $50,000, apologized to the voters of Washington, then had the chutzpah to solicit money from the same crowd to pay him a salary and cover his legal expenses! These kinds of shenanigans do untold damage to anti-tax movements everywhere.

I-695 prided itself on its grassroots organization, using volunteers to get enough signatures to qualify for the ballot, and being vastly outspent by the competition. That's what these movements are all about. In Tennessee, the contrast between the two organizations on each side of our tax fight was also striking. Tennesseans for Fair Taxation raised hundreds of thousands of dollars from big-money interests and paid their executive director. Tennessee Tax Revolt, on the other hand, was made up entirely of volunteers. Nobody got paid, and they raised several thousand dollars a few bucks at a time. Howard Jarvis in California proved that you don't have to spend a ton of money to win, nor do you have to turn it into a business or a racket, as it appears to have become in Washington State. Once grassroots becomes big business, it's no longer grassroots, and its claim to represent the people must be relinquished.

I-695 in Washington became a victim of its own success. Tim Eyman gave the opposition the hammer with which they could beat him over the head. And they've taken every opportunity to do just that. Take this passage from an article about Eyman, for instance: "Anti-tax activist Tim Eyman used campaign donations to pay himself a salary, solicit business for his watch company, replace the windshield in his Lexus, and reimburse himself for a contribution to the Republican National Committee, according to an investigation by the Public Disclosure Commission released yesterday."[20] Ouch! As the reporters began to smell blood in the water, before the full story broke, Eyman arrogantly wrote in the (Spokane) *Spokesman-Review:* "Reporters could run front-page stories telling people that I smoke crackpipes and frequent prostitutes, and voters would still support our initiatives."[21]

Eyman then made a deal with the public. If they would support his next two initiatives, he would take it as a sign they wanted him to draw a salary. The initiatives both failed to get the requisite number of signatures, but Eyman went forward with plans to draw salaries for himself and two others anyway. He formed a salary fund called "Help Us Help Taxpayers," which would pay him, along with father-and-son team Jack and Mike Fagan of Spokane.[22] Shameless, no doubt.

There are valuable lessons to be learned from the Washington State experience. The most important one is to keep these movements on the grassroots level. That's what is so enticing to the public. They love being the underdog. That's where these movements draw their strength. When they eventually do win, it gives everyone involved a feeling of accomplishment. To turn it into a business is to become exactly what they protest. Anti-tax movements are about accountability. That accountability starts with the movement itself.

Summary

Low taxes, a good economy, and a great quality of life can certainly coexist. Colorado, Tennessee, and other low-tax states are proof of that. In fact, Americans demonstrated that with their moving vans during the 1990s. I did a little research and found something quite interesting. I took the five highest-taxed states for 2000 and the five lowest-taxed states for 2000 and compared population growth during the decade of the nineties. Here's what I found: the highest-taxed states averaged a rate of 12.3 percent for state and local taxes. Those states had an average population growth of just 6.5 percent. On the other hand, the five lowest-taxed states had an average state and local tax per capita of only 7.9 percent, and their average population growth was 16.5 percent! That's well over twice the rate of growth of high-tax states!

After I completed my informal study of tax and migration, I discovered a much more in-depth study conducted by The Taxpayers

Network. In their study, they concluded that during the nineties, 2,611,000 Americans moved from high-tax states into low-tax states. That works out to about a thousand people per business day for ten years! Mind you, these are Americans moving from one state to another. This doesn't count immigrants from other countries. The state that saw the most migration was Florida, with a net increase of 1,109,000 new people. Florida, by the way, doesn't have a state income tax. Before you blame the move on the nice climate, consider that California had a net *decrease* in population of 2,171,000.[23]

Low-tax states attract people in droves. Or, I should say, high-tax states are driving people away in droves. Tennessee ranked forty-seventh out of fifty states in low taxes in 2000. Our governor was ashamed of it. Governor Sundquist found it embarrassing that our tax rate would be so low, yet our rate of growth was three times that of states like New York and Maine, which topped the list of high-tax states. There definitely was a correlation between the two, but the pro-income-tax politicians of our state could not see the forest for the trees. I announced that I was embarrassed, too. I thought we should be fiftieth! I suggested we make that our goal, then emblazon on our license plates "Lowest Taxes in the Nation." It wouldn't take but one swing through the Rust Belt and you'd have people following you home like the Pied Piper.

During the tax debate, I often asked my listeners to honestly complete a mental exercise for me. I'd ask them to list in their minds the top five reasons they live where they live. You can do it right now. Think of the real reasons you live where you live. Some were just born in a certain place and never moved, but our society is getting increasingly mobile. Even if you were born where you live, think of the top five reasons you like it and don't move. You may like the climate. You may like the vibrancy of the city. You may find the terrain beautiful. If three of your top five have to do with the government, you're too dependent on it. If four of five have to do with the government, you're a socialist. If all five reasons you live where you live have to do with the government, you're most likely a communist! I say that about halfway tongue-in-cheek, but there's a lot of truth to it.

It's an amusing exercise, but it really is an eye-opener. I think of my own reasons for living where I live, and I think of things like the fact it's a great place to raise a family. The hills around Nashville and the natural beauty are exceptional. I enjoy the excitement of the music industry and all the entertainment available. There's a tremendous family atmosphere and sense of community where we live. We're also zoned for very good schools. In all my reasons, only one really has anything remotely to do with the government—the schools.

Try this simple exercise yourself to determine how dependent *you* have become on the government. If you draw a government check, paycheck or otherwise, depend on NPR for your news and information and PBS for your entertainment, never buy books but merely check them out from the library, and love your home because it's just two doors down from the city bus stop, you have a government dependency problem. The good news is, there's probably a government program that will pay to get you unhooked.

Not that all government services are bad. I certainly visit the library, even take in a play or the symphony on occasion, which are taxpayer-supported. But my life doesn't revolve around only things doled out by the government. The trouble is, the lives of too many people do. Those whose lives don't revolve around the government are fighting these state and local governments and their ever-increasing taxes. They still have a sense of what our founders envisioned for us. They still understand that the government that governs best is the one that governs least.

The people who fought these modern-day tax revolts also understood that lower taxes and smaller government add up to a higher quality of life. If you truly want to help the children, you'll allow their parents to keep more of their own money. One who advocates otherwise presumes the government can spend your money better than you can.

Although the fight for lower taxes is best fought on the local and state level, that doesn't mean it's easy. It also doesn't assure you'll win. But taking your cause to a politician who has to drive home each night to the district he or she represents instead of back to some Washington-area residence increases your chances. Perhaps if congressional sessions were shorter and congressmen were required to log a certain number of hours in their districts, we might see a more responsive federal body. Until then, citizens across the nation continue to fight the good fight where they can. For now, the states are the battlegrounds for reining in the size of government and getting control of taxes, and more and more of these battles are being won.

Seven

"WE NEED TROOPS"

After the tax revolt sneak attack in the summer of 2000, Darrell Ankarlo left the Nashville market. He had succeeded me in the morning slot at WTN when I headed to Philadelphia in 1996. With Ankarlo gone, WTN's management approached me about coming back to the morning show. I reluctantly agreed to meet with them, although I had no desire to return to getting up at three o'clock in the morning. Also, having experienced the heavy-handedness of management there regarding issues I chose to champion on the air, I was hesitant to put myself in that position again. They apologized for their prior conduct, insisting they had matured and now understood talk radio much better. Still, I didn't want to take the chance that the income tax issue would fall from favor with the corporate bigwigs, encouraging them to pressure me to keep my mouth shut. I politely declined their offer and chose, instead, to sign a three-year deal with WLAC. I would return to WTN in 2004 after an ownership change and new management.

Steve Gill was offered the position and left for the morning show at

WTN. I was sad that Steve would now be working for the competition, but I certainly understood his reasons for taking the job. Still, we would be competitors at a crucial time in the battle against the income tax, and I feared that would dilute our efforts. In retrospect, however, it probably helped. The competition only drove us to work harder to keep the people informed. It made us both more tenacious. Although we were competitors, there was an unspoken pact of solidarity when it came to the income tax issue. Steve and I continued to talk often by phone about the issue and, in many cases, coordinate our protest efforts.

Like a stubborn case of acne, income tax plans began to pop up again in February of 2001. Senator Roscoe Dixon and Representative Tommy Head proposed a graduated income tax topping out at 8 percent.[1] What was so incredible was this was the very same Tommy Head who had proposed a 4 percent income tax two years before. Back then, proponents of the tax insisted that it would never increase, yet the percentage had already doubled and the tax hadn't even been passed yet! Tommy "The Head," as he came to be known on talk radio, had tried to maintain a low profile, but it was evident that he was one of the primary sources for the repeated attempts to pass the income tax. The Head/Dixon plan wasn't the only income tax plan being floated. Senator Bob Rochelle was busy filing a version of his own. It was shaping up to be another busy legislative session.

After two years of fighting the income tax, news of the tax revolt in Tennessee had spread across the country. I was invited to address the National Taxpayers Union convention in St. Louis on June 16, 2001. Taxpayer advocates from around the nation and several from other countries had assembled to discuss ways to beat back encroaching taxation. Attendees sat in rapt attention as I recounted the events of the past two years. They were fascinated with what the citizens of Tennessee had been able to accomplish. Many stopped me afterwards to learn more about how their particular organizations could replicate what the people had done in Tennessee. I answered their questions with cautious enthusiasm. I was immensely proud of the citizens of our state, but I knew it was far from over.

In reality, the issue was still very much alive. Naifeh and Rochelle continued to weave their web in the General Assembly, and more and more lawmakers were being caught up in it. Between the two of us, Steve and I had a pretty good grasp on what was going on. Still, the element of surprise lurked in the shadows. We never knew when those income tax proponents running the show might pounce, and we faced each day with caution and suspicion. No matter where we were, no matter what we were doing, we had to be ready at a moment's notice to alert the public. Organizations like Free Republic and the Libertarian and Republican Parties stood at the ready with their e-mail lists to help spread the word. The guns on both sides were cocked. We just waited for them to fire first.

The So-called "Riot"

July 12, 2001—It was a Thursday afternoon. Johnny B and I were doing a remote broadcast from a cellular phone store in Brentwood, just south of Nashville. We had absolutely no inkling about what was going on at the State Capitol. As many times as they had tried their sneak attacks, we should have known they would try to pull one over on us when they thought we couldn't respond. A remote broadcast, I'm sure, seemed like the perfect roadblock to rallying the citizens into action. After all, broadcasting for a paying client would prohibit us from immediately pulling up stakes and heading down to the Capitol for another horn-honking escapade.

Remote broadcasts aren't nearly as involved as they were when I first started in the business in 1979. Time was when you hauled all sorts of heavy equipment into a business. Often special phone lines were installed, and it took several people and lots of time to pull it off.

Nowadays it's a completely different story. It's not like music radio, where people envision the disc jockey setting up CD players and commercial racks and establishing the entire radio station on-site. Truth is, that's just something you'd see on a TV show like *WKRP in Cincinnati*. Very few remotes were ever done that way. Almost always, the music and commercials were run back at the station and the personality just talked from the remote location.

Nowadays the broadcast equipment consists of a small mixing board, about the size of a laptop computer, and a couple of microphones with cords carried in a separate bag. Most times there's an engineer or a promotions person who sets up the equipment, hangs station banners, and preps the remote with the client, but even that's not always necessary. I've done plenty of remotes at political conventions or newsworthy events in Washington or New York where I'm all alone. I check the equipment through the airport like luggage and wheel it in myself, all contained in a rolling suitcase. Most people outside the business still have this image of some elaborate set-up and don't realize just how easy it is these days. I suspect the folks behind the income tax push had no idea either. They thought if we were on remote, we wouldn't have time to get down to the Capitol before the vote. They probably also didn't realize that with our cluster of five radio stations we had multiple remote broadcast units. Even while I was broadcasting from one location, engineers could be setting up another.

Johnny B and I arrived at the cellular store in our usual manner, about five minutes before broadcast time, and sat down to do the show. While we conducted our show, State Senator Marsha Blackburn sat at her desk on the Senate floor. Something was going on. She could tell something was in the air, but she was not privy to the details. As it turned out, several senators were conferring with Senate majority leader Bob Rochelle over a compromise to the budget impasse. Again, these meetings were taking place out of view of the public. Lawmakers like freshman legislator Donna Rowland continued to complain about the way the state's business was being conducted. "We feel we're doing the public's work, and, as far as I'm concerned, the meetings should be open and accessible for the people who want to be involved," she said.[2]

Since there are no records of what actually transpired in the negotiations, stories conflict. Some maintain that those senators opposed to the income tax were close to reaching a compromise with Rochelle, a compromise that did not include an income tax. Others claim Rochelle was setting them up. They claimed afterwards that if the anti-income-tax senators had taken the bait, a state income tax would've been inevitable. Rochelle, they reasoned, would have agreed to bring both measures to a vote. Once both measures were on the table, he would have shot down the alternative to the income tax, leaving the income tax as the only way out. State Senator David Fowler was one of those at the meeting. He confided to me later that they were close to forcing a vote on the income tax, and he thought it wouldn't pass.

My other sources told a different story. As well-intentioned as Fowler was in trying to force the issue to a vote, they thought he was playing with fire. They knew Senator Bob Rochelle to be extremely savvy in the ways of the Senate and felt he would never agree to anything that would result in the income tax being killed. Either way, Marsha Blackburn acted upon the information she had, which was quite convincing.

At around 4:15 PM, Lieutenant Governor John Wilder, the elder politician, meandered by Blackburn's desk. Pausing, he rubbed his face as he glanced around the room. To no one in particular, he muttered under his breath, "They're getting ready to run the income tax." Then he casually walked away. Senator Blackburn sat there for a moment digesting what she just heard. Wilder was the lieutenant governor, after all. She took his comments as a warning from someone with the knowledge and power that comes with the job. The income tax was, by this time, a volatile issue. He wouldn't mention it if he didn't know something she didn't. Wilder was a hard character to figure out. He seemed to play both sides of the fence. Nobody was really sure where he stood on the issue. I'm not even sure he knew where he stood. At any rate, she took the warning at its face value. Wilder had told her because he knew she would jump into action. And jump she did.

E-mail communications between Blackburn and her assistant, Judi Butler, told the story of what was going on inside. Not allowed to use a telephone from the Senate floor and afraid to leave her voting button, Senator Blackburn e-mailed Butler to alert me. At 4:20 PM, she wrote to Butler, "We need troops at 5:00 PM." Much would be made of the word "troops" in the days ahead, as if Blackburn were calling for violence. Democrat State Representative Larry Miller, a pro-income-tax lawmaker from Memphis, suggested a censure of Blackburn several days later saying, "Sometimes the tone of the language can incite people. To me, if you say send 'troops,' that says this is a battle, this is a war."[3] In a figurative sense it was. Each attempt to pass the income tax was looked upon by each side as a battle. Each side had a strategy. Each side attempted to read the other, to outmaneuver the other, to win the day. We had often referred to the protesters as troops, and the other side had used war analogies as well.

Three minutes after her first e-mail, Senator Blackburn sent another. She wrote, "Income tax vote should be around 5:00. Need support if they want to stop it."

Meanwhile, Judi Butler called our hotline at the radio station and talked to the board operator, who passed the message along to me. She then informed Senator Blackburn of her actions. She told Blackburn that she told us, "Rochelle was fixing to run the income tax bill and that we needed honkers if it's not too late."

Judi Butler's message was forwarded immediately to me at our remote location. I, in turn, went straight to the air with the information. Although I wouldn't be able to be there for another ninety minutes, I encouraged my listeners to head to the State Capitol and begin honking their horns. I sent Johnny B ahead to broadcast from our usual spot in front as soon as the equipment was in place.

At 4:28 PM, Judi Butler informed Senator Blackburn on the Senate floor that she had received a phone call from Pamela Furr, Steve Gill's producer at WTN. Furr had heard the news about the income tax on my show and wanted details to pass along to Gill. Butler brought her up to speed, and she passed the information along. The decision was made to continue the sports show on WTN and merely allow Gill to do "cut-ins" from the Capitol. By a little after 5:00 PM, our equipment was in place, and Johnny B was reporting what was going on. The horn-honkers had turned out in droves. Honking horns had become the trademark of our protests. "It was just amazing as a tool," Ben Cunningham of Tennessee Tax Revolt admitted, with glee. "You could be so assertive without getting into trouble." Of course, that was about to change.

Knowing that searching for a parking place downtown would eat up valuable time, I asked my wife, Susan, to come by our remote location and pick me up. We reached Charlotte Avenue, which runs in front of the State Capitol, at around 6:10 PM. I could hardly believe what I saw. Traffic was backed up a mile or more down Charlotte on the way up the hill to the Capitol. After sitting in traffic for a few minutes, I decided to get out and hoof it the rest of the way. As I ran up the hill, weaving in and out of traffic, motorists began to recognize me and yell encouragement from their windows, blowing their horns.

I trotted up the hill jabbing my fists in the air like Rocky with each inspiring shout from the car windows, absolutely giddy at the enormous turnout. It was a very uplifting experience as the folks looking in their rearview mirrors realized what was happening and cheered me on as I passed their vehicles. The cacophony grew more intense as I made my way up the hill. By the time I reached our broadcast site, the whole area was a large traffic jam, with motorists circling in both directions. One of the first people I saw in the crowd was Steve Gill. We gave each other a high-five, and I headed to our broadcast position. As I attempted to catch my breath, I relayed what I was seeing to my listeners.

People of all ages and from all walks of life had turned out. Senior citizens, single adults, families with young children, some with strollers. They all gathered in front of the Capitol to show their disdain for the income tax. It was a very peaceful assemblage. Loud, mind you, with all the honking horns, but peaceful. As I've made the analogy before on the air, it really reminded me of a church picnic. People laughed and talked and drank in the excitement of such a patriotic moment. Susan, who had parked the car and joined me, was taken by the camaraderie and exemplary behavior of the crowd. People gathered around our location to find out what was going on inside.

Suddenly, a motorcycle cop came barreling through the circling honkers, blasting his siren in annoying spurts. He would stop momentarily, taking out his ticket book. Bob Stratton, a local attorney, got the first ticket. The motorcycle cop pulled alongside his car and warned, "If you don't stop blowing that horn, I'm going to give you a ticket." Stratton looked over at the cop and told him, "You better go get your ticket book." Bob's wife jumped out of the car and ran over to my broadcast position to inform me of what was going on.[4] I watched in disbelief as this hotdog officer, not at all typical of most of the officers we had encountered, wrote tickets for disturbing the peace. I reported this to my listeners, and the callers were incensed.

Then the police began pinching off the traffic in both directions. They were barricading the street in front of the Capitol. Emerging from the backside of the Capitol, state troopers in riot gear trotted in single-file down the steps and took their places across the front of the building, between us and the front door. A Tennessee National Guard military police unit was alerted for possible mobilization.[5] State Safety Commissioner Mike Greene and Tennessee Bureau of Investigation Director Larry Wallace set up a command post in the governor's outer office.[6] No citizens were allowed into the building. However, when a lobbyist would approach, the troopers would part and allow them in. This only served to infuriate the assembled protesters, who saw this as a slap in the face.

Nashville police on horseback waded into the crowd on Charlotte Avenue in front of the Capitol. If the move was meant to intimidate the crowd, it had virtually no effect. In fact, most within the close perimeter of our broadcast location were insulted that they were being treated like out-of-control reprobates. The crowd, by and large, was made up of responsible, taxpaying adults who were fed up with the antics inside the State Capitol. They had grown tired of seeing money wasted through irresponsible stewardship of their tax dollars while these same greedy politicians schemed to take more of their hard-earned money. They were there to take a stand, and they would not be swayed by the usual crowd-control tactics of the police. They had a legitimate grievance, and they would be heard.

Thinking that blocking traffic would quell the protest, the police found they had created a much bigger crowd. Those who were blocked from driving by simply parked their cars and joined the pedestrian protesters. The crowd of several hundred on foot swelled to several thousand in a matter of minutes. As the stranded motorists reached the top of the hill on foot, I began to hear stories of a couple of police officers out of control. One involved a gentleman named Tom Jackson who dared ask a cop his name after he witnessed him verbally abuse a woman in her car. Jackson was taken from his car, handcuffed, and temporarily detained. Another involved a mother riding with her husband and three-year-old daughter. When the officer told the lady to go home, she replied that it was her constitutional right to protest. The officer allegedly shot back, "I'll show you a constitutional right." He jerked the woman from the passenger side of the car, then handcuffed her, and threw her in the back of a squad car in front of her hysterical little girl.[7]

I had seen the handcuff marks on Tom Jackson with my own eyes, yet in an interview with me the following day, a Nashville police spokesman denied that anyone was handcuffed. It wasn't until after the show that the spokesman called me at home to change the story. He admitted then that people had, in fact, been handcuffed. Why that wasn't known by the spokesman before he went on air with me is still a mystery.

I must point out that there were over one hundred police officers present that day. The fact that two or three may have overstepped their bounds is not bad given the tense situation. What I found ironic was as hard as reporters were looking for, even fabricating, clashes with police, these two incidents were totally ignored by the press. The clashes they were looking for were out-of-control citizens, not overzealous cops.

The most egregious incident of police abuse was actually caught on videotape by WVLT-TV in Knoxville, yet there was no mention of it in the *Tennessean* the next day. Steve Rogers, one of the protesters, was inside the Capitol. He was angry, as many were, at the sneaky way in which the General Assembly was going about trying to pass the income tax. Apparently, there were some words exchanged between Rogers and Tennessee State Trooper Harold Gooding. In the video, you see Sergeant Gooding grabbing Rogers by the throat. The natural reaction would be to grab your attacker's arms to try to loosen the grip, but, to Rogers' credit, he passively held his hands against his chest. Gooding loosened his grip and Rogers simply turned to walk away. Gooding followed him. As Rogers passed the WVLT cameraman, he looked at the camera, held his hands out to his side, and shrugged his shoulders as if to say, *See, I didn't do a thing.* Gooding, who was still following him, grabbed him from behind and pushed him to the floor. He grabbed Rogers by the feet and upended him, slamming him down on the floor. Having turned his feet toward the door, Sergeant Gooding then proceeded to drag him from the room. All the while, Rogers put up no resistance.

As I recall, Steve Rogers called my show to relay the incident. My listeners were enraged, as was I. It wasn't until the next day or two that the video of the incident surfaced. We posted still shots from the video on our Web site. Despite the coverage on the local television stations of the incident, it wasn't until a full week later that the *Tennessean* decided to run a story on it, and that was only because they could no longer ignore it. Sergeant Gooding had been placed on administrative leave. In all their sanctimonious hand-wringing over violence at the Capitol, here was violence caught on tape, and they had totally ignored it.

Steve Rogers wasn't the only one to incur the wrath of Sergeant Gooding that night. Rodney Alexander, a fellow protester, told WKRN-TV that Gooding had grabbed another protester and pulled his arm up behind his back. When Alexander asked the trooper, "What are you doing? Why are you doing this?" Gooding turned on him. "He lets off this guy, and then he gets right in my face and starts verbally abusing me," Alexander said. Alexander quickly stepped outside to call 911 to alert them about Sergeant Gooding. That's when a friend of his came out and said, "This guy just threw a man to the floor and physically drug him by his heels."[8] That man was Steve Rogers.

Sergeant Gooding, who had been disciplined twice before in his nine years with the state patrol, was eventually suspended for ten days without pay, reassigned from his post at the Capitol, and ordered to undergo "anger management classes," which included a class called "Coping with Difficult People."[9]

State Representative Carol Chumney, a pro-income-tax Democrat from Memphis, who claimed to witness the event, wrote to the Department of Safety defending the trooper. "From my observations," she wrote, "Sergeant Gooding conducted himself professionally and exercised appropriate judgment and restraint."[10] From the video, a woman, who appears to be Chumney, is actually talking to someone else with her back to the trooper when the abuse took place. All she saw was Gooding following Rogers and throwing him to the ground, then dragging him out by his feet. To her, that was exercising appropriate judgment and restraint.

I don't know Trooper Gooding, nor have I ever spoken to him. For all I know, he's not a bad person, but he certainly overheated that night. The biggest outrage though of the Trooper Gooding incident was that it, along with the other isolated abuses by police, was not widely reported. In fact, the other police abuses were not reported at all. And I doubt the Gooding incident would've been reported had it not been for the videotape. Can you imagine if these protesters were demonstrating against a war or a nuclear facility or any other pet issue of the media? The police abuse would be splashed all over the front pages.

That night, as I reported incredulously the events unfolding in front of my eyes, we began receiving eyewitness reports from points around the Capitol. We got our first report that a rock had been thrown through the window of the outer room of the governor's office. Authorities claimed to have no idea who did it. I was immediately suspicious. With all these people, with all these cops, with all of us looking right up at the Capitol building, someone would've seen a person heave a rock through a window. Nobody saw anything. Nobody heard anything.

At the time of the rock-throwing incident, State Representative John Mark Windle was cowered in the governor's outer office as the protesters arrived. "They kept coming," he said. "I walked into the center, inner office and sat down, and a rock came through the window about half the size of a football and landed at my feet."[11] Half the size of a football? From a marble and concrete expansion devoid of rocks? Television reporters were allowed into the room to report the incident. Although I didn't have access to a television, reports I got from personnel back at the radio station indicated it looked like the window was broken from the inside. Others told me it looked like it came from the outside. Regardless of the facts—rock or no rock—television reports began crying that a riot had broken out at the Capitol. Mind you, just because riot police are present doesn't mean a riot has broken out, but that's what was being reported.

Governor Sundquist, who was not in his office when the alleged "rock-throwing incident" occurred, was quick to blame talk radio. "I am particularly critical of some radio talk show hosts and at least one legislator who encouraged disruptive behavior and destructive acts," he said. Since our show was the only one set up in front of the Capitol and continuously broadcasting the events as they happened, I assumed he was talking about me. Of course, I had not encouraged anyone at any time to commit "destructive acts." In fact, I had strongly *discouraged* it. The governor was taking the opportunity of the chaos to exploit the situation. He added, "My top priority has, and continues to be, the welfare of Tennessee's children." Oh, brother.

Meanwhile, protesters next to the front door of the Capitol were knocking on the door chanting, "Let us in! Let us in!" These were the same citizens who repeatedly saw police allow lobbyists to pass through only to have the door slammed in their faces. Ben Cunningham of Tennessee Tax Revolt was walking the perimeter of the building at the time of the alleged rock-throwing incident. He met the news with the same skepticism as I. He stood, for a time, watching the protesters at the front door of the Capitol. "What really got to me," he said, "was the look of the security guys. They were looking at us with such arrogance and contempt." One protester, who was pounding her fist on the window next to the door, cracked the window. That window, and the one allegedly damaged by a rock, were the only things out of the ordinary. Sure, there were protesters inside and outside, but most were very well-behaved. Ironically, the only confirmed violence had been on the part of the police officers.

Johnny B talked to his wife, who was watching live reports on television. She was in a panic thinking his life might be in danger. He assured her that whatever she was seeing on TV was not indicative of the real situation. He encouraged her to come down and see for herself, which she did. Once she arrived, she saw how well-behaved the crowd was. My wife, Susan, had joined us in the middle of the action. Ordinarily not one to go for a lot of controversy, she was really enjoying herself. She conversed with all sorts of nice people, saw some of her own friends who had come down, and watched as the events of the evening unfolded. She listened to the stories of the people who had been removed from their cars. She especially sympathized with the lady who had been handcuffed in front of her little girl. Susan could relate, having three children of her own.

Being at the epicenter of these protests had its advantages and disadvantages. One disadvantage was not being able to decipher all the information that was coming in at once. Some reports were conflicting. It was hard to get a clear picture of exactly what was taking place on the floor of the Senate. My usual contact with state senators was sporadic since they were actually in session and couldn't take calls. One state senator, Tim Burchett, came marching out to our table at one point and urged the audience to remain calm. He had just been informed about the alleged rock-throwing incident and was mad. I assured him on and off the air that no one was being encouraged to riot. In fact, I warned listeners that anyone who got out of line would answer to me. I wasn't about to allow anyone to sully what we had worked so hard to accomplish.

I didn't know if any of these stories of riots were true. I had no first-hand reports of any violence except for the woman who cracked the window with her fist. All I knew was what I saw and what was being reported to me. I did know that the police had completely overreacted, spurred on by the report of the alleged rock-throwing incident. Those flames were being fueled by the governor's office, not by us. Although Burchett appeared to be mad at us, he was actually exasperated with the pro-tax forces in the General Assembly. He defended the protesters to a reporter who asked him if he thought the protesters were getting too angry. "They've got every right to be angry," Burchett said. "This is democracy in action and these people are getting something crammed down their throats that they don't want."[12]

If you could've seen what I saw, you would understand how ludicrous and insulting the police action was that day. We literally had grand-mothers and grandfathers, young mothers strolling their children, busi-nessmen and businesswomen in suits, clergy, pillars of the community, all being backed down by police in riot gear and cops on horseback and motorcycles. Understand, I'm not blaming the cops. They were just following orders, and for all they knew there was a riot breaking out. They were getting their information from the very people who were trying to destroy the collective reputation of the anti-tax movement. It was a blatant attempt on the part of the pro-income-tax forces in power to exploit an emotional situation and score political points at the risk of hurting law-abiding citizens in the process.

Ben Cunningham even attempted to allay the fears of the police that a real riot was about to break out. He walked down to a group of officers standing at the foot of the Capitol and introduced himself. Then, in a fatherly manner, he gently placed his hand on one of the officer's shoulders and said, "Hey, everybody's being nice. I hope you guys will show restraint." The cop looked at him and said, "Get your hand off me." So much for diplomacy. As Ben pointed out, the overkill show of force only served to insult the peaceful crowd.[13]

I learned later that some of the cops were upset with my depiction of police abuse by the two officers who got out of hand. There tends to be a rally-'round-the-flag mentality with police officers, and I respect their loyalty to one another. It's that dedication and trust that helps keep them alive on the streets. However, they have to be frank enough with themselves and other cops when someone among their ranks crosses the line. I will defend other talk show hosts and their right to free speech, too, but when one crosses the line of decency, I'm the first to blast them.

I was extremely critical of the way the whole situation was handled by the police that day but I also acknowledged that they were just following orders. The other incidents I cited were not in the course of following orders. You don't jerk ordinarily law-abiding citizens from their cars just because they ask you your name. You don't handcuff young mothers in front of their children just because they espouse their constitutional right to free assembly. I even believe the motorcycle cop who was hotdogging it through traffic and writing tickets was not conducting himself properly. A judge, by the way, ended up throwing all of those tickets out. As most Nashville cops know, I have the utmost respect for what they do. I appreciate the risks they take. I appreciate the dirty job they sometimes have to do. I also know abuse when I see it and hope they learn to recognize that and not defend bad conduct from what may have been ordinarily good cops. People make mistakes. Some very good police officers sometimes screw up. I believe a few did that day.

Earlier in the day, when I was still broadcasting from the cellular store down in Brentwood and had gotten word from Marsha Blackburn about the impending income tax, I made an offhand comment that was bent and twisted by the media. A listener from Lebanon, Tennessee, Bob Rochelle's hometown, called in to say she was so frustrated that she wouldn't be able to get down to the Capitol. I told her that we would miss her, but if it made her feel better, "just drive by Rochelle's office in Lebanon and blow your horn." We both got a chuckle out of it and moved on, but the pro-tax people seized on the comment. By the time it hit news reports, I had been encouraging people to drive by Rochelle's *home!* The *Tennessean* reported the next day, "Valentine also suggested that listeners go to Sen. Bob Rochelle's Lebanon home and protest. State troopers were sent to Lebanon as a precaution."[14] No fewer than three stories in the *Tennessean* carried the same erroneous information. Of course, they never checked with me to see if it was true.

As the setting sun faded behind the tall buildings downtown, the protest continued to build. The State Capitol was illuminated by large outdoor lights. Protesters crammed onto the steps, waving signs and chanting. On the wall to the right of the front steps, a protester stood waving the American flag. Alongside him, another protester waved the Tennessee state flag. Still another protester stood in the middle of the steps waving a Tennessee Tax Revolt flag. The spotlights on the ground surrounding the wall cast shadows of the protesters against the limestone facade of the Capitol. Elongated, dark figures danced in the summer breeze as ordinary citizens demanded their grievances be heard. The honking horns had been relegated to the streets several blocks down the hill on either side of the Capitol. Police barricades prohibited motorists from coming any closer. Still, the horns could be heard in the distance, the symbol of a struggle against those who would silence every single horn had they the power to do so. But they could not silence the crowd outside. Citizens by the thousands filled the massive steps leading up to the Capitol doors and spilled out onto the sidewalks and across the street to Legislative Plaza. Chants would begin in one quarter of the loud crowd and would quickly spread across the mass of humanity. Protesters' faces were highlighted sporadically throughout the throng, lit by the lights atop television cameras.

Tax supporters, who had hoped the choking off of traffic on the street below would stem the crowd and the distracting noise, peered out the Capitol windows in mortal fear. The thoughts of *what have we done?* must have been racing through their minds. Architects of the tax deal huddled together in an effort to alter their strategy in hopes of salvaging the income tax. The compromise deal that had been shaped that afternoon began melting away under the hot lights of public scrutiny. Whatever deal was being struck was slipping through their hands as the angry voices penetrated the inner sanctum. Like adolescents trying to sneak a smoke behind the barn, the members were safe as long as they were not found out. As they heard the voices of authority growing closer, they attempted to extinguish their plan and wave their hands across the air in front of them in hopes the smoke from their scheme would dissipate before anyone drew close enough to detect it. Pro-tax forces in the general assembly feverishly tried to hold their troops in line. This was their precious sandcastle, and high tide had come unexpectedly. The fragile coalition they had built was washed away in a wave of taxpayer outrage. Faced with the angry protesters outside, the income tax simply collapsed.

I got word of its demise from inside and eagerly announced the news to the crowd. Cheers erupted in front of our position, and I watched as the news spread quickly through the crowd like wildfire. Soon the whole multitude roared with delight. Photographers for various news-papers across the state fired off flash after flash, capturing elated protesters against the breathtaking backdrop of a lighted State Capitol. Television news crews snaked through the crowd, grabbing protesters for interviews. Others staged stationary stand-ups with reporters beaming the festivities live to their respective audiences as protesters celebrated in the background.

The failure of the income tax was only part of the bad news for the income tax supporters. Legislators grew decidedly anti-income-tax in the face of the angry crowd. They knew they had to take steps to ensure they wouldn't have to face that same crowd again. Not only did the income tax go down in flames, the General Assembly passed an alternative. Instead of the income tax, they passed what critics called the "bare-bones budget." Sundquist had asked for almost $20 billion, an increase over the previous year's budget of over $2 billion, or a 10 percent increase, when the average increase in states across the nation was around 2.3 percent because of the economic slowdown. Instead, he got a $19.6 billion budget, still a sizeable increase over the previous year of $1.6 billion.[15] Legislators had gotten the message and they weren't about to take the heat for the Axis of Upheaval.

A pitiful pro-tax protester outside whined to a reporter after the vote, "The fact that they passed a bare-bones budget on top of that [defeating the income tax] is, it's, it's cruel. It's cruel to our children, it's cruel to our families who are trying to, you know, have opportunities."[16] According to these folks, only the government can make you happy. Forget that an income tax would've taken *more* away from "our families."

THE AFTERMATH

When I arrived home, a scathing e-mail from State Senator David Fowler was waiting for me. He was furious that I had alerted the public when, according to him, he was close to forcing the income tax to a referendum. "The activities of the talk-radio people and Senator

Blackburn have killed the right of the people to vote. I think the mob effectively killed their opportunity to vote on this issue," he told the press. Fowler was in negotiations with Senator Bob Rochelle to allow the income tax to pass with a mandatory referendum on the issue before it went into effect.[17] I believe his heart was in the right place, but you can't outfox the fox. There's no way Rochelle was going to come that close and risk his precious tax being nullified by the voters. I believed Fowler was being had, and I respectfully told him so.

My wife, Susan, who had been with me during the entire affair that night, turned on the television to catch the late news. Her mouth fell open as she watched the reports. As we flipped through the various local channels, reporters were talking about the riot that had taken place down at the Capitol. She was in utter disbelief. Having experienced the media bias for quite some time, I was less surprised, yet no less disgusted. "I was there," she said. "There wasn't any riot down there." She commented that she would've felt perfectly safe having our children attend the protest. She had found it invigorating and exciting. She had met and talked with some of the nicest people you could ever want to know. These mothers with strollers, these grandmothers and grandfathers, these respectable citizens of Tennessee that she had just met were being depicted as a mob. I had bent her ear on numerous occasions about the gross bias in the media and the unbelievable slant they put on the news. In the past, she simply rolled her eyes. Now she knew.

As he had done in his historic move the year before, Governor Sundquist once again took his veto pen to the so-called "bare-bones" budget. On August 7, the General Assembly returned to vote on the veto. Hundreds of protesters returned as well. The police were out in full force making sure there wasn't a repeat "riot." Tennessee state troopers formed a ring around the Capitol, and a state police helicopter circled overhead. "I feel like I'm in Genoa," one TV reporter remarked, referring to the riots that marred the G8 summit in the summer of

2001.[18] In short order, the veto was overridden by the General Assembly. Even the pro-tax propaganda machine with its claims of riots and threats and sinister anti-income-tax forces couldn't dislodge the people's money from their wallets. Their ploy to turn the events to their favor had failed. Even many of those who believed there actually was a riot were unmoved in their opposition to the income tax. After the way the governor and the tax supporters had conducted themselves, they figured, who could blame those downtown for getting angry?

Eight

HOW TO STAGE A REVOLT

The so-called riot in the summer of 2001 was far from the most action the historic Tennessee State Capitol has seen. Designed by Philadelphia architect William Strickland, who served as an apprentice to Benjamin Latrobe, architect of the U.S. Capitol, the Tennessee Capitol has witnessed several hot-tempered skirmishes since its cornerstone was set in 1845.

One such clash occurred just after the Civil War. Union sympathizer William Brownlow was named governor of Tennessee in 1865. Brownlow was eager to see Tennessee readmitted into the Union, but the state first had to pass the Reconstruction Acts. The legislature refused on grounds the acts violated constitutional rights of due process by seizing property. Brownlow sent the Tennessee militia out to round up all the legislative members and forced them to hold session at gunpoint. When the legislature refused to act, legend has it that Brownlow ordered the militia to fire on the body. No one was hurt, but they were scared into submission. The chip marks from the bullets can still be seen in the marble banister and column inside the Capitol.

Several years after the Brownlow incident, an altercation between a prison warden and a chairman of the Marshall County Democratic Executive Committee resulted in the warden's pulling his gun and firing on the chairman in May of 1895. Missing the chairman, the warden instead mortally wounded a dear friend. He was charged with murder and later found not guilty.[1]

Considering the sometimes-raucous history of that building, our demonstrations were certainly mild by comparison. However, demonstrations don't come naturally to me. Having been an establishment child instead of a child of the sixties, I was wholly unfamiliar with how to throw a good protest. Sure, I'd seen them on television. Didn't much care for them, to be quite honest. I'd always associated protests with the liberal left because most of the protests I had seen were on the wrong side of the issue for me. I'm sure I'm not alone. That's probably why you don't see more establishment, suit-wearing types at protests.

I've given a lot of thought to some commonalities in the various successful revolts, especially tax revolts. One point is central to success. It *has* to be something the people care about. That may sound obvious, but it is not central to many protests. Protests have become so commonplace in our society that few people pay them any attention. That's because most of them are over issues nobody cares about. But the tax issue was a hot button. Everyone pays taxes. Most people feel overtaxed. Naturally, when the General Assembly is about to foist a whole new tax on you—one that sucks money out of your paycheck before you even see it, no less—folks are going to be a bit upset.

The very first protest I ever participated in was not a tax protest at all. We were fighting a movement by the mayor and city council of Nashville to put a landfill on some pristine land inside the city down by the Cumberland River. Being a big fan of clean air and clean water, and knowing the Cumberland was already polluted to intolerable limits, I signed on to help the protesters. To add insult to injury, the site was an ancient Indian burial ground. The Indians from around the area joined the fight. My morning show partner, Terry Hopkins, and I ginned up support for a tractor procession from the site of the proposed dump to the council chambers. Of course, this was music radio, so we naturally had to add a little theater to the event. I dressed up as "Lady Landfill," a knock-off of the Statue of Liberty, complete with a torch and bed sheet for a gown. Terry dressed as "Chief Nodumpum," certainly politically-incorrect these days. Come to think of it, my dressing as a woman would now be in vogue.

We met at the proposed dump site, met the neighbors, met the Indians, hopped aboard the tractors, and headed for downtown. We got a lot of press and a lot of talk, and eventually the plan was abandoned. I'm not suggesting Terry and I had anything to do with *that*, but the point is, it was an issue that people cared about. Whether you lived there or not, nobody wanted to see that area ruined by a landfill. When we talked about it on the air, people responded.

The "Honkers"

The very first anti-income-tax rally staged at Legislative Plaza in Nashville was a demonstration I held with activist/singer/songwriter Gene Cotton on May 25, 1999.[1] Gene had a string of hit songs back in the seventies, including "Before My Heart Finds Out" and "You're a Part of Me," a duet he sang with Kim Carnes. I've known Gene almost since I first hit town in 1985. His was the first interview I conducted on the air in Nashville. Although still active in the music business, Gene had, by that time, become more famous locally as an opponent of State Route 840, a bypass that cut through pristine sections of farmland. State Route 840 was designed to connect the area's interstate system in a loop many miles from the traffic-snarled downtown area. Gene, a bleeding-heart liberal by his own admission, didn't want to see the congestion around these interchanges, which is what had happened in Atlanta when they tried a similar tactic. As he told me, these areas became more of a nightmare in Atlanta than the downtown traffic they were trying to divert.

Although I didn't have much of an opinion on the 840 issue, we had a common enemy—a bloated TDOT, or Tennessee Department of Transportation. With control of this department left to the governor, TDOT had become, in the opinion of many, extremely wasteful. In my view, it was part and parcel of the whole budget problem. The General Assembly appropriated the money based on what the governor asked for, and it was left to the governor to decide where the money was spent. It was all too often used as a dangling carrot or blunt instrument for getting legislators to toe the line.

Gene and I coordinated a demonstration at the very spot that would become our home away from home on Legislative Plaza, right in front of the state Capitol. We billed it as "The Tennessee Tea Party" and invited listeners to come join us. Groups as diverse as the Tennessee Conservative Union, Tennessee Reform Party, Tennessee Christian Coalition, and Citizen's Action Group were in attendance. Gene entertained the crowd with a song he had written called "Road Rage," which poked fun at TDOT, as I broadcast my show from underneath our tent. Always famous for underestimating our crowds, the *Tennessean* put the number at seventy-five. I recall there being more people than that, but certainly not the thousands we would draw in future rallies.

That particular protest was important in two respects. First, it demonstrated that people who disagreed on a wide variety of issues could come together on this single issue. The media would try to pigeonhole our protesters in the future as right-wing, Lexus-driving nuts. This protest proved otherwise, and it was one of the only times—perhaps the only time—the *Tennessean* would admit that in print. It also drove home the reality that we weren't going to get a ton of people to respond unless there was an immediate crisis—like a vote coming down on the income tax. I had, quite frankly, hoped for a better showing and thought twice about doing something like that again unless there was some urgency.

That's why Steve Gill and I have repeatedly said that the people deserve the credit for stopping the income tax. I can set up a tent and broadcast equipment and complain about pretty much anything. It took the people getting revved up enough to act to stop the income tax. Our rally that day did serve the purpose, however, of getting people accustomed to the idea of coming out and being heard. It got a nice placement on the front page of the paper, and people saw we were serious about fighting the income tax.

The Birth of the Horn-Honking

The key ingredient missing from that protest with Gene Cotton was the horn-honking. All of our protesters that day were on foot. They had to go to the trouble of finding a parking space, then walk up the hill to Legislative Plaza, too much of a hassle for most people. We had to find a way to make it easier to demonstrate. How the horn-honking protests got started is an interesting story in and of itself. As I mentioned before, there was no secret backroom meeting that hatched the income tax issue as a talk show host cause. We just knew, innately, that it was very important to our listeners because it was very important to us. However, once we were in the thick of the struggle, we made sure we worked together in order to maximize the effect. Many aspects of those protests after the first horn-honking—where we learned the importance of organization—were carefully planned by Steve and me. Much to the dismay of our bosses, even when he left for the morning show at WTN, we continued to talk regularly, plan strategies, and coordinate our efforts.

To many in the radio business, that kind of collaboration is verboten. In our competitive world of broadcasting, it's all about winning. To Steve and me, it was about winning, too, only we were determined to win the war against the income tax, not against each other. We both knew we were much stronger working together than we were apart. That's not to say that we did everything in lockstep, either. But, overall, we understood we were involved in a noble cause and remained focused on winning the bigger fight.

The horn-honking turned out to be one of those magical things that pretty much took on a life of its own. Steve, who was there on that November morning in 1999 when the honking began, recalled for me the chain of events that led up to it: "They [the legislators] were saying, 'We're not going to answer the phones anymore.' They [the listeners] were e-mailing. Legislators were saying, 'I'm not going to even look at my e-mails.' The faxes, they were turning off. So, basically they were saying, 'We don't care what you say, we're not going to listen.'"

As Steve pointed out, those of us who had opposed the income tax on radio had become frustrated, even angered, by the prevailing attitude at the Capitol. Even with all the commotion made by the phone calls and e-mails and faxes, they had still voted the income tax out of committee. We had to find a way to get their attention. Steve and I had been pounding the point home, he in the mornings, still at WLAC at that time, and me in the afternoons. Darrell Ankarlo and Dave Ramsey over at WTN had been doing the same.

"Big Wally" Londo, the program director for our sister station, The Rock, had been listening to my rant the afternoon before and Steve's rant that morning. He, as a citizen, was outraged that the legislators were being so arrogant. He asked Steve to come on his station after the morning show and explain what was going on to The Rock's listeners. When Steve did, the phone lines went nuts. Wally then wanted to know what else they could do to get the message through. Steve informed him that WLAC had planned a remote broadcast for the next morning at The Arcade, an open-air shopping center just a few blocks from the Capitol, and invited The Rock to join them.

Wally then suggested the rest of the five stations in the cluster get involved. The Rock had just purchased a big Hummer with their station's logo and colors painted all over it. This thing was definitely an attention-grabber. Steve suggested they bring the Hummer downtown, set up on Broadway—the main drag through downtown—and hold up a sign that read, "Honk if you're against the income tax." Wally suggested he actually bring the vehicle down to Legislative Plaza and get right up in the faces of the legislators.

Wally quickly coordinated the other stations and got them committed to coming down the next morning, and we began promoting it on my show and the other stations that afternoon. Steve recalls that I started calling it a "drive-by honking." All I knew was I thought it was a wonderful way to get their attention, but, as Steve pointed out, we merely envisioned motorists driving by the sign, honking once or twice, then driving off. The citizens actually deserve the credit for turning it into what it became. Instead of driving by and honking once or twice then heading off to work, hundreds of cars began honking as they passed the sign on Legislative Plaza, then wouldn't stop! Not only that, they circled the Capitol over and over and over, constantly laying on their horns.

I remember driving down that morning with intentions of parking my car and joining Steve at his broadcast position. However, when I was several blocks from the Capitol, I could hear the deafening blare of the horns, so I fell right in with the rest of the motorists and circled the Capitol with them. Darrell Ankarlo from WTN had been down at Legislative Plaza the morning before. He brought his show back downtown that morning, also urging his listeners to come down and honk. Between all six stations, practically anybody who had a radio on that morning got the word, and they flocked to the Capitol.

That first horn-honking was really a shot across the bow of the income tax ship. Even though the measure had made it out of the Senate Finance Committee, the votes simply weren't there to pass it. However, we were not prepared to take that chance. We wanted to make sure they got the message that the people of Tennessee did not want an income tax, just in case there was any question. If they weren't going to listen to the phone calls to the Capitol, if they were going to ignore the faxes and e-mails, we were going to bring the people to them. The fact that the horn-honking caught on so quickly demonstrated, with a fevered pitch, the discontent of the voters. After that morning, we knew we had a powerful weapon, and we waited for the opportune moment to break it out again. It would be seven months before we felt the need, but when we did, it made quite an impressive statement.

THE GRASSROOTS

Steve Gill and I both made it clear time and time again that the fate of the efforts to defeat the state income tax rested in the hands of the citizens at the grassroots level. We could continue to alert people, but eventually apathy would creep in unless there was an organization to hold the various people and groups together. Steve and I could disseminate information, but we didn't have time to organize a group. This tax fight might take years. I was hoping someone would step up to the plate. In July of 2001, I got my wish.

Cheryl Whitsell was a regular listener to my show and an avid horn-honker. "One day, while I was listening and heard people calling in, I was struck with the idea to call in and give out my e-mail address and see if anyone thought the way I did about organizing the effort officially," Cheryl said. She called my show with the idea of forming an organization called Tennessee Tax Revolt. "I am an administrator, I organize things for a living," she explained. "I knew that if this group of people did not get together outside of this horn-honking endeavor that we would be unable to sustain organized resistance to this and would not make a lasting impact on the tax debate in Tennessee. I knew I had the ability to get people organized and set in the right direction, but I had no idea how to accomplish that."[2]

She gave out her e-mail address and invited listeners to join her. She organized the first meeting to plan strategy. Ben Cunningham heard her plea on the radio and responded. He was one of the founding members and became a driving force behind the group. In an interview, he recalled for me those early days and why they felt it was important to organize. "You were calling the troops together," he said, "but we needed some way for taxpayers, as a group, to get together and carry the banner." Many of their members became familiar faces at our protests. This, for most of the members of Tennessee Tax Revolt, and for most of the horn-honkers for that matter, was the first demonstration in which they had ever participated.

"You could see the evolution," Cunningham said. "The first time they came down there, everybody was very tentative. It was like, 'Where's the State Capitol?'" he recalled. "Then the next time they came down there they were a little more assertive. Then about the third time it was like, 'Let me at 'em.'"

The protestors grew into their roles very quickly. Homemade signs, banners, even flags were put together with slogans and clever phrases. "Ax the tax" became a popular slogan, but some were even more creative. One college student wore a sign that said, "Yes, I go to college. Yes, I work my way through school. No, I don't want an income tax!" A station wagon rolled by with "Taxation *with* representation isn't so great, either!" written on its window. Some middle-school kids held a sign on the sidewalk that read, "Get a budget! Gee, what a concept!!!" Another car drove by with the passengers holding signs that read, "It's the spending, Stupid." One guy held up a sign that said, "We came, we saw, we kicked your tax!"

These signs were in stark contrast to the professional signs made up at the print shop that were sported by the pro-tax people. They were well-funded and organized through their labor unions and other big money interests. Some were even paid to be there. On at least one occasion, they were bussed in. Everyone on our side was volunteering their time. Some took the day off from work. Others came down during breaks or lunch hours. During the summer protests, hundreds of kids would come down with their parents. It was a beautiful thing to see.

I can't overemphasize just how impressed I was with the people who came down to those protests. It was their fight. As Steve Gill says, "We just supplied the volume." This grassroots movement was awe-inspiring. They had created the horn-honking. They had created the signs. They had created a collective voice, and they were determined to be heard. Whether those inside the Capitol would listen remained to be seen.

MOVED TO SERVE

Several participants of that grassroots movement ended up running for office. Donna Rowland was, for the most part, a political novice who was energized by the income tax issue. Her representative was Mary Ann Eckles, a four-term rep with deep connections to the House hierarchy. Rowland had challenged Eckles in 1998, and Eckles won that race with 54 percent of the vote by outspending Rowland better than two-to-one.[3] Eckles was so confident her seat was safe she openly supported the income tax and encouraged others to do the same. She insisted supporting the income tax would not harm legislators in their reelection bids and cited a Mason-Dixon Research poll as her evidence.

In the poll, 40 percent said they would be less likely to vote for a candidate who supported the income tax. Talk about seeing the glass half full. Eckles saw this as hard proof that lawmakers would not be damaged at the polls if they joined her in supporting the income tax. "Other members need to know they can get reelected if they do the right thing," she said. "I would hope that the [poll numbers] would give some of them confidence to know that a majority of their voters would forgive them if they voted for an income tax."[4]

In 2000, I was first formally introduced to Donna Rowland at a rally for Congressman Van Hilleary featuring Charlton Heston in Pulaski,

Tennessee. I had seen Donna at our horn-honking protests and had corresponded with her numerous times via e-mail. It wasn't until we met that I realized what a dynamo she was. Her enthusiasm was contagious. Up until that point, I had believed that Mary Ann Eckles was destined for reelection, despite her pro-income-tax stance. She had done an incredible job building her political network and ingratiating herself with the well-connected. She certainly had a war chest that would intimidate the most seasoned politician. Donna, however, was not deterred. She pressed forward with her campaign that year.

Eckles outspent Rowland by more than four-to-one, the bulk of that coming from PACs and lobbyists.[5] But this time, Rowland had the income tax issue to make hay with. Because of the income tax issue and the presidential race, twice as many people showed up at the polls. Donna Rowland shellacked Eckles with 60 percent of the vote. A stunned Eckles was belligerent after her humiliating defeat. "I think 60 percent of the people don't believe there is a problem and if they get rid of me it will go away," Eckles said. "I think people didn't want to hear the truth. They want people to think it is a spending problem instead of a revenue problem."[6] That's right, Mary Ann. You're the smart one, and the people are just stupid. Eckles couldn't quite tear herself away from the state Capitol. After getting booted out, she went directly from her lost House seat to become a lobbyist.

In 2002, protesters like Jim Bryson, Phillip Johnson, and Susan Lynn, among others, entered the political fray. Bryson won the Republican primary for State Senate over an established candidate who admitted after the election that he had not gone far enough to the right. Both came out against the state income tax. Bryson ran unopposed in the general election and took over the seat vacated by Marsha Blackburn when she was elected to the U.S. Congress. Both Lynn and Johnson won open House seats against their Democratic opponents. The grassroots movement had begun the transition from outside antagonists to inside reformers. No longer were they satisfied to merely stand on the sidelines and cheer. They wanted to get in the game and make a difference, and these fresh voices were beginning to make inroads in dismantling the political machine that had run the state for generations.

Keep It Simple

One of the keys to getting people to care is to explain the problem in the simplest of terms. Don't overcomplicate the issue. The points of the tax revolt were pretty straightforward. State income tax. You're not paying it now. You *will* pay it if it passes. It's unconstitutional. They're already wasting your money. Don't let them get any more. Boom. Pretty simple. The first tax Sundquist tried was the tax on LLCs (or limited liability companies, which allows individuals or separate legal entities, such as corporations, to avoid personal responsibility for debts or obligations the business incurs). It was, as you can see, much more complex. In retrospect, there wasn't that much of an outcry about it, and Sundquist would've been better off pursuing that for three years rather than the income tax. The LLC issue was much too complex for most people, including me at the time, to fully understand. Besides, most people don't own an LLC (although the tax would've been passed on to them, regardless, through increased prices on goods or services). The LLC tax was killed, not by the people, but by concerned business interests who put pressure on the General Assembly.

Why they thought it would be easier to fight the people instead is anyone's guess. Perhaps they thought we wouldn't be paying attention. Maybe they thought by starting with folks making over $100,000 a year they could pit us against one another. Who knows? The truth is, once they went for a tax everyone could get their mind around, it made our job on the radio much easier.

That wasn't the only mistake they made. The fact that Governor Sundquist was stupid enough to say there was absolutely no waste in his proposed budget set him up for the inevitable. There's *always* waste in government. After I started delineating it on the air and on our Web site, what could he say? Instead of trying to refute it or just ignoring it, he blundered into another mistake by saying those who opposed him were Neanderthals. That *really* endeared him to the public. It wasn't just the fact that he was calling us names. It was his whole attitude. Since we didn't agree with him, we were somehow backwards, dumb, a people who had not evolved. Southerners are kind of sensitive about that sort of talk. We get hit with cheap shots all the time. Southerners are about the only group of people still in open season in our rigid world of political correctness. To have some guy from Illinois saying that we were, essentially, not sophisticated enough to understand his proposal, did not make him any friends.

That's lesson number two. Learn to exploit the other side's mistakes. As soon as Governor Sundquist referred to anti-income-taxers as "Neanderthals," the anti-income-taxers sailed on that gaffe and made as much political hay from it as they could. If the opposition makes a dumb comment, especially such a condescending one, play it for all it's worth. If there's one thing that infuriates even the fence-sitters, it's someone in authority looking down their nose at them. Use it.

Another common thread in most of these tax revolts is communication—getting the word out. From the time of the American Revolution, revolts have depended on communication. Thomas Paine riled up the people of his day with his pamphlet *Common Sense*. Revolutionary plans and ideas were committed to paper and distributed via a loose network of patriots that came to be known as the Committees of Correspondence. We informed everyone via talk radio, which can be a very powerful medium. Consumers of talk radio tend to be more passionate than consumers of other radio formats. They also tend to be better educated, not necessarily in terms of schooling, but in terms of knowing the issues. They're a very pro-active bunch. They care deeply about the issues of the day, and they get involved. That's borne out by the fact that they vote in much greater numbers than listeners to other formats. If you can tap into the talk radio audience, you have a much better chance of moving your agenda forward.

The trick is getting a talk show host or hosts interested in your issue. There are some hosts who feel uncomfortable participating in advocacy radio, even when they're passionate about the issue. However, most hosts are looking for a good angle. They're looking for ways to involve their listeners. The freedom rallies that were staged by us in Nashville, Darrell Ankarlo in Dallas, and Glenn Beck and Sean Hannity on a national level have drawn thousands upon thousands of people together. That started from a simple idea Ankarlo had in Dallas just before the Iraq War began in 2003. Other talk hosts picked up on it, and it swept the nation.

Talk show hosts and program directors know that camaraderie can translate into a loyal listener base, and most are eager for a good cause. But capturing and keeping the attention of a host or station can be difficult. I know from personal experience that I'm going one hundred miles an hour every day. The news is fluid. Hot stories cool in a hurry or get bumped by something hotter. It's sometimes difficult, if not impossible, for a host to stay focused on one thing for very long. If your issue is important enough, make sure you keep it out front.

Here are some tips from my own experience as a host. E-mail the host or producer, or both, but don't bombard them with frivolous press releases, and don't subject them to document dumps. Choose your press releases carefully. I get tons of press releases each day from people who think if they're not sending out X amount per week, they're not doing their job. There are some I've wasted my time reading so many times that they're automatically deleted. Experience tells me that there's nothing useful inside that e-mail, even though they may, at last, have something interesting to say.

Personalize the e-mail. Don't send it from a mass mailing list. For one thing, I'd like to think I'm talking about something nobody else knows about. If I'm on a list with a bunch of other talk show hosts as well as MSNBC, Fox News, and Oprah, I don't bother. If it's that big, it'll make it to Fox or the Internet news sites, and I'll see it there. I delete hundreds of those every single day without ever reading them. Some get my attention with a clever subject line and I'll open them, but I'm almost always sorry I did. With all the e-mail I get, I have to have a system for getting rid of large volumes of e-mail that I'll never read. Most hosts are in the same boat. E-mail is a great tool, but it is also quite time-consuming. We tend to look for ways to instantly reduce the volume and get to the important ones.

That's not to say that there's anything at all wrong with e-mailing lists. We have one for *The Phil Valentine Show,* the FOP list (Friends Of Phil). Those are fine. They're lists people have signed up for, and I don't mind getting something I asked for. In fact, I welcome those. But when it comes to unsolicited items, I'm looking for "newsworthy" e-mails that suggest I'm getting a scoop. Most talk show hosts would like to think they're special enough that someone would offer them an exclusive story. Even if you're not, make them feel that way.

Another way I cull my voluminous inbox is by deleting most everything with "FW:" in the subject line. That means someone has forwarded something to me. I don't have enough time to read all the original e-mails specifically addressed to me, much less something that was forwarded from someone else. Unless I know the person, those don't get read. Besides, most of the time, it's the same old junk that's been circulating the Internet for years. You've seen them: things like Hillary and the Black Panthers or a patriotic message from George Carlin or the same message from Bruce Willis or any of a variety of other celebrities credited as the author. Avoid forwards.

Another tip. Never send an attachment unless you've cleared it with the host first. Many politicos and agency types love to include PDF files because they can dress up their press releases and make them look pretty. I *never* open them. I've had at least one computer destroyed because I opened an attachment and unleashed a virus. It was a nightmare! I no longer open anything from anybody unless I'm specifically expecting it.

I'm sure you're asking yourself, "What the heck kind of e-mail *do* you open, Phil?" I open direct one-on-one e-mails that have a concise but interesting subject line. That may sound a bit ambiguous so let me cite some examples. In the case of the tax revolt in Tennessee I would certainly open one with a subject line, "Phil, here's evidence of fraud in the state computer system," or, "Phil, here's the answer to a question you asked on the air today." Notice the inclusion of "Phil." That usually tells me that it's not a mass e-mailing. Sometimes I get ones stating, "Phil, get larger breasts in just two weeks," so that rule doesn't always apply. Most of the time it does.

Once you get a host curious enough to open your e-mail, make it count on the inside. I look at the little scroll bar on the side. If it's really small, I know I have a novel ahead of me. If it's large, I know the message is concise. Concise is nice. Get directly to the point. If you've met the host before, refresh his or her memory: "Phil, we talked yesterday about taxes at the library." Don't assume the host remembers you. And, please, no "Hey, Phil, remember when I called your show in 1998?" messages. Be realistic. Most hosts don't remember the last caller, much less someone who called in years ago. That's not said to make you believe talk show hosts are special; in fact, it's to say that they're just like you. You talk to dozens of people in a week's time and don't remember most of them. It's gratifying to most hosts if their listeners feel close to them, but just because you feel like you know the host, don't assume the host remembers you. When I e-mail other talk show hosts or media personalities that I've only met a couple of times, I make sure I reintroduce myself. I leave nothing to chance. If you have a connection with that person, you have a better chance that they'll take time to read your message. Even then, you want to get directly to the point.

If you have air support, that's a big piece of the puzzle, but you need more. To really pull off something like a tax revolt you need an organization. Howard Jarvis and his band of twenty-some citizens realized this early on in their fight to limit property tax increases. They formed an umbrella organization and included tax advocates from all across the state of California. The Tennessee Tax Revolt organization that was started on my show as the anti-income-tax movement began to build up steam. Now Tennessee Tax Revolt boasts a membership of thousands across the state, and they've been very active on tax issues far beyond the income tax fight.

Ben Cunningham, one of the founding members of Tennessee Tax Revolt, offers some tips for organizing such a group. First, "Have a very clear, short message," he advises. Many groups get bogged down in too much information and try to foist that on the politicians. Like the document dump I warned about, too much information can be as useless as none at all. Second, "Always assume that the most powerful unit of government is the individual citizen and that as individual citizens you hold the keys to power." Too often groups are timid. Are we allowed to talk to so-and-so? Are we allowed to visit such-a-place? You are the boss. Keep that in mind, and, in a respectful way, remind the politicians you're dealing with if they ever forget that salient point. Third, "Get to the decision-makers quickly and make your presence felt." That's certainly a lesson learned from the tax rebellion in Tennessee. Pretty soon, the politicians knew exactly who Tennessee Tax Revolt was. They either feared, loathed, or respected them, but they knew who they were.

I'd also add a piece of advice I heard from a speaker at a taxpayers' convention a few years ago. He said, "Be known for something." For example, Citizens Against Government Waste is known for its annual Congressional Pig Book Summary, or "The Pig Book," as Washingtonians call it. Each year this book itemizes and summarizes the year's wasteful pork-barrel legislation, providing names and details. Wisconsin Senator William Proxmire used to issue the Golden Fleece

Awards for the most egregious wastes of taxpayers' money. With his blessing, Taxpayers for Common Sense picked up the mantle in 2000 and, once again, began issuing the Golden Fleece Awards. Americans for Tax Reform issues Friend of the Taxpayer and Enemy of the Taxpayer Awards. The National Taxpayers Union gives "Taxpayer-Friendly" rankings. If you're looking to get some media attention, you may want to consider coming up with a hook like those mentioned above. These types of ideas help your organization stand out.

However, if you have an issue as hot as the income tax issue was in Tennessee, you might not need anything to catch the attention of the media and the public. But once the media attention around the income tax died down, so did the attention around Tennessee Tax Revolt. And yet the efforts of Tennessee Tax Revolt didn't stop when the income tax issue was off the front pages. They became even more vigilant, attending budget meetings and offering their acquired knowledge and expertise to anyone across the state who might be fighting higher taxes all alone. "We try to assist those who are acting as citizens and as taxpayers trying to get involved in the process," Ben Cunningham explained. "The system does work if people will get involved."[2] It also helps to stay plugged in on a regular basis instead of just mobilizing when there's a crisis. If you have an infrastructure in place, it makes it much easier to jump into action.

Nine

SMEARING THE OPPOSITION

One of the tactics employed by the pro-income-tax forces was not atypical of the desperation employed in other political battles. When the opposition discovers they no longer have any facts to back up their argument, they resort to smears and name-calling. I described this particular stratagem in my previous book, *Right from the Heart*, as the verbal equivalent to running out of bullets then throwing your gun at your opponent. We had, quite successfully, boxed the opposition in by demonstrating their hysterical call for an income tax as mere theatrics unsupported by facts. The colossal waste in state government had been amply documented, and the people had responded with understandable outrage. The only thing left to do was to try to discredit the spring from which most of this information flowed, and that was talk radio.

State Representative Keith Westmoreland, a Republican from Kingsport, Tennessee, was a rather low-profile lawmaker. Up until his name hit the headlines, I don't recall ever hearing of him. But hit the headlines he did, not in the way he would've hoped. WSMV-TV broke a story on June 17, 2002, that would set in motion a chain of events allowing those in favor of the income tax to exploit a tragic situation in order to vilify talk radio. The television station reported to its viewers that Representative Westmoreland had been arrested the prior weekend in Florida on charges of exposing himself to young girls at a Sandestin hotel hot tub. I logged in my journal that evening:

What kind of idiot would do such a thing? With all the political scandals it stuns me that politicians continue to be so dumb. If this turns out to be true, this guy needs to resign.

I echoed that same sentiment on the radio. As it turned out, Westmoreland was on record as voting for the income tax. I hadn't checked that fact at the time I went to air, nor did I care, though some would claim that was my motivation. It wasn't. Whoever this guy was, he needed to go. On June 19, just two days after the Florida story broke, Nashville police held a news conference to announce that the Florida incident apparently wasn't isolated. There were at least two more incidents of improper conduct by Westmoreland being investigated in Nashville. I commented on-air that elected office was no place for a pervert and that he ought to resign. Still, Westmoreland showed up at the legislative session that morning as if it were business as usual.

Friends and colleagues began to rally around Westmoreland. I began to catch heat from them because I was convicting him on-air before he was ever tried, despite the fact that I was always careful to say "alleged" and to preface my comments with "if this is true" before outlining what I thought should happen. Like it or not, that's what we do. We talk about the hot issues of the day. I don't recall anyone waiting for a jury verdict before forming an opinion about O. J. Simpson. Even after his trial, commentators, talk show hosts, and ordinary citizens voiced their doubts about his innocence. People also make all sorts of assumptions based on their best information regarding presidents and other politicians, both Democrat and Republican, without the benefit of a trial. As long as these opinions are just that, and are couched that way, it's part of the national dialogue of the country and should not be impeded. However, there were those who, in spite of the mountain of evidence, refused to believe Westmoreland was guilty.

As it turned out, Westmoreland returned home after that day's session and killed himself. The next morning, I arrived for another broadcast in front of the State Capitol. They were threatening to run the income tax again, and we were out in full force. I did not know at the time about Westmoreland's suicide and only learned of it after we started the show. I was truly saddened by it. I thought Westmoreland was a rogue, but I don't like to see anyone take his own life. It was tragic, and I wish he had chosen another alternative to solving his problems. Still, the General Assembly was in session, and I thought it possible that the tax supporters would use the tragedy to run a vote on the income tax. We held our position, awaiting word that they had adjourned. Until they did, I planned to stay right where we were.

The mood of the show, mind you, was quite somber in light of the sad news. Having been going at Westmoreland pretty heavy the day before, I thought it appropriate to recount a story my father told of my grandfather. It seems a scoundrel in my hometown had died. One of my grandfather's friends rushed into his law office to gleefully share the news, knowing my grandfather didn't care for the man. After ridiculing the deceased man and laughing at his demise, my grandfather looked sternly across the desk at the man and said, "The pale face of death is a flag of truce for me." The man sheepishly withdrew from the room.

That was the tone of my broadcast that day. Whatever Keith Westmoreland had done no longer mattered. He had been punished by his own hand, and I saw no sense in belaboring the issue. I did, though, see a need to remain vigilant outside the Capitol since those in charge of the state government had already demonstrated they could not be trusted. Inside, unbeknownst to us, an impromptu memorial service was taking place. One lawmaker began the service with a hymn, then representatives rose to reflect and take stock of Westmoreland's life. One in particular, Representative Chris Newton, a fellow Republican from Cleveland, Tennessee, was livid. "You hounded the man to death," he scolded, his face red with rage.[1] Most believed his comments to be aimed at talk radio, Steve Gill and me in particular. Newton would confide in me later that he was referring to the television reporters. No matter the target of his rage, the pro-tax forces saw their opportunity: Saddle Valentine and Gill with the death of Westmoreland, and the pro-taxers might garner some sympathy with the public.

Some weren't waiting for Newton's cue. I got word that another talk show that morning had specifically fingered Gill and me for the death. Conflicting reports named either host Teddy Bart as the culprit or one of his guests. Either way, it was certainly below the belt and, on its face, absurd. In my mind, the fact that Westmoreland committed suicide settled the argument over his guilt. I didn't drive him to do it. He came face-to-face with his own demons and decided on his own course of action.

Despite the obvious absurdity, the pro-income-taxers had a field day with the issue, shamelessly exploiting the man's death for their benefit. The first printed salvo was being written even as I was doing my show the day Westmoreland's suicide hit the news. Edith Wright, a reporter from the *Tennessean*, stopped by our broadcast position that morning to get my reaction to the news. I was on guard. I tried to choose my words carefully. She asked what I thought about it, and I quickly relayed my grandfather's story. She then pointed out that I had been "ridiculing" him just one day prior. I acknowledged that fact but pointed out that today's news cast our discussion of him in a whole new light.

She then asked if I felt guilty about ridiculing him. "No," I answered. "People need to understand that if you run for public office there's going to be more scrutiny than normal. If you don't want to be ridiculed, don't get in the public light, but the situation is entirely different today. I feel very sorry for his family and hate that he chose to end his life like this." "What do you think Keith Westmoreland will be remembered for?" she asked. I told her that I had never really heard of him until the scandal surfaced. I was sure he had done some good things in his life, but the way the media operates, unfortunately, most people will associate his name with the scandal. "If he was alive today, would you still ridicule him?" she asked. I was getting frustrated with her fixation on the "ridicule" angle. I thought for a moment and said, "Well, if he were alive today, knowing what we know about the Florida arrest and the investigation by Nashville police, I would continue as I was yesterday, but that's not the case. He's gone now and we need to put this behind us." Satisfied, she moved on. I turned to Johnny B and said, "I'm going to be real curious to see how that comes out in the paper."

The next morning, I grabbed a copy of the paper. The front-page story detailed the Westmoreland memorial service inside the Capitol. After the details of the service, the kind words by his colleagues, even a description of the flowers placed on his desk, came this stark, out-of-place inclusion. "On WLAC-am 1510 yesterday, talk show host Phil Valentine defended the media coverage. 'If you don't want to be ridiculed, don't get in the public light. We will forever remember him for exposing himself to children. If he was still alive today, I would still ridicule him.'"[2] No mention of my grandfather's touching story. No mention of the tenor of my show that day. No mention of my concern for his family or wanting to put the issue behind us. She had prodded me until she got enough quotes to piece together what she was there to do—make me the villain. An old producer of mine joked once that reporters can make you say anything they want you to say. Then he handed me a sheet of paper with this headline. "O. J. Simpson: I . . . killed . . . Nicole." I was laughing then. This, however, wasn't funny.

The attacks began almost immediately in the letters to the editor. One letter stated that Steve Gill and I should, "own up to their role in helping to push a disturbed man to a tragic end."[3] Another opined, "These two bloody stains on our city need an escort out, along with their hate radio."[4] These rantings by misinformed readers are almost understandable given the information they were spoon-fed by the *Tennessean*. What was inexcusable was the editorial run by the *Tennessean's* competitor, the *Nashville City Paper*. Their editorial board saw fit to run the headline, "Radio hosts dance on Westmoreland's grave." I rarely let criticism get to me, but that was absolutely outrageous. They accused Gill and me of linking Westmoreland's perversion to his support of the income tax. "They cynically attempted to use the Westmoreland scandal as a weapon in their on-air battle against a state income tax," they wrote.[5] I did nothing of the kind. How ironic that *they* were using the man's death to garner support *for* the income tax. I had to keep reminding myself that this was all designed to discredit Gill and me over the income tax issue. Still, I thought it was a cheap shot. I had been in informal discussions with the *City Paper* about writing a column for them. I decided, at that point, to discontinue any further discussions.

The first to fire a shot my way in the "Who Killed Westmoreland?" debate was Teddy Bart, a talk show host on a competing radio station. Teddy and I have a long history, dating back to the time he hosted a talk show on WLAC-AM when I was working the FM. Despite the barbs he's thrown my way over the years, I've always liked Teddy. Besides, talk radio is all about opinions, and if I'm big enough to espouse them, I should be big enough to accept those of others. After the Westmoreland story, Teddy invited me to be a guest on a local television show he was hosting at the time. I accepted. Teddy asked if I had gone "beyond the pale" by calling Westmoreland a pervert. I thought it an odd question. I answered him with a question. "What do *you* call a grown man who exposes himself to little girls?" He then accused me of convicting Westmoreland in the press without a trial. I asked him if he thought Richard Nixon was guilty. He said, "Yes, but Nixon was impeached for his crimes." I pointed out that Nixon was neither impeached nor convicted of anything. Teddy had made my point for me. He had convicted Nixon, as most Americans had. Keith Westmoreland, on the other hand, had convicted himself.

'BIG MONEY' BACKS THE TAX MOVEMENT

The counterpart to Tennessee Tax Revolt over on the pro-income-tax side was the group Tennesseans for Fair Taxation. Actually, it was a mouthpiece for the various government unions. While Tennessee Tax Revolt was a true grassroots organization with thousands of members making small contributions, Tennesseans for Fair Taxation, or TFT, was a bureaucratic behemoth akin to the bloated government it fought to perpetuate. The coffers of Tennessee Tax Revolt filled to no more than about $3,000. The largest contributions were a couple of $500 checks from two of the founders. Tennesseans for Fair Taxation, on the other hand, was a conglomerate with over $236,000 in revenue and well over $243,000 in expenses. Even as a pro-tax organization they were running a deficit!

Its board members read like a who's who of union activists and advocates for larger government. Board member Tony Garr was also the executive director of the Tennessee Health Care Campaign, which lobbies the General Assembly to further fund the black hole boondoggle known as TennCare. One of Tennessee Health Care's board members, Gordon Bonnyman, has sued the state countless times in order to extract more blood from the turnip. These groups are infested with people who believe the government, at all levels, should do everything for everyone. They're also aligned with some of the most leftist groups in America, including the National Organization of Women.[6] This group openly derided not only me but also my listeners, referring to them as "hate radio groupies."[7] TFT was not only in bed with some of the whacked-out leftist organizations, they had aligned themselves with the Nashville Peace and Justice Center, which, until I exposed them on the air, counted the Communist Party USA as one of its member organizations. The CPUSA even shared the same address as the Nashville Peace and Justice Center. Tennesseans for Fair Taxation had no problem enlisting the help of the NPJC, even with their dubious history of communist ties, which the news media predictably ignored.

Soft Bias

Efforts within the news media to discredit the anti-tax movement, and in particular talk radio, were subtle. When the horn-honking protests first began, some reporters, like Lydia Lenker, refused to even acknowledge that talk radio was behind them. I remember one reporter commenting, as she stood on the street corner with cars honking in the background, "Nobody knows where these cars are coming from." That's not to say all the reporters were like that. There were many television reporters who did an admirable job. One in particular made it a point to feed me information from down at the Capitol. I dare not give his name here for fear of jeopardizing his job. It wasn't so much that he was on our side. Frankly, I couldn't say for sure where he was ideologically, but he listened to my show for information. He felt moved to pass along tidbits he thought I might find of interest.

In addition to little subtleties like Lydia Lenker labeling the horn-honkers as the "Lexus Brigade," there were attempts to downplay the size of the crowd. I noted on one particular day the newspapers, in various articles within the same paper, estimated the crowd from "three hundred protesters" in one news report to "over a thousand" by a more objective columnist. It was also the newspapers that turned a peaceful demonstration in 2001 into a "riot," even though only one window was cracked, by accident, and a very questionable "rock" was supposedly thrown through a window in the governor's office.

The headline in the *Tennessean* the day after the big protest in July of 2001 read: "Crowd hurls rocks, shouts to protest tax." Rocks? Suddenly the infamous "rock" had become plural. It conjured up images of wild-eyed hippies from the sixties throwing rocks and burning cars. Reporters used inflammatory language like "mob of tax protesters" to describe the protest. Paula Wade, a rabidly pro-income-tax reporter from the *Commercial Appeal* in Memphis, wrote that legislators were "almost drowned out by the clamor of violent tax protesters." Violent tax protesters? No mention, of course, of the violent cops.

The papers tended to be the most biased of the media sources. They spoon-fed the public the propaganda coming out of the governor's office, especially when it came to figures. Either they didn't check the numbers or they didn't want to. Reductions in runaway growth were labeled "drastic cuts." Outrageous claims of multimillion-dollar deficits were never questioned, just printed. Despite the wealth of information available from talk radio and the budget analyses posted on my Web site, reporters ignored it all.

I must give credit to one columnist from the *Tennessean* who was man enough to admit years later that we were right and he simply had ignored us. Tim Chavez, whom I have watched transform over the years from an ideologue to a realist, wrote his mea culpa in June of 2004. "I believed the spin from the governor and the Democratic legislative machine. I allowed myself to be blissfully ignorant and willingly arrogant about a complex topic. Now I understand how taxpayers feel," he wrote. "Plenty of people have been sounding the warning. Steve Gill, Phil Valentine, and [Bill] Hobbs have been asking people like me to wake up for years. It's hoped that we'll accept the spin. We must not. We must demand better of ourselves in knowledge, then from the candidates we choose in November."[8] I thought it was a courageous admission.

Chavez wasn't the only one who was "blissfully ignorant" in the media. Others were not only ignorant but downright arrogant. It was during one of our protests down at the Capitol that a *Nashville City Paper* reporter, Joe White, approached our broadcast table with the intention of embarrassing me. He parted the crowd that had gathered around our tent and walked up to me carrying two state budgets. Obviously, he had bragged to the woman with him that he was going to make me out to be a fool. In front of the crowd, he held up the budget documents, one in each hand, with his fingers covering the dates. The covers for the budgets each year were issued in different colors so you could quickly discern one from the other. I had laboriously gone over each budget since Sundquist first proposed his tax plan in 1999. I knew these budgets inside and out.

White turned to the woman and said, "Watch this." Then he asked loudly, "Hey, Phil. Which one is this year's budget?" The crowd nervously looked at me. I smiled and pointed to the one in his left hand. "That's this year's budget, Joe. The other is last year's." The cocky smile drained from his face. He quickly lowered the two volumes, turned without saying a word, and walked away. The crowd erupted in laughter. It was illustrative of the impertinence of many in the media, especially the print medium. He truly believed that all the information I imparted to my listeners was simply made up. He couldn't fathom that someone in radio was possibly smart enough to have actually read and digested the information within the budgets. Many of these media types harbored the same contempt for our listeners. To them, they were just saps, mindless robots who were too stupid to think for themselves. They would soon learn that we were smarter than they gave us credit for.

How Dare You Promise To Keep a Promise

The "no income tax" pledge spearheaded by Steve Gill was becoming extremely effective. Known tax-backers were reluctantly signing it in order to hang on to their seats. Dozens of lawmakers from both chambers had signed, and it was seriously affecting the income tax movement. Tax proponents decided they had to do something, but what they chose to do took them to new heights of audacity.

Gene Elsea, a pro-tax Republican in the Senate, filed a complaint with the Senate Ethics Committee and sought to have senators who signed the pledge expelled for violating their loyalty oath. Elsea asked the committee to determine whether the pledge constituted, get this, "a breach of trust in office." A breach of trust?! Instead of just paying lip service to not voting for the income tax, we were asking them to put their promise in writing. Of course, there was no legal obligation in signing and there was nothing to keep them from going back on their promise, but it put lawmakers on record. "I believe this type of agreement to be harmful to the integrity of the Senate and unethical based on the code of ethics for the Senate," Elsea said.[9] Unbelievable! He had said it for the whole state to hear. Pledging to do something then actually doing it ran contrary to the ethics of the Senate. Perhaps we needed to reassess those ethics.

The threat to boot out members of the Senate who actually kept their word was symptomatic of the whole problem with the General Assembly. It demonstrated the level of frustration and desperation to which these pro-income-taxers had risen. They knew the clock was ticking on their time to pass the income tax. Despite their propaganda machine within the media and the vast amount of money being spent by the unions and Tennesseans for Fair Taxation, the issue was slipping away from them. The window of opportunity was passing. They needed to act, and they needed to act soon.

Ten

THE FINAL SHOWDOWN

By 2002, the tax issue was far from resolved. We had been fighting it since the Spring of 1999. Although we had repeatedly beaten it back, the pro-income-tax forces were getting stronger—not in terms of popular support but in terms of special interest money and the pressure that money brings to bear on less-resolved lawmakers. All sorts of deals were being made to bring the income tax to fruition.

The pity train rolled back into Nashville in February. The *Tennessean* portrayed the struggle as a diversity of opinions on both sides of the tax issue, but the meat of their story unintentionally demonstrated it was an all-out effort on the part of those dependent on the government to pressure the lawmakers into continuing to shovel coal into their endlessly consuming pits of fire. Education unionists whined that they were cutting education when, in fact, they were only talking about slowing the out-of-control growth. The governor was pushing an additional $100 million just to teach kids how to read by the end of third grade! Excuse me, but isn't that why we have elementary school? Our kindergartens spend weeks teaching kids about the

Rainforest, even having them make "Save the Rainforest" t-shirts and recite a pledge to do just that! I argued that if we still had kids in third grade who couldn't read, we might want to consider teaching them *that* instead of indoctrinating them into some eco-freak, activist subculture.

Don't get me wrong—all three of my kids are in public school and I support the public schools whole-heartedly, but the union activists inside the teachers' unions don't give a damn about your children. They care about funneling more money into education so they can raise union dues and line their pockets and craft silly socialist indoctrination curricula to brainwash your children. Most teachers I know despise the union but only pay dues because they consider it a necessary evil to keep receiving benefits. What these teachers don't realize is they can get the benefits without joining the dominant unions.

It wasn't until later that we learned from a NewsChannel 5 investigation by reporter Phil Williams that some of Sundquist's buddies stood to rake in millions from his $100 million reading initiative. Sundquist buddies John Stamps and Al Ganier controlled a company called Education Networks of America. ENA received a no-bid contract in 1996 to connect Tennessee schools to the Internet. When the contract was put out to bid two years later, ENA got the business once again, despite the fact that they were not the lowest bidder. Little did we know that the Sundquist administration had already signed a contract with ENA to carry out the reading initiative even before the governor had presented the idea to lawmakers.

I had opposed the reading initiative plan simply on the principle that we shouldn't have to spend that kind of money to teach what should already be taught in schools. But I have to tell you, I came unglued when I learned Sundquist's buddies were poised to pull down over $40 *million* from the deal! Unfortunately, I didn't learn that little tidbit until Sundquist was almost out of office. Neither did the lawmakers. "Had we been privy to this information, we would have raised some eyebrows," said House Majority Leader Gene Davidson. "I think this would have sent up red flags—I know it would have."[1]

Sundquist and the pro-tax advocates in the General Assembly became masters at pressing the hot buttons. Not only did they hold education hostage, they threatened to close state parks and, in fact, did just that. They went to a fee-based system, thinking the people would be outraged, but relatively few complained. I thought it was a splendid idea. I don't use the state parks too often, but when I do, I don't mind paying a couple or three bucks to do it.

To demonstrate how out-of-touch the pro-tax lawmakers were, they proposed a bill that would implement the income tax first, then allow voters to decide on the measure if they voted to call a constitutional convention. That had mischief written all over it. "They are asking us to OK an income tax first and allow the public to vote on it later," said Senator Mike Williams. "That's not democracy. That's dictatorship."[2]

Meanwhile, as the state parks closed and the so-called "budget crisis" intensified, Governor Sundquist and his transportation commissioner, Bruce Saltzman, went yachting. They jetted off to the Caribbean for a long weekend cruise along what one travel guide calls the "most magnificent coast on earth." They were guests of an East Tennessee trucking executive, Scott Niswonger. Niswonger was—coincidentally, I'm sure—lobbying the governor to fork out $7 million for a runway extension at his local airport to accommodate his $30 million private jet. Saltzman, who owned stock in Niswonger's companies, headed up a meeting on the runway expansion proposal.[3] Saltzman also purportedly exerted his influence to help the builder of Sundquist's retirement home in the mountain town of Townsend, Tennessee. When the builder needed a parking lot for his rafting business, he began to build a lot on the state right-of-way next to his business. City officials ordered him to stop. That's when Saltzman allegedly intervened. One witness recalled Saltzman's attitude. "He said, 'I only have two hundred and something odd more days in office. I was appointed to this office. I may never come up here again, but the parking lot is going in.'"[4] Not only was the builder allowed to have his parking lot on the state right-of-way, the state of Tennessee constructed it for him at no cost to him! All this when the governor was whining about a budget crisis.

TAX ME MORE

In December of 2001, a few anti-income-tax lawmakers borrowed an idea from Arkansas Governor Mike Huckabee when they created the Volunteer Tax Me More Fund. Representatives Mae Beavers and Bobby Carter, along with Senators Marsha Blackburn and Jeff Miller, introduced a bill to allow those who didn't feel the state had enough money to make charitable contributions to the state. It was a blatant "put up or shut up" move.

"In this season of generous giving, we invite, no, we urge all the income tax advocates who feel guilty to go ahead and give before the end of this calendar year so that they can achieve equity in taxation through deductibility," Beavers said. The bill, in part, would "note that charity in general is a good thing, note that this year Tennessee was listed as second in the nation in charitable giving, and cite the Internal Revenue Code which provides for the deductibility of gifts to states."[5] Typical of big-spending liberals who want to spend your money instead of their own, the Arkansas Tax Me More Fund reported contributions of less than $3,000 its first year.[6] In Tennessee, pro-income-tax advocates scoffed at the fund. Citing lack of support for the measure, Senator Jeff Miller withdrew the bill three months later. Guess those advocating higher taxes don't really mean what they say.

SPREADING THE NEWS

The income tax fight spilled over into the General Assembly session of 2002. By that time, the citizens were well-educated on the issues and knew exactly what was going on. It was extortion, plain and simple, and they knew it. Organizations like Tennessee Tax Revolt were well-organized by then, and they became a tremendous asset in our efforts. Web sites like TaxFreeTennessee.com sprang up and updated their readers each day on what was going on. Steve Gill and I were, of course, still updating listeners on the radio. Our struggle had captured national attention, and Web sites and newspapers like WorldNetDaily.com, NewsMax.com, and the *Washington Times* were running stories. John Fund at the *Wall Street Journal* ran at least one piece on the battle, as did the *L.A. Times*.

The *L.A. Times* story is a funny aside. The reporter came to town shortly after the so-called "riot" in 2001 and did a piece featuring Steve Gill and me. He took a nice picture of the two of us standing in front of the Capitol. Somehow, during the course of his investigation in Nashville, he heard that I had once crashed a Clinton/Gore campaign rally while dressed as Elvis. The story was true, of course. It's a humorous story I'll have to save for another book. Anyway, when the story hit the *L.A. Times*, it described me as "Phil Valentine, radio talk-show host and Elvis impersonator." You put on an Elvis costume one time, and you're branded for life! I took it as the reporter's subtle way of portraying me and, in turn, the protesters as a bunch of clowns. No matter. It got a great deal of attention on the West Coast, and I ended up on several radio shows out there describing what we had gone through. We apparently made an impression.

By March of 2002, an alternative to the income tax was being floated—a sales tax increase. The proposal aimed to raise a good chunk of money. The numbers we were hearing were somewhere over $1 billion. We were certainly in an economic downturn by then, and September 11th only exacerbated the problem. Monthly revenue figures were down over the previous year, but nothing to panic about. The difference would turn out to be a 2.5 percent downturn from the year before, but other states were being hit much harder, especially states like California with state income taxes. The pro-income-tax forces seized the opportunity and began painting a picture of unprecedented disaster. With our state sales tax at 6 percent and counties allowed to tack on up to 2.75 percent more, our sales tax was already high enough. The politicians used the possibility of raising the sales tax to scare the pants off the public. It was beginning to have an effect.

One lady wrote in the *Tennessean's* "Equal Time" column, "Spending cuts must come first, realistic cuts. I am against any kind of tax increase, and although I can't believe that I am saying this, I'd rather see an income tax than an increase in sales tax—Phil Valentine forgive me."[7] I understood the reader's concern, but it was not an either/or situation. We ended up being short just under $200 million for the fiscal year out of $7.4 billion in state-collected revenue. Many Tennessee families were having to cut back at least 2.5 percent, why couldn't the government? In fact, in times of economic trouble, the government needs to take the lead in trimming its budget to make due with what they have. No one could convince me that reducing the budget by 2.5 percent across the board was going to bring government to a standstill, but the income tax proponents kept railing that we were going to have to shut down the government. What a bunch of bovine scatology.

If the pro-income-taxers in Tennessee weren't listening, the rest of the country sure was. "The economic slowdown of 2001 and 2002 led to fewer tax hikes than the shallow recession of 1990/1991 largely due to politicians across America remembering the cars circling the State Capitol in Nashville loudly honking their horns, honking so loudly they were heard even years later in Montgomery, Alabama, and Sacramento, California," said Grover Norquist, president of Americans for Tax Reform.[8]

The panic-button pushers were frustrating enough, but what was really maddening was the fact that we had been warning them for years that they were growing the budget too fast. We pointed out again and again that economic good times don't last forever and we needed to be prepared for a downturn. The politicians stuck their fingers in their ears and kept on spending and spending and spending. Many programs had been growing at a double-digit annual rate through the nineties when inflation was hovering around 2 or 3 percent. They continually busted the constitutional cap on spending so they could burn off all the extra money that was coming in. Now these same folks were working the public up into a lather over a 2.5 percent drop in revenue!

Freshman State Representative Donna Rowland, who had been swept into office on a wave of anti-income-tax sentiment in her district in 2000, set up a Web page to enable those with knowledge of waste, fraud, and abuse within state government to submit their tips anonymously. Donna promised to investigate each tip. Those that appeared to have some validity would be forwarded to the appropriate commissioner of the department in question. The commissioner would have ten days to respond, or Rowland would post on the Web site that they had not responded. She began to get dozens of tips and set about the task of tracking them all down.

On March 11, 2002, a temporary one-cent jump in the sales tax passed the Senate. Advocates of the income tax were furious. They had pushed the idea of a sales tax increase to the forefront merely to scare the people. Now the Senate was actually going forward with it. When the bill hit the House side four days later, finance chairman and income tax supporter Matt Kisber killed it.[9] A week later, Kisber announced that he was not seeking reelection. Although the news reports said he wanted to spend more time with his family, pursue other interests, et cetera, et cetera, I suspected I knew the real reason. Despite his having signed a "no income tax" pledge, I knew he was going to renege on that pledge, going out in a blaze of glory on a political suicide mission—a kamikaze politician. He joined nine other House members who had announced they were stepping down after the current session. Of those nine, at least five, all Democrats, turned out to be kamikazes.

On March 22, State Representative Mae Beavers announced she would challenge the man thought at one time to be invincible—

income tax architect Bob Rochelle.[10] Ironically, she had worked for Rochelle a few years prior as a freelance court reporter.[11] Now she was taking on the powerful senator, and the income tax issue was where she was drawing her strength. The income tax had already left carcasses scattered all across the political landscape. The big question was, could Mae Beavers, who had become a leader in the anti-income-tax movement, slay the chain-smoking, all-powerful, speaker pro tem of the Senate? It was a formidable task, indeed. Despite his push for the tax—and in some cases, because of it—Rochelle was still a giant in Tennessee politics.

Let the Games Begin

In early April, pro-taxers in the Senate began picking off any and all other proposals to raise more revenue. A plan to increase the state's car registration tax, a bill to repeal a tax break on aviation fuel, and others were shot down.[12] The pro-taxers were trying to wear the General Assembly down. Members were losing their patience. "We could be close to finishing if we had just buckled down and done our work," argued State Senator Jeff Miller. "Everyone knows the situation we're in, and everyone knows what needs to be done. All the options are out there before us. I don't see a real reason for procrastination."

Then, Naifeh had his lieutenant, Matt Kisber, create a bill that would freeze state spending. They named the budget "Downsizing Ongoing Government Services," or DOGS. The DOGS budget was meant to frighten the people of Tennessee into supporting the income tax. State Representative Steve McDaniel, a Republican who had sold out to Naifeh, said if the anti-income-taxers forced the General Assembly to pass the DOGS budget it would "terrorize people of the state," as if the DOGS budget was the only alternative to the income tax.[13] If that weren't comical enough, State Senator Doug Jackson and Representative Frank Buck would come out with the CATS budget some time later, which stood for "Continuing Adequate Taxes and Services."

As the cat and dog fight continued in the House, Bob Rochelle over in the Senate was biding his time, waiting to get closer to the end of the fiscal year at the end of June to create a crisis environment, hoping lawmakers would resort to his graduated income tax as a way out. By mid-April, the pity train rolled back into town again. College students held a "bake sale for higher education" on Legislative Plaza. Governor Sundquist applauded their efforts saying, "Those kids are trying to help us raise money for higher education." What a crock. It was a publicity stunt, but the governor used the occasion to try to scare the citizens of Tennessee once again. "I am worried that a solution can't be found," he said. "I'm worried about what happens on July 1, 2002. Do prison guards go to work? Are state troopers going to be out on the highways if we don't have a budget? We are beyond where it is a problem. It is a crisis."[14]

Of course, it never occurred to Sundquist to suggest that if these students really wanted to stay in college, they get jobs to help out. Obviously, they had enough time to drive the three hours from Knoxville and spend all day selling ding-dongs and marble cakes in front of the state Capitol. Why didn't they put that energy to good use and get a job after classes and stop whining to the government? The answer is, of course, they had been brainwashed by their professors into believing that a college education was their God-given right, that someone owed them an education. I got so sick of seeing those snotty-nosed brats with their hands out, I didn't know what to do. There are plenty of people working in high-paying jobs right now who either paid their own way or secured student loans and paid them back when they went into the work force. And it sure never hurt them one bit. In fact, it's extremely helpful. It gives people a sense of ownership in their own education, a sense of pride and accomplishment. Besides, the taxpayers were paying for the bulk of their education already. Imagine thinking that somebody owes you a college education! Apparently, the university wasn't teaching classes in humility.

Right on cue, Speaker Naifeh followed the college bake sale by introducing an income tax in the House. Remember how those pro-tax people were saying the income tax would only affect the rich, those making over $100,000? We, on the other side, warned that they'd be coming after the rest of the citizens soon after that. They didn't even wait to get the "tax on the rich" passed. Under Naifeh's plan, all those making over $15,000 a year would pay! In other words, everybody.

Over on the Senate side, Bob Rochelle and his income tax cohort, Jim Kyle, said the House plan would put pressure on the Senate to pass the income tax. Just as we had predicted, the sales tax proposal was a red herring designed to put the squeeze on the lawmakers. The squeeze was on. Kyle laid it on the line. "Members are being asked to choose between a sales tax of 9.75 percent or an income tax. You have to choose one of those two," he said.[15] In an unprecedented move, Speaker Naifeh addressed the House Republican Caucus and pitched his income tax proposal. He told them we faced a $480 million deficit in the current fiscal year, which was a lie. The deficit turned out to be less than half that figure. He then turned around and admitted that his plan would generate $1.1 billion in new revenue![16] I thought we just needed $480 million! His scheme became painfully transparent. He wanted to grow the state revenue by 15 percent in one year! And, of course, take all that largess out of the pockets of anyone making $15,000 or more.

In the meantime, State Senator David Fowler was drumming up support for his plan to send the income tax to the voters and let them decide. That, of course, meant that the people's will would be done, and they couldn't have that, so pro-taxers in the Senate made sure the Fowler plan never got off the ground. As I would learn later, Fowler had another trick up his sleeve.

In early May, the income tax was voted out of a House committee on a surprise voice vote. The question was, when would it hit the full

House? The gun was cocked. It was just a question of when Naifeh would pull the trigger. He wasn't showing his cards, but we were paying close attention. This is one of the only times when Steve Gill and I didn't fully coordinate our two stations. We had held our fire as far as the horn-honking was concerned for many months. Now that the measure was loose and could come up at any time, Steve felt we needed to be back down at Legislative Plaza with the horn-honkers. I agreed but thought we should wait until early afternoon when the General Assembly was set to go back into session.

It was my feeling that we shouldn't overdo the horn-honking. If we showed up in the morning when there was nothing to honk about, we could lose our impact. I preferred to start the broadcast at 1:00 PM. By then, we would have a better idea of when, or even if, the vote was coming down. Steve decided not to take any chances, and he rallied his listeners down at the Capitol early in the morning on May 15. I held to my plan of beginning in early afternoon. Some were puzzled and questioned my judgment, but I felt strongly about waiting until the right moment. I came down a little after noon to find only a handful of protesters still there.

Johnny B and I began our broadcast at 1:00 PM, just before the afternoon session began, and the crowd began to grow. In the afternoon, the General Assembly went back into session. I called for people to come down, and they did, but not nearly in the numbers we had seen in the past. Many folks had come out that morning and couldn't come back. Besides, there wasn't the urgency of the other protests since a vote was not imminent. The protest drew about two hundred people. The *Tennessean* and the governor used the occasion to poke fun at the smaller crowd. The paper printed Sundquist's reaction to the protest: "'I had trouble finding them out there,' he said, an apparent jab at the size of the protest."[17] One thing we learned from that experience was, we needed to be unified. We had to get all the people down there at the same time. We tried not to make that mistake again.

As we worked on our coordination skills, I was surprised to learn that Speaker Naifeh had received what the legislators perceived as a death threat. A guy called the speaker's office and said, "If he [Naifeh] continues with this, he'll have to die." Hard to take seriously a guy who was easily tracked down by Caller ID. The man was not arrested and later apologized for his stupidity. The person who took the phone call said that the guy had my show on in the background, thus I was accused of "inciting" violence. Of course, nothing could've been further from the truth. I never advocated violence. For one thing, I knew it would damage our cause. Naifeh and Sundquist longed for us to do something violent, and we were very careful not to give them that card to play. Even though I had not incited anyone to call Naifeh's office and make any kind of a threat, he said some tax opponents and the radio talk-show hosts that incite them "have no morals" and "are the lowest class I can think of."[18] That was a helluva note coming from a man who had repeatedly lied to the citizens of Tennessee, had abused his power by using state aircraft for golf junkets and other frivolous trips, and was trying to ram an unconstitutional income tax down the state's throat.

OUTFOXING THE FOX

About a week later, I got a call from State Senator David Fowler. He had a secret plan that he was playing very close to the vest. It was similar to the plan he said he was trying to carry out the summer before when we showed up in droves and the so-called "riot" occurred. Fowler had written me an angry e-mail that night saying we had thwarted his efforts to force a vote on the income tax and kill it for the session. Whether or not his plan ever had a chance of succeeding is a matter of debate. I tended to agree with Marsha Blackburn that the goal was to keep the measure from ever coming up. Bringing it to a vote in hopes of seeing it shot down was a calculated risk, a risk I wasn't sure I was willing to take.

David Fowler had been quietly conferring with other senators and members of the House. His plan was to bring a revenue bill to a vote. As of late, they had been making a practice of killing other revenue measures in order to leave only the income tax as an alternative. Fowler aimed to beat them at their own game. He knew they were suspicious of him in the Senate, so the plan would be hatched in the House. The revenue bill would be introduced, then the bill's sponsor would accept an amendment to substitute the income tax. At that point, Naifeh would be forced to call for a vote, even if he didn't have the votes to pass it. According to the rules, once a revenue bill is killed, it can't be brought up again that session. He wanted my blessing so I wouldn't marshal the troops again and foil his attempt to force a vote. I was quite reluctant and had numerous questions.

I told Fowler I thought it was a tremendous gamble. What if the income tax actually passed? He told me he had considered that but reasoned that the tax was going to pass on Naifeh's timetable anyway. He pointed out that Naifeh obviously didn't have the votes or he would've called for a vote. Fowler wanted to force the issue before he could line up the votes. But if it passed, the blood of the income tax would be on his hands. Was he willing to take that risk? He was acutely aware that he would take the fall for the income tax if it passed but was willing to take that chance. I thought long and hard about his idea. Fowler was right in that Naifeh would eventually run the income tax. That much we knew.

The storm clouds were gathering. The pressure was building. All other alternatives were being systematically disposed of in a concerted effort to force the lawmakers into the income tax corral. Perhaps it was best to try and beat Naifeh to the punch. If we waited until he had the votes, it would be too late. This way, we could be reasonably sure that he didn't have the votes—otherwise he would call for a vote himself. I reluctantly agreed to hold off rallying the troops if I saw Fowler's plan taking shape. However, I couldn't promise the same for Steve Gill. I was not about to drag him into this, nor would I betray Fowler's trust by alerting the other anti-income-tax lawmakers. It was a decision I agonized over. Win or lose, I would have to come clean afterwards. If it went according to plan, it would be hailed as brilliant. If the income tax passed, I would have to take my share of the blame. But I kept coming back to the salient point in Fowler's argument. The income tax was going to come to a vote eventually. This might be our only chance to force it before Naifeh was ready.

It's awfully hard to keep secrets at the Capitol. By David Fowler's own admission, he had brought several legislators and senators into his confidence about his plan to force a vote on the income tax. Jimmy Naifeh was no fool. He hadn't held onto his speaker's position for those many years without being a savvy politician. I don't know if he got wind of the Fowler plan or if it was pure coincidence, but on May 21, just four days after the call from David Fowler, I got the call we had been dreading since that hot June day two years before. After all the cajoling and arm-twisting and promising, Naifeh had fifty-three votes, three more than the fifty he needed to pass the state income tax, and Rochelle was ready with his votes in the Senate. They were beating David Fowler to the punch.

I hung up the phone and sat there in stunned silence at my office desk. My source was sure of the count. The votes were there. I wearily rubbed my face as I worked through the inevitable actions we would need to take. My phone continued to ring. State Representative Mae Beavers called to share the news, then Representative Donna Rowland. They were solemn but still hopeful. Anything could happen. We had fought this fight before. Yes, but could we win again? I wasn't at all sure we could, but we were going to go down swinging.

I carried the cordless phone from my office into the bedroom to tell my wife, Susan, what was up. We were in for another long day down at the State Capitol, and I wanted to prepare her for it. These protests had become particularly taxing on my family life, but I was far from alone in that department. There were many others who were sacrificing family *and* work time by coming down to protest. At least my role in this whole affair was deemed work by my employer and I didn't have to beg off time to be there.

Just as I made my apologies to Susan, the phone rang again. It was Steve Gill calling to make sure I'd heard the news. He admitted it didn't look good for us. If Naifeh was actually going to run the tax, he had the votes. No way was he going to expose all these people to a vote on such a volatile issue only to have it lose. Besides, he wasn't about to run the tax knowing that it would be rejected and knowing he couldn't bring it up again this session. There hadn't been a vote on the state income tax in Tennessee since 1931, when it was eventually thrown out by the courts as being unconstitutional.[19] There was a good reason it hadn't been brought up since. There hadn't been support in the General Assembly for the despised tax, and no speaker of the House was willing to try it again . . . until now.

I walked back into my office and sent out an FOP (Friends Of Phil) mass e-mail alert to let the thousands of people who had signed up for the periodic e-mails know what was going on. We had no way of knowing exactly when the vote would come down, but in all likelihood it would be sometime the next afternoon. Although the vote wasn't scheduled until afternoon, we were out in full force the next morning, May 22, 2002. Steve was on WTN; I was on WLAC. Unlike the blistering hot weather of that June day in 2000 when Rochelle attempted his sneak attack, this day was unseasonably cool, about seventy degrees during a time when temperatures usually hit close to eighty. There wasn't a cloud in the sky. A perfect day for a protest. Steve and I sounded the alarm, and citizens from all walks of life from all over the area headed down to the Capitol.

The crowd started slowly, not the mad dash we saw the previous year. We felt comfortable that, if the vote happened, it wasn't going to be quickly. There would be debate, then the vote would be tallied. Therefore, people began to arrive in strong numbers by midmorning.

At first, the state troopers were in regular uniforms, and they casually stood at the midway point up the front steps. They had orders not to let protesters up close to the Capitol because of the "riot" the year before. Protesters gathered at the bottom steps, some carrying on conversations with the troopers while the noise from the horn-honkers began to grow. There was even enough room on the level in front of the troopers for protesters to march in a circle, carrying homemade signs and chanting slogans. One protester, who decided to join those on foot after he wore out his horn, carried a sign that read, "Horn broke . . . Watch for finger." Another protester wore a colonial costume and rang a cowbell. There were homemade signs throughout the crowd that read, "Ax the Tax, Enough Is Enough" and "No Tax, Talk Radio Is Our Voice."

As the crowd grew, the state troopers formed a line across the steps, leaving about two feet of space between them. One trooper, a sergeant, showed up with a helmet on, and troopers in riot gear stood waiting in the wings. This only insulted the crowd, which was made up of ordinary citizens, many in casual clothes, but a few in business attire. There were also children carrying signs, lots of children, ranging in age from toddlers to teenagers. People carried American flags and Tennessee flags and chanted, competing with the horn-honking on the street below.

As the crowd filled up the mezzanine level of the Capitol steps, things began to get rather cramped. There were probably ten steps between the mezzanine and the cops, so one lady, a soccer-mom type, about thirty- or thirty-five-years-old, moved up to the first step. The sergeant in the helmet came down to tell her to move back down into the crowd. She looked frightened but determined. She was going to make her stand. The noise and the crowd had become rather loud, and the trooper tilted his head toward the woman's mouth to hear her better. A protester by the name of Remo Circo, who had become a regular fixture at our protests, tried to make peace. He attempted to coax her back down that one step as the cop grew impatient. Almost in tears she responded softly, "But it's my right." The other protesters in the front encouraged her to step down. Up until then, it looked like the woman was going to step down; then a television news reporter moved in to interview her. The sergeant began to lose his patience and demanded that she step down. Someone in the crowd then shouted, "Why don't you drag her off like you did last time?" Another yelled, "Freedom of assembly! Freedom of assembly!" The trooper had had enough.

The helmeted cop signaled the riot police who waited in the wings. The uniformed troopers parted, and the "storm troopers," as they were derisively called, trotted into place, to the boos of the protesters. They wore full riot gear, including helmets with plexiglass shields and billy clubs. They lined up shoulder to shoulder, two men deep, standing there, stone-faced, with the butt of their billy clubs in their gloved right hand and the business end in their left.

The protesters were infuriated. There was absolutely no cause to bring out the riot police. It was obvious someone much higher up than the sergeant was trying to provoke a confrontation. Suddenly, the front row of protesters simply sat down, an indication that they were not going to be intimidated and they weren't going anywhere. Rachell Willhite, one of the most devoted anti-income-tax protesters, became a regular fixture. She was known for her signature rusted-out '74 Chevy pickup with over 575,000 miles on it. She decorated the old truck with anti-tax messages spray-painted on the side. She was also known for her bullhorn, which she used regularly to penetrate the thick walls of the Capitol. As the storm troopers lined up, she led the crowd in chanting "Our House! Our House!"

"Go home, Gestapo!" Rachell yelled, through the bullhorn above the chants. The crowd by then was packed into the mezzanine area. People filled the sidewalks on both sides of the street as horn-honkers drove slowly by in both directions blowing their horns at deafening levels. Reporters covered their ears to try to hear their respective studios in their earpieces. It was almost impossible.

At our position on Legislative Plaza, right across the street from the ongoing confrontation, Johnny B and I relayed the events to our audience. Steve Gill did the same under his tent right next door. Dave Ramsey had come down for moral support and periodically joined Steve for their broadcast. In addition to the wonderful display outside, we tried to keep people updated on what was going on inside, although reports were sketchy.

Inside, legislators were debating the income tax bill. There was a little matter of the income tax being unconstitutional. Matt Kisber, a man who signed the "no income tax" pledge just to get reelected, was carrying Speaker Naifeh's water on the bill. He stood at the Well of the House to explain how they had gotten around the obvious unconstitutionality of the income tax. The Tennessee State Constitution says, "The General Assembly shall not authorize any municipality to tax incomes . . . or to impose any other tax not authorized by . . . this Constitution." In other words, municipalities can't tax incomes because the *state* can't tax incomes. In another part of the constitution, it lays out what *can* be taxed, and personal income is not among those items. The state Constitution does say, "The Legislature shall have power to tax merchants, peddlers, and privileges." This is where the pro-income-taxers chose to strike, and this was the most egregious example of their arrogance and disregard for the working citizens of Tennessee. *They were categorizing income as a privilege!*

Representative Bill Dunn, a Republican from Knoxville, rose to address Representative Kisber, and the pro-tax coterie gathered behind him in the Well. "Does that mean we're defining any work or income as a privilege?" Dunn asked, incredulously.

Kisber conferred with his henchmen for a moment, then tepidly approached the microphone. "In the construction of this language," he said, "in order to accomplish the goals as set out in the speaker's presentation, our legal staff consulted with the attorney general's legal staff, and it was this language that was determined to be the most effective." In other words, the constitution be damned, they were going to redefine terms within it to pass their income tax. Suddenly your paycheck wasn't your rightful, hard-earned money; it was a privilege.

Dunn tried to keep his composure. "I understand that, but I'm trying my hardest to get somebody to say that it's still a *right* to work, as opposed to a *privilege* to work, in the state of Tennessee." Kisber looked at him sheepishly. Surely he knew he was treading on thin ice, constitutionally.

Representative Jack Sharp, a Republican from East Ridge, stood to be recognized. Sharp was visibly perturbed by the masquerade that was taking place before the House members. "My colleague from Knoxville brings up a good question," he began. "Is this bill constitutional? We've heard that five attorneys general have ruled that, properly worded, this would be a constitutional bill. *Fifteen* Supreme Court justices have said it is *not* constitutional."

The anti-income-taxers in the gallery applauded. Naifeh pounded the gavel and patronizingly thanked the citizens for their attendance, then asked them to please be quiet. Representative Sharp was not finished. "In the manner of Tennessee law," he continued, "I will take the word of fifteen Supreme Court justices before I will take the word of five attorneys general. It's time to do something. Ladies and gentlemen, it is *not* time to do the wrong thing. It is *never* time to do the wrong thing."

With that, further debate on the bill was cut off, and Naifeh moved toward a vote. Before he called for a vote, he allowed several more pro-tax legislators to plead their case. Representative Zane Whitson, a Republican from Unicoi, pled passionately that, "We've been struggling with this issue for four years. We were told at that time that the sales tax would decline and continue to decline in the state of Tennessee, and it has."

That was an outright lie, and Whitson knew it. Sales tax revenue from fiscal year 1998–99 through fiscal year 2001–02 had grown by $329 million![20] This whole notion that sales tax receipts were dramatically declining overall was the big lie. Everyone pushing the income tax knew it, but they were trying to scare the citizens into believing that our tax structure was a failure and we were facing insolvency. They had extracted a few bumpy months during the economic slowdown and paraded them around as an apocalyptic trend. What they weren't telling the people was states relying on the income tax were being hit much harder.

Outside, the protest had swelled into the thousands. The home-made signs were getting more and more colorful. "Sundquist: A Legacy of Lies," read one, with a picture of Governor Sundquist sporting a Pinocchio nose. Another had a standard "House for Sale" sign at the top. In the space reserved for filling in the price, they had written in "$1.2 billion." Underneath, it read, "Several spacious backrooms. Perfect for dealing." The battle-garbed riot police stood at attention with their batons at the ready. As the protesters chanted and waved their signs in front of them, one protester approached a stone-faced trooper. As if joking with the palace guards of Buckingham, the man made faces and tried to make the cop laugh. The trooper simply stared straight ahead, seemingly looking right through him.

A wide variety of vehicles continued to circle the Capitol with horns blasting. Even an off-duty ambulance joined the parade. Scott Couch, a reporter for WTVF-TV, hitched a ride with one of the protesters. Dave Cole had been given the day off by his employer so he could come down. Couch asked him, "Are they listening this time?" Cole responded, "They're *hearing* whether they're listening or not."

A few *pro-tax* protesters stood holding their signs, almost completely obliterated by the anti-tax signs. Kathy Jeffers, a state employee, made the outrageous statement, "The low income people in Tennessee have been paying. A hundred percent of their income has been taxed with the sales tax. The people who are making all the money and are on the radio getting everybody stirred up, they don't want you getting into their money."[21] One hundred percent of the income of poor people was being taxed by the sales tax? What did she think the rich people were doing with their money, hiding it under a mattress? The rich people were paying far more in sales tax than the poor, plus they were being taxed on their investments. Jeffers demonstrated the utter ignorance of those on the pro-tax side. The real reason she was there, I'm sure, was that, as a state employee, she stood to get a hefty raise if the income tax passed.

The riot police continued to stand their ground on the steps midway to the top of the Capitol. The citizens continued to hold their ground as well and were increasingly agitated at the overkill of police force. They continued to shout and wave their signs. "Uphold the constitution or get the hell out!" one protester yelled. The horn-honkers were lined up around the block in both directions. One guy in a Jeep drove by the protesters lined on the sidewalk blasting "We're Not Going To Take It" by Twisted Sister from his car stereo. The protesters jabbed their fists in the air and cheered.

Anti-tax protesters who wanted to enter the gallery of the House Chambers were being stopped at the entrance and told to remove all stickers and buttons and leave their signs at the door. Protester Rick Meyers was told to take the wooden stick from his small Tennessee state flag. "The stick could possibly be a weapon," he scoffed. However, in the gallery, tax proponents were allowed to wear their stickers and buttons.[22]

After the parade of pro-tax speeches on the House floor, Jimmy Naifeh decided he had pushed as far as he could push. His people out on the floor assured him they had rounded up more than the requisite number of yeas to pass the measure. Confident and cool, he called for a vote. The huge electronic boards on either side of the chamber lit up. Naifeh eyed the results with House Speaker Pro Tem Lois DeBerry at his side. They watched as the light beside each name illuminated. It was a slow process, but gradually Naifeh and DeBerry began to look like a couple watching a scary movie. Naifeh stared at the results in stunned silence, his face blank and expressionless. DeBerry squinted her eyes, hoping a closer look would tell her something different than what she was actually seeing. *What the—?* This couldn't possibly be. Naifeh could not believe his own eyes. The board showed forty-four in favor, fifty-three against. DeBerry muttered something to Naifeh, but he said nothing, continuing to just stare at the board.

Steve McDaniel, the Republican in charge of bringing in the Republican votes in favor of the tax, approached the speaker. He looked like a whipped puppy. How could this be? Naifeh was sure he had the votes, or he wouldn't have run it. He leaned down to allow McDaniel to whisper something in his ear, then popped back upright, still looking at the board. He was in shock. This was not the way he had planned things. He leaned forward toward the microphone. Maybe those yes votes just needed a little prodding.

"Any member wish to change their vote?" Naifeh asked, in a monotone, his voice belying the panic inside. He looked at the board. There was no change. He paused. "Any member wish to change their vote?" he asked again. Still no change.

Representative Bill Dunn, who had questioned their definition of the word "privilege" just minutes before, huddled with a couple of anti-tax legislators. They all three stared at the board, as stunned as Naifeh. Then they broke into hushed but giddy laughter. They could not believe their good fortune. This was not supposed to happen. Passage was a sure thing, or the speaker wouldn't have called for a vote. Naifeh was in serious trouble, and everyone in the chamber, including Naifeh, knew it.

Shelby Rhinehart, the crusty old pro-income-tax Democrat from Spencer, meandered up to the Well and adjusted the microphone. With a cigarette burning in his left hand, he boomed into the microphone, "Mr. Speaker, I'd like to move, sir, that we reconsider our actions on Bill 2646." The room erupted in laughter with a loud "No!" echoing from the back of the room. It was a feeble attempt to undo what had already been done, contrary to the rules of the House.

Speaker Naifeh gently reminded Rhinehart that his motion was out of order. He could not stop a vote once it had been taken, even though Naifeh would've given just about anything to make it so.

Representative Tommy Head, who had sponsored the bill on Naifeh's behalf, conferred with Representatives Rob Briley and John Arriola, both of Nashville. Head and Briley attempted to convince Arriola to change his vote, but he just shook his head.

The vote remained unchanged at forty-four in favor, fifty-three against. Like the stubborn protesters who refused to budge outside, the results stared resolutely down at Naifeh. Ordinarily, the vote was taken and the clerk recited the results, all in a span of a few moments. It had been far longer than the standard time taken, and the vote was still open. Naifeh slowly stepped down from the podium like somebody who had just crawled out of a wrecked car. He parted a group of legislators, then stopped in front of another small group clustered together. They looked at him with dazed expressions, shaking their heads. Naifeh turned and looked, bewildered, around the crowded room, not quite sure what to do next. All the time, the vote was still open.

Reporter Ben Hall had been covering the historic moment from up in the press box above the House floor for WTVF-TV. Democrat Gary Odom, an income tax opponent, came up to talk with Hall. "This is unprecedented," Odom said, referring to the vote being held open. "I've never seen this happen. I'm not aware anyone has ever seen this happen." He was obviously not happy with the stunt. "We do not have a specific rule that deals with this issue, and, certainly, maybe, that's something that needs to be considered," he added. When he left, Hall pointed out the obvious. "It might be hard to dream up a situation that would be worse for Speaker Naifeh and supporters of his plan at this point," he told his viewers.

Outside, it was bedlam. The police in riot gear and billy clubs stood nervously, ready to rebuff the thousand-plus protesters who carried five American flags and the banner of the state of Tennessee, as well as countless homemade signs and banners. The protesters faced off with the police chanting, "The whole world is watching! The whole world is watching!" The street overflowed with protesters on foot as hundreds of cars continued to circle and honk their horns. Steve and I continued to report the events in real time. I'm sure the police fully expected the income tax to have passed by that point and that they would be left to deal with the angry crowd.

Then we got word that Naifeh had fallen short of the requisite fifty votes and was holding the vote open. Word quickly spread through the crowd. They began chanting, "Close the vote! Close the vote!" Television crews from all across the state buzzed around the periphery and inside the crowd, capturing the event on tape. The horns grew even louder, the shouts from protesters more passionate. It was a good sign that he had fallen short, but no one was underestimating Naifeh. As long as the vote remained open, he was within striking distance of passing the tax. Leaving the vote open meant that he felt he could change some minds, and Naifeh could be quite persuasive.

As reporter Ben Hall commented on hearing the horns from inside the chamber to his television audience, Naifeh strode over to Representative Frank Buck, one of the votes he was counting on to put his tax plan over the top. Buck dropped his head and shook it back and forth. Democrat Rob Briley, who was in charge of securing the Democrat vote for the measure, stood nervously to the side, listening to their conversation. Buck looked up and began his explanation of why he voted against the measure as Naifeh sternly stared back at him. Before he could finish, an exasperated Naifeh walked off. It wasn't over, however. Not by a long shot. The vote was still open, and Naifeh still had some cards to play. He abruptly left the House floor. A few minutes later, Frank Buck left as well.

The listeners to my show who couldn't make it down to the Capitol were outraged. This unprecedented holding open of the vote represented another blatant example of excessive abuse of power to them.

They began calling for Naifeh's removal. It was an hour after the vote had been opened, and Naifeh was nowhere in sight. Those not able to get inside the House chamber or even close to the Capitol steps huddled around our tent to hear what was going on. As we impatiently waited, the protest stayed at its fevered pitch. I tried desperately to reach legislators on their cell phones, but they were all on the floor of the House. Then I got a call from Mae Beavers who had stepped outside the chamber to update me. Naifeh had left the House floor with several legislators—legislators who had voted against his precious income tax. He was obviously not a happy man when he left. Heaven only knew what was going on behind his closed office door.

I relayed the situation as I knew it to my listeners and to those gathered close enough to our tent to be able to hear over the noise of the crowd. Those who heard the news were livid. They were smart enough to put two and two together. Naifeh had been betrayed by somebody, and they were apparently feeling his wrath. The vote was still open, and lawmakers could still be browbeaten into submission. The front line of the protesters pushed slightly closer to the riot police who could feel the heat of their breath and the rage in their voices.

Inside, the scene was much more subdued, solemn even. Some legislators made small talk in groups of three or four while others made sandwiches at their desks. Some, mostly those who had voted for the tax, sat silently at their desks. Their faux pas loomed large over the room, staring down at them in bright lights from the two electronic tote boards, which still showed the ugly truth. Then, as suddenly as he had left the chamber, Speaker Naifeh reemerged looking like somebody had just shot his dog. The room fell almost silent, and legislators scrambled for their desks as if the principal had just entered the room. Naifeh strode toward the podium but stopped, momentarily, at Steve McDaniel's desk. McDaniel said nothing as Naifeh whispered something to him across the desk then proceeded up to the podium. McDaniel looked relieved, but it wasn't clear why.

Frank Buck entered from the front of the chamber and made a beeline for his desk. He was detained, briefly, by another legislator, but didn't stop. He walked backwards for a few steps, angrily chopping the air with his right hand, then headed for his desk. He had been to the principal's office, and when he surfaced, the normally talkative Buck abruptly told reporters, "Not now."[23]

After an hour-and-forty-minutes absence, Naifeh finally resumed his post at the podium. He started to speak into the microphone, then was tapped on the shoulder by another legislator. All eyes were on Naifeh. Lawmakers sat in rapt attention, waiting for the first words to drip from Naifeh's mouth. Naifeh left the podium again for a moment, then stepped back up to the microphone. Matt Kisber and Lois DeBerry sat, dejected, at his side. Naifeh squinted, looking out on the floor, then mouthed something to someone in the chamber and again looked up at the board. Three votes changed from "no" to "present but not voting." Naifeh waited. He looked out across the room, then spoke into the microphone. It was not on, but, obviously, whoever he was talking to could hear him. "We need one more," he said, holding up his index finger. He backed away from the microphone and looked at the board. Another "no" vote magically switched to "present but not voting."

"Mr. Clerk, take the vote," he barked in his country drawl.

The clerk announced, "Ayes 45. No's 49. Four present, not voting."

Then Naifeh bellowed, "Bill 2646 having failed to receive a constitutional majority, I hereby declare re-referred to the committee on calendar and rules. Next bill."

In an instant, it was over. Business appeared to get back to normal on the floor of the House, but it was anything but normal. This was a historic moment, no matter which side you were on. Never had a vote been held open for more than just a few minutes. There hadn't been a vote on the income tax in seventy years, and it had never ended like this. Speaker Naifeh kept up appearances from the podium, but this was no ordinary vote that could be forgotten over cocktails and small talk. This was a defining moment for many members on the floor who had stuck their political necks out under the assumption there would be spoils to take home to present to their people and soothe the savage talk of expulsion. Now they were branded with the scarlet letter "Y" for "Yes," having voted for the detested state income tax with nothing or no one to protect them from their own constituents. News reporter Ben Hall had been so right. It was, indeed, nearly impossible to dream up a scenario that would be worse for Naifeh and his pro-income-tax supporters. Several of them sat silently at their desks, heads bowed as if praying, pleading that God would turn back the clock, but it was not to be.

I got the call outside at our position. I relayed the incredible news to the crowd, and they burst into uproarious cheers and celebration. We could scarcely believe our luck. What looked like a sure thing just two hours before had evaporated like a drop of water on a hot August day. The scene in front of the Capitol looked like a town whose team had just won the Super Bowl. I relaxed for the first time all day, sitting back and soaking up the excitement. Johnny B and I high-fived one another. Elated listeners took turns at our tent with their hugs and handshakes and congratulations. Happy motorists squealed their excitement between their long bursts of the horn. The protesters who had held their ground in front of the riot police turned on their heels and followed the mass of humanity back down the steps and into the sea of happy citizens below. The police relaxed too, loosening their grips on their billy clubs and allowing them to playfully drop to their sides as if they never intended to use them in the first place.

This day was a long time coming. We had waged a three-year battle against the income tax. All of these people, many of whom had been at our protests through scorching sun and drenching downpour, had doggedly stuck with this cause to see it to fruition. Familiar and not-so-familiar faces had become compatriots in a cause as old as our republic—a cause of government rule by the people and for the people, not in spite of the people. By sticking together, we had slain the beast of big government. What had started out as a loose confederation of like-minded citizens had grown into a statewide movement. Against all odds and to the aggravation of the political elite and the academics who looked down upon the common citizens, we had overcome insurmountable obstacles and a gargantuan propaganda machine and prevailed. David had just killed Goliath.

Tim Chavez, a columnist for the *Tennessean*, had already begun his transition over to our side. He came down that day to see firsthand what all the fuss was about. If he wasn't already a convert, he was certainly in awe of the founding fathers' spirit he saw in action. He wrote this in his column the next day:

> *The people of Tennessee were not supposed to win yesterday. Working people like those who drove by the state Capitol in their big rigs honking horns. Stay-at-home moms who stood at Legislative Plaza with signs in one hand and children on the other. Men in suits and women in dresses who kept looking at their watches as they took long lunch hours from their white-collar jobs. The news media said that House Speaker Jimmy Naifeh had 53 votes to pass his income tax. The media said that protesters—fatigued from continual appearances outside the state Capitol—wouldn't muster more than 200 people. Yesterday was invigorating. Protesters have something behind them that the lawmakers and most of the media can't comprehend—the thrill of regularly standing up for what they believe. They know the law is on their side in the state Constitution, which says an income tax is illegal. They know the flags of this nation and state they carry are on their side. Ours are supposed to be representative governments of the people. A majority of Tennesseans oppose an income tax. Naifeh and the media will blame protesters for ignoring what they call the inevitability of an income tax. But their anger is like that of a druggie learning he won't have any more financial support for his habit. It all didn't matter. The people still won.[24]*

Eleven

POST SCRIPT

The income tax battle had residual effects in the makeup of the General Assembly. Because of their stand on the tax, many pro-tax lawmakers saw the handwriting on the wall and bowed out rather than face defeat in November. State Representative Mae Beavers had taken a calculated risk by giving up her House seat to run for the state Senate against political powerhouse Bob Rochelle, the speaker pro tem. I kept in close contact with Mae during that tumultuous time. They threw everything they could at her, including a trumped up investigation into her residency. She and her husband had built a home outside her district as a spec home for resale. Her opponents attempted to make it appear that she was living in the house as a permanent resident and filing false documents in order to show her residency inside her legislative district. The accusations were false, of course, and she was fully exonerated after the investigation.

Meanwhile, Mae confided in me that her internal polling showed her way ahead of Rochelle. He had not counted on such a formidable opponent when he exposed himself as a blatant income tax supporter.

He also denied publicly that his campaign was in trouble. However, on July 5, 2002, just six weeks after the income tax was defeated, Rochelle announced that he was suspending his campaign. He cited "violent, threatening" phone calls to his home as the reason. A reporter's call to his wife revealed that there had been no death threats against Rochelle or his family. A check with the police and the Tennessee Bureau of Investigation confirmed that there was no investigation into any threats against Rochelle or his family.[1] The truth was, the twenty-year veteran of the Senate knew he was facing a humiliating defeat. Four days later, he made it official when he formally dropped out of the race. Rochelle joined about a dozen other pro-tax lawmakers who had decided not to seek reelection.

The Democrats scrambled feverishly to find a write-in candidate for the August primary. They backed Sherry Fisher, a Carthage business-woman, who captured the nomination. Former Vice President Al Gore campaigned feverishly for Fisher, but to no avail. She went down to defeat in November, and Mae Beavers, who Rochelle had labeled a "do-nothing legislator," took over his seat in the Senate.

Mae's biggest challenge would come in 2004 when she was diagnosed with breast cancer. Being the fighter she is, she was determined to win. Mae was able to announce later in the year that she had won that crucial first battle. Like fighting the income tax, Mae understood that fighting cancer is a constant struggle. She added the push for a cure to her list of passionate causes.

Marsha Blackburn left her State Senate seat to make a run for Congress in 2002. She entered a crowded field of seven candidates in the Republican primary. Due in part to the reputation she built as an anti-income-tax crusader, Marsha handily defeated her six opponents in the primary and glided to victory in the general election. Once in place in Washington, she went to work on sales tax deductibility for states without an income tax to put states like Tennessee on an equal footing when it comes to filing federal tax returns. I happened to be in her office in Washington the day the measure passed the U.S. House of Representatives. It was signed into law by President Bush in October of 2004.

Political novice Jim Bryson, who became a fixture at our tax rallies down at the Capitol, sought and won the Senate seat vacated by Marsha Blackburn. He immediately began work on a taxpayers bill of rights for Tennessee, similar to the law passed in Colorado. As for those legislators voting for the income tax, all-in-all, thirteen either stepped down or were defeated in elections in 2002. One, Keith Westmoreland, committed suicide and another, Shelby Rhinehart, died after a long illness.

Even though, officially, the Republican Party of Tennessee never separated itself from Don Sundquist, he was persona non grata with any Republican who ever wanted to get elected. That was brought into sharp focus when I attended a fundraiser for Lamar Alexander, who was running for U.S. Senate in 2002. President Bush was the draw, and he gave a noontime speech to several thousand supporters. Everyone who was anyone in Republican politics was there. Conspicuously absent was the sitting Republican governor of the state. Not only was he not there, no one even mentioned his name from the stage! I thought at the time, what a powerful statement that was to have the president of the United States, a president from your own party, come to your state and your capital city and totally ignore you, the sitting governor of the state. The good news for the Republicans was, as Sundquist blew up his own political career, it was mostly Democrats who were standing close by.

The tax rebellion in Tennessee was not limited to the state's borders. Grover Norquist, president of Americans for Tax Reform, a cheerleader early in the struggle, saw the Tennessee tax rebellion as the impetus for true tax reform across the nation. He helped coordinate the anti-income-tax pledge that helped hold many lawmakers' feet to the fire. "The Tennessee victory over Sundquist's inexplicable drive to impose a state income tax is the father of the 2003 victory over Alabama Governor Bob Riley's $1.2 billion tax hike, the 2001 and 2002 Oregon tax hikes that were defeated through referendum, and the recall of Governor Davis of California," Norquist said. "The struggle against a Tennessee income tax sent shock waves throughout the nation. As in California's property tax revolt and Proposition 13, the Tennessee state fight had nationwide consequences. It emboldened taxpayers in other states—you can fight the state legislature. Taxpayers don't have to lose to the hydra-headed monster of teachers unions, government bureaucrats, collaborators in the media, and the hate and envy crowd pushing class division."[2]

In California, during the height of the recall effort against Gray Davis in which Arnold Schwarzenegger became governor, I was doing a simulcast with talk-show host Roger Hedgecock out of San Diego. He had one of the organizers of the recall effort on the phone with him. He introduced me to him, saying, "This is the guy I was telling you about in Tennessee." The gentleman then gushed that they were inspired to try the recall by what they had seen our citizens do in Tennessee. I thought it was an interesting ripple effect of citizen involvement and was pleased to hear our stand had made a difference elsewhere.

The downside of the Tennessee story is the fact that the one-cent sales tax that was bandied about to scare legislators into the income tax was passed a few weeks later. Sold as a temporary solution to our budget woes until we came out of the economic slowdown, it naturally became permanent. As repugnant as that tax increase was, it still was not the income tax, which would've opened up a great big door for the politicians to walk through. It was also rather ironic that the same people in the General Assembly who pushed the sales tax increase were the same ones who cried all those years that the sales tax was regressive and tortured the poor. When it came time to choose between saving the poor from this dreaded tax or raking in more walkin'-around money for the General Assembly, I guess we saw who got thrown in front of the bus. It just proved my point that all that talk about the poor was simply a guilt trip, a scare tactic, a way to finagle more cash out of the citizens' wallets.

In November of 2002, Speaker Naifeh came dangerously close to losing his seat when a political novice, retired Air Force Colonel Tony Lopez, garnered 47 percent of the vote. Naifeh retained his seat, but many of those he left out to dry weren't so lucky. In addition to the fifteen legislators who either stepped down, died, or were defeated, another five legislators either called it quits or were defeated in 2004, including Tommy Head, who had carried Naifeh's water on the income tax in the House. Of the original group voting for the income tax in 2002, twenty were gone just two years later.

Lt. Governor John Wilder survived a stiff challenge in 2004 and was reelected at the age of eighty-three. However, his reelection was bittersweet as the Republicans seized control of the State Senate for only the second time since Reconstruction. After the election of '04, there was speculation that Wilder might switch parties in order to hold on to his power. It would certainly not be out of character for a man who had played both sides of the aisle for so long.

Ever since his dramatic transformation in 1999, those of us who had supported Governor Don Sundquist mused as to what could have caused such a change. Perhaps some of the pieces of the puzzle began to fall into place in September of 2002. Just four months after the demise of the state income tax, the FBI and the Tennessee Bureau of Investigation (TBI) launched a joint criminal investigation into the Sundquist administration over insider contracts awarded to friends of the governor.[3] Eighteen months later, a former Sundquist Labor Department official, Joanna Ediger, who arranged a state contract for a company in which she later became part-owner, was indicted for influence peddling. She was charged with mail fraud, wire fraud, bribery, and lying to investigators.[4] Two months later, a jury found Ediger guilty on the mail fraud and wire fraud counts. The lead prosecutor in the case, Zach Fardon, indicated that federal investigators would expand their investigation in search of "bigger fish."[5]

They landed one of those "bigger fish" in November of 2004. Longtime Sundquist friend, Al Ganier, was indicted on two counts of obstruction of justice. He was accused of accessing an employee's computer to destroy, conceal, and cover up documents that could have been damaging to him and/or the Sundquist administration. Investigators believed the destroyed e-mails pertained to a contract his company obtained from the Sundquist administration worth $106 million.[6] As 2004 came to a close, that investigation into state contracts was ongoing. Many speculated that it may ultimately reach into the upper echelon of the Sundquist administration.

Instead of building a legacy of government reform, as many had hoped from his first term, the Sundquist administration will forever be remembered for its stubborn fight for the income tax. His former press secretary, Beth Fortune, wishes he would have handled things differently. "I wish he could've said something like, 'While I still believe it's the best thing to do, the best way to go, I have heard the will of the people and will move in another direction.' I really wish that could've happened." On the prospect that the corruption investigation could reach the former governor, "I don't think there's a smoking gun there," she said. "I believe with all my heart that he did it because he thought it was the right thing to do."[7]

So did the city of Memphis. Despite a clear constitutional ban on the income tax, Memphis politicians managed to get a city payroll tax on the ballot in 2004. This was to be a small-scale test of the income tax. If the pro-income-taxers could get a toehold in the Democratically-dominated Memphis area, they might be able to spread the income tax throughout the state. Even though 58 percent of the residents of Shelby County voted for John Kerry, a whopping 73 percent voted against the payroll tax.

Other tax increase initiatives suffered a similar fate thanks to Tennessee Tax Revolt. Capitalizing on their success in helping to defeat the state income tax, the folks at Tennessee Tax Revolt managed to get a wheel tax increase referendum on the ballot in nine Tennessee counties. They achieved this through the grassroots effort of gathering petition signatures instead of standing idly by as county officials quietly passed the tax increases with impunity. In all but one of the counties, the citizens overwhelmingly rejected the tax increase. Knox County was the only exception, and that was due to the fact that the arrogant county commission and the mayor had already told the voters if the wheel tax increase was defeated, a property tax would automatically go into effect. For the voters of Knox County, it was a matter of choosing between the lesser of two evils.

Much of the consternation over wheel tax increases came about when Governor Phil Bredesen, who succeeded Don Sundquist, balanced the state budget, in part, by withholding some of the shared sales tax revenue with the counties. In his vow to fix the state's financial problems, Governor Bredesen vowed to reform the troublesome TennCare program, believed by many to be at the source of the state's budget woes. Bredesen, a former healthcare executive, tried to keep the program alive through reform, but social leeches and perpetual litigators like attorney Gordon Bonnyman refused to budge. When Bredesen wanted to end such absurd practices as providing rental cars for meth addicts to go to clinics, TennCare advocates took the state to court. There, mouths were agape when Governor Bredesen finally announced he was pulling the plug on the program and going back to Medicaid, thus dumping some four hundred thousand people off the program. Bonnyman and the troublemakers then launched an eleventh-hour plea to save it, reminiscent of union leaders who made ridiculous demands on companies, then stood in shocked amazement as the factories closed.

As for Bob Rochelle, who suddenly withdrew from his State Senate race against Mae Beavers in 2002: he got himself appointed to a task force on taxes in 2003. In a last gasp effort to ensure the income tax wouldn't die, outgoing Governor Don Sundquist joined with the other principal members of the Axis of Upheaval—Lt. Governor Wilder and Speaker Jimmy Naifeh—to choose members of the Tax Structure Study Commission. Rochelle, of course, was one of the first people named to the panel. This farce of a commission was stacked with pro-income-tax members. Their recommendation on what to do about Tennessee's tax structure was a foregone conclusion.

In September of 2004, as the commission busily went through the motions of looking at the state's tax structure, a fresh survey on taxes surfaced. The study by the Massachusetts Taxpayers Foundation confirmed the pro-income-taxers' worst nightmare. It found that Tennessee had dropped to fiftieth in the nation in taxes as a portion of income.[8] The pro-income-taxers tore their garments, and there was much weeping and gnashing of teeth. They cried that the state was hopelessly doomed. I, on the other hand, found much cause to celebrate and proceeded to break out the bubbly. Despite their Herculean efforts to saddle us with an income tax, despite their passage of a one-cent increase in the sales tax, we had managed to attain my goal of becoming the lowest taxed state in the union. It was time to begin work on those license plates I had dreamt of years before—the ones that read "Lowest Taxes in the Nation." From the looks of the legal woes of some of our income tax friends, it appeared we'd have no shortage of people to make them.

ACKNOWLEDGMENTS

This project was truly a labor of love. The history of beating back an unwieldy government is an American story that needed to be told. I was privileged to be an eyewitness to the Tennessee component of it. So many people aided in its telling.

It would not have been possible had Nelson Current publisher David Dunham not approached me about writing this book. I appreciate his confidence in me and his excitement for this project. Senior editor Joel Miller and managing editor Wes Driver offered invaluable advice that helped weave this intriguing tale. I'm honored to be part of Nelson Current and the more than two-hundred-year-old tradition of Thomas Nelson Publishers.

Johnny B, my longtime producer and sidekick on the radio, was there by my side through the jubilant highs and discouraging lows. The long and trying hours we spent on the radio during the tax protests passed more quickly because he was there. Johnny, I appreciate your friendship.

Steve Gill was my "co-conspirator" in the Tennessee tax revolt. His political savvy and knowledge helped sort out friend from foe and expose those who worked so diligently to take more of our money.

A special thanks to the generous people at the Thomas Jefferson Foundation. Andrew Jackson O'Shaughnessy, Saunders Director at the International Center for Jefferson Studies, graciously opened the doors of the Jefferson Library at Monticello to me. Eleanor Sparagana helped dig through the massive volumes of Jefferson's writings, which gave me a unique insight into his and the other founders' thoughts on taxes.

I'm always grateful for and ever-cognizant of the inconvenience my family endures while I'm sequestered for long spans of time researching and writing. My wife, Susan, and my three sons—Carr, Campbell, and Douglas—put up with quite a bit in allowing me this indulgence I so love. Thank you.

And thank you, God, for all with which you have blessed me. I am always mindful of your presence.

ENDNOTES

Prologue

1. Cato Policy Analysis No. 261, October 22, 1996.
2. "Budget Message of the President, Fiscal Years 1981–1989"; Budget of the United States, FY 1993, Part 5, Table 1.3, pp. 5–18.

Chapter 1— The Sneak Attack

1. Source: Catalogue for Philanthropy, "Generosity Index 2004," Giving Rank.
2. Interview with Marsha Blackburn, June 17, 2004.
3. Karin Miller, "Income Tax Pusher Bob Rochelle Hangs It Up," Associated Press, June 14, 2000.
4. Phillip Langsdon, *Tennessee: A Political History* (Hillsboro Press, 2000).
5. Interview with Steve Gill, June 15, 2004.
6. "Sundquist Seeks a 'Season of Compromise,'" Text of State of the State speech, *Tennessean*, February 9, 1999.
7. Phil West, "Incentives Not Enough To Convince Businesses on Sundquist Tax Reform Plan," Associated Press, April 2, 1999.
8. Interview with Beth Fortune, November 8, 2004.
9. Paula Wade, "Graduated Income Tax Gets Senate Panel's OK," *Commercial Appeal* (Memphis), November 17, 1999.
10. Source: "Review of Tuition Authority and Support for Higher Education," Washington Research Council, March 27, 1998.
11. Bonna de la Cruz, "Study Raises Stir over UT Salaries," *Tennessean*, March 30, 2000, p. 1B.
12. Bonna de la Cruz, "Audit: TennCare Paid $6M To Insure Dead People," *Tennessean*, July 9, 1999, p. 1A.
13. Duren Cheek, "Sundquist May Allow Income Tax," *Tennessean*, April 16, 1999, p. 1A.

14. Duren Cheek and Bonna de la Cruz, "Session Ends with No Vote on Tax Reform," *Tennessean*, April 23, 1999, p. 1A.
15. Bonna de la Cruz and Jon Yates, "Budget Cuts Tossed Back to Governor," *Tennessean*, May 13, 1999, p. 1A.
16. Tom Sharp, "GOP Senators Chided by Governor To Offer Ways To Handle Finances Respond," Associated Press, May 6, 1999.
17. Bonna de la Cruz, "Senators Trash Tax-Reform Talk," *Tennessean*, August 30, 1999, p. 1B.
18. Bonna de la Cruz, "Income-Tax Debate Heats Up," *Tennessean*, September 22, 1999, p. 1A.
19. "The Government Performance Project," *Governing Magazine*, February 2003.
20. Source: Tennessee Department of Revenue, July 2001–June 2002.
21. Duren Cheek, "E-mail Block Is Suspicious, Anti-Tax Legislators Warn," *Tennessean*, October 29, 1999, p. 10A.
22. Bill Hobbs, "Tennessee Legislature Aims To Break Spending Cap—Again," HobbsOnline.com, May 3, 2004.
23. Mae Beavers, "The Connecticut Game," *Tennessean*, February 24, 2002, p. 18A.
24. Tom Humphrey, "Sundquist Blasts Critics of His New Stance on Income Tax," *Knoxville News-Sentinel*, October 31, 1999.
25. Tom Humphrey, "Income Tax Issue Bound to Return," *Knoxville News-Sentinel*, November 21, 1999.
26. John Commins, "Lawmakers Study Tax Options," *Chattanooga Times-Free Press*, November 2, 1999.
27. Interview with Beth Fortune, November 8, 2004.
28. Stephen Moore and Richard Vedder, "The Case against a Tennessee Income Tax," Cato Institute, No. 53, November 1, 1999.
29. Moore and Vedder, "The Case against a Tennessee Income Tax."
30. Maclin P. Davis Jr., "The Constitutionality of the Proposed Tennessee Income Tax," Tennessee Tax Revolt (TNTaxRevolt.org).
31. Bonna de la Cruz and John Shiffman, "Sundquist 'Senses' Support," *Tennessean*, November 4, 1999, p. 1B.
32. Paula Wade, "Wilder's Role in Tax Debate a Flash Point for Both Sides," *Commercial Appeal*, July 23, 2001, p. A1.
33. Wade, "Wilder's Role in Tax Debate a Flash Point for Both Sides."
34. Richard Locker and Paula Wade, "Tax Reform in Jeopardy as Wilder, GOP Balk," *Commercial Appeal*, November 18, 1999.
35. John Shiffman, "Rowdy Day in Legislature Ends Tumultuous Special Session," *Tennessean*, November 19, 1999.

Chapter 2— Rich Heritage of Revolt

1. "Thomas Jefferson on Politics and Government," compiled and edited by Eyler Robert Coates Sr., Metairie, Jefferson Parish, Louisiana.
2. Dall W. Forsythe, *Taxation and Political Change in the Young Nation 1781–1833* (New York: Columbia University Press, 1977), p. 25.
3. Richard B. Morris, *Alexander Hamilton and the Founding of the Nation* (New York: The Dial Press, 1957), p. 341.
4. Internal Revenue Service, tax year 2002, figures compiled by the National Taxpayers Union.
5. Joseph Curl, "Blue State Buzz over Secession," *Washington Times*, November 9, 2004.
6. "Indicators of Welfare Dependence: Annual Report to Congress," 2003; Appendix A—Program Data, Tables 8 and 12.
7. Catalogue for Philanthropy, Generosity Index 2004.
8. Letter to Edward Carrington, December 1787; Source: *The Jeffersonian Cyclopedia: A Comprehensive Collection of the Views of Thomas Jefferson*, edited by John P. Foley (New York: Russell & Russell).
9. Forsythe, *Taxation and Political Change in the Young Nation 1781–1833*, pp. 59, 123.
10. Forsythe, *Taxation and Political Change in the Young Nation 1781–1833*, p.7.
11. Paul C. Light, *The True Size of Government* (Brookings Institution Press, 1999).
12. Thomas Jefferson, note in Destutt de Tracy's "Political Economy," 1816; Source: *The Jeffersonian Cyclopedia*.
13. Thomas Jefferson, note in Destutt de Tracy's "Political Economy," 1816; Source: *The Jeffersonian Cyclopedia*.
14. Dean Stansel, "Sales vs. Income Taxes: The Verdict of Economists," Mackinac Center for Public Policy, 1994.
15. Source: MSMoney.com.
16. Thomas Jefferson's letter to William Short, November 1814; Source: *The Jeffersonian Cyclopedia*.

Chapter 3— Storm the Bastille

1. Richard Goode, *The Individual Income Tax*, rev. ed. (Washington D.C.: The Brookings Institution, 1976), p. 3.
2. Tom Humphrey, "Legislator Wants To Use Current Budget Next Year," *Knoxville News-Sentinel*, February 13, 2000.
3. Emily Phillips and Knight Stivender, "Protesters Fear Income Tax Will Target Them Next," *Tennessean*, June 11, 2000, p. 1A.
4. Richard Locker and Paula Wade, "Income Tax Stalls in Chaotic Session," *Commercial Appeal*, June 11, 2000, p. A1.

5. Source: Interview on WTVF-TV NewsChannel5 in Nashville.
6. Source: Interview on WTVF-TV NewsChannel5 in Nashville.
7. Locker and Wade, "Income Tax Stalls in Chaotic Session."
8. Bonna de la Cruz and Jay Hamburg, "Governor Spent Saturday Doing Some Horse Trading to Line Up Votes for Tax Plan," *Tennessean*, June 12, 2000, p. 1A.
9. Locker and Wade, "Income Tax Stalls in Chaotic Session."
10. Duren Cheek and Bonna de la Cruz, "Income Tax on the Ropes; Pivotal Session Tomorrow," *Tennessean*, June 11, 2000, p. 1A.
11. Phillips and Stivender, "Protesters Fear Income Tax Will Target Them Next."
12. Jim East and Drew Sullivan, "Middle-class Retirees Gain Most under the Proposed Income Tax," *Tennessean*, June 12, 2000, p. 1A.
13. Duren Cheek, "Tax Plan Draws Constituents' Fire," *Tennessean*, February 21, 1999, p. 1A.
14. Richard Locker and Paula Wade, "State Tax-the-Rich Plan Advances/Stress Sends Three Lawmakers to Hospital," *Commercial Appeal*, June 13, 2000, p. A1.
15. Interview with Diane Black, June 14, 2004.
16. Tom Humphrey, "State Shutdown Not Ruled Out as Lawmakers Seek Budget Fix," *Knoxville News-Sentinel*, June 18, 2000.
17. Kate Miller, "Protesters Send Message in Many Ways," *Tennessean*, June 13, 2000.
18. Interview with Steve Gill, June 15, 2004.
19. Patrick Poole, "Tennessee v. Talk Radio," WorldNetDaily.com, June 16, 2000.
20. Duren Cheek and Anne Paine, "Budget Impasse Could Shut Down Services," *Tennessean*, June 15, 2000, p. 1A.
21. Duren Cheek and Bonna de la Cruz, "Budget Veto, Tobacco Lawsuit Settlement," *Tennessean*, June 28, 2000, p. 1A.
22. Phil Valentine's journal, January 22, 2002.
23. FollowTheMoney.org, Tennessee Governor's Race, 1998.
24. Interview with Marsha Blackburn, June 17, 2004.

Chapter 4— Historic Tax Fights

1. Source: Founding.com, Parliament passes the Sugar and Currency Acts, respectively.
2. "Prelude to Revolution, 1763–1775," HistoryPlace.com.
3. "The Sons of Liberty," USHistory.org.
4. Charles Adams, *Those Dirty Rotten Taxes* (Free Press, 1998), p. 37.
5. Source: U-S-History.com.
6. Source: U-S-History.com.

7. Source: TheHistoryPlace.com.
8. Boston Massacre Historical Society, BostonMassacre.net.
9. Adams, *Those Dirty Rotten Taxes*, pp. 44–45.
10. Source: InfoPlease.com.
11. The Boston Tea Party, North Park University.
12. George Hewes, "Boston Tea Party: Eyewitness Account by a Participant," HistoryPlace.com.
13. Source: InfoPlease.com.
14. Source: HistoryWiz.com.
15. Leonard L. Richards, *Shays's Rebellion: The American Revolution's Final Battle* (Philadelphia: University of Pennsylvania Press, 2002).
16. George R. Minot, *The History of the Insurrections in Massachusetts* (Da Capo Press, 1971).
17. Michael A. Hoffman II, Loompanics.com, 1996.
18. Source: Fact-Index.com.
19. "Whiskey Rebellion-Whiskey Insurrection," WhiskeyRebellion.org.
20. Dall W. Forsythe, *Taxation and Political Change in the Young Nation 1781–1833* (New York: Columbia University Press, 1977), p. 40.
21. Forsythe, *Taxation and Political Change in the Young Nation 1781–1833*, p. 41.
22. C. M. Ewing, "The Causes of that So-Called Whiskey Insurrection of 1794," paper written by head librarian of Washington and Jefferson College, 1930.
23. Joe Smydo, "Rebellious Notions," *Pittsburgh Post-Gazette*, July 15, 2001.
24. Ewing, "The Causes of that So-Called Whiskey Insurrection of 1794."
25. Smydo, "Rebellious Notions."
26. Murray N. Rothbard, "The Whiskey Rebellion: A Model for Our Time," *The Free Market*, September 1994.
27. Source: MarketplaceSolutions.net.
28. Source: JamesMannArtFarm.com.
29. Adams, *Those Dirty Rotten Taxes*, p. 88.
30. Letter from Abraham Lincoln to Joshua Speed, August 24, 1855.
31. Source: Scott Moody, senior economist, the Tax Foundation, InfoPlease.com.
32. Source: The Tax Museum, tax.org.
33. Adams, *Those Dirty Rotten Taxes*.

Chapter 5— Threats, Bribes, and Intimidation

1. Duren Cheek and Bonna de la Cruz, "Your Tax Bill Is in Their Hands," *Tennessean*, March 21, 1999, p. 1A.
2. Interview with Diane Black, June 14, 2004.
3. Tom Humphrey, "Allegations against Gov. Lead FBI To Investigate," *Knoxville News-Sentinel*, November 13, 1999.
4. Interview with Diane Black, June 14, 2004.
5. Interview with Beth Fortune, November 8, 2004.

6. Interview with Marsha Blackburn, June 17, 2004.
7. Humphrey, "Allegations against Gov. Lead FBI To Investigate."
8. Larry Bivins, "State Near Bottom on Lobby Rules," *Tennessean*, May 15, 2003, p. 9A.
9. John Gerome, "Income Tax Backers Pack Up, Sadly Leave 'Camp Reform,'" Associated Press, July 4, 2002.
10. Warren Duzak, "Tax Foe Tells Police His Life Was Threatened," *Tennessean*, August 7, 2001, p. 1A.

Chapter 6— Modern-Day Tax Revolts

1. Source: Tax Foundation.
2. Howard Jarvis, *I'm Mad As Hell* (Times Books, 1979).
3. Jarvis, *I'm Mad As Hell*.
4. Jarvis, *I'm Mad As Hell*, p. 57.
5. Jarvis, *I'm Mad As Hell*, p. 59.
6. Jarvis, *I'm Mad As Hell*, p. 87.
7. "Proposition 13: A Look Back by Joel Fox," Howard Jarvis Taxpayers Association.
8. Michael J. New, "Proposition 13 and State Budget Limitations: Past Successes and Future Options," Cato Institute, No. 83, June 19, 2003.
9. New, "Proposition 13 and State Budget Limitations."
10. New, "Proposition 13 and State Budget Limitations."
11. Source: Tax Foundation.
12. Michael J. New, "Fiscal Trail Blazer," National Review Online, November 4, 2002.
13. New, "Fiscal Trail Blazer."
14. Chris Frates and Julia C. Martinez, "Put 2 Laws on Hold, Owens Says," *Denver Post*, March 13, 2004.
15. Interview with Douglas Bruce, June 8, 2004.
16. Peter Blake, "Bruce Playing the Game," *Rocky Mountain News*, May 19, 2004.
17. Source: Tax-Cut.org.
18. Rich Yukubousky, MRSC Executive Director, "Initiative 695—Local Government Impacts," MRSC News, September 1999.
19. Source: Tax Foundation.
20. David Postman, "Eyman Investigation: 2 Years of Deception," *Seattle Times*, April 6, 2002.
21. David Postman, "Eyman's Words Haunt Him," *Seattle Times*, February 10, 2002.
22. David Ammons, "Eyman Creates Salary Fund: 'Help Us Help,'" *Seattle Times*, July 7, 2003.
23. Richard Vedder, "Taxation and Migration," The Taxpayers Network.

Chapter 7—"We Need Troops"

1. Duren Cheek and Bonna de la Cruz, "Income Tax Bills To Appear Again in Legislature," *Tennessean*, February 16, 2001, p. 1B.
2. Kirk Loggins and Noble Sprayberry, "Lawmakers Confident Closed Meeting Privilege Will Not Be Abused," *Tennessean*, January 13, 2001, p. 1A.
3. Richard Locker, "'WE NEED TROOPS,'" *Commercial Appeal*, July 20, 2001.
4. Interview with Bob Stratton, June 26, 2004.
5. Richard Locker, "Talk Stays Hot in Wake of Tax Protest at Capitol," *Commercial Appeal*, July 14, 2001, p. B1.
6. Richard Locker, "Riot Police Block Tax Protesters Threatening Lawmakers at Capitol," *Commercial Appeal*, July 13, 2001, p. A1.
7. Carl Limbacher, "Tennessee Radio Talker Sets Record Straight on Tax Protest," NewsMax.com, July 17, 2001.
8. Nancy Hauskins, "Witness of Protest Abuse Speaks Out," WKRN-TV, July 14, 2001.
9. Dwight Lewis, "A Fair Deal for Officer in Tax Protest Row?" *Tennessean*, August 23, 2001, p. 13A.
10. Sheila Burke, "State Trooper Suspended for Actions at Tax Protest," *Tennessean*, August 11, 2001, p. 1B.
11. Locker, "Riot Police Block Tax Protesters Threatening Lawmakers at Capitol."
12. Source: WTVF-TV NewsChannel5 in Nashville.
13. Interview with Ben Cunningham (of Tennessee Tax Revolt), June 9, 2004.
14. Duren Cheek, Bonna de la Cruz, and Rob Johnson, "No-Tax Budget Passes as Protesters Swarm Capitol," *Tennessean*, July 13, 2001, p. 1A.
15. Source: Governor's Budget 2002-03, actual total state budget figures from 2001–02 and 2002–03, p. A-4.
16. Source: WTVF-TV NewsChannel5 in Nashville.
17. Cheek, et al, "No-Tax Budget Passes as Protesters Swarm Capitol."
18. Jason Zengerle, "Nashville Dispatch. Radio City," *The New Republic*, August 9, 2001.

Chapter 8— How To Stage a Revolt

1. Ted Guillaum, essay: "A Mortal Shooting in the Tennessee State Capitol."
2. Duren Cheek, "Tennessee Tea Party Small but Steamed over Budget," *Tennessean*, May 26, 1999, 1A.
3. Interview with Cheryl Whitsell, June 10, 2004.
4. Source: *Knoxville News-Sentinel*, campaign finance data.
5. John Shiffman, "Poll: Income Tax Supporters Not Destined To Lose Favor," *Tennessean*, April 26, 1999, p. 1A.
6. Source: *Knoxville News-Sentinel*, campaign finance data.
7. Duren Cheek, "Tennessee Democrats Hold Senate," November 8, 2000, p. 19A.

8. Interview with Ben Cunningham, June 9, 2004.

Chapter 9— Smearing the Opposition

1. Duren Cheek and Edith Wright, "Special House Service Honors Westmoreland," *Tennessean*, June 21, 2002, p. 1A.
2. Cheek and Wright, "Special House Service Honors Westmoreland."
3. Pete Barnham, "Time for Talk Radio To Be Held Accountable," letter to the editor, *Tennessean*, June 22, 2002.
4. Harold Lowe Jr., "Radio Hosts Need Escort out of Town," letter to the editor, *Tennessean*, June 23, 2002.
5. City editorial, "Radio Hosts Dance on Westmoreland's Grave," *Nashville City Paper*, June 24, 2002.
6. Source: Tennesseans for Fair Taxation Web site at YourTax.org.
7. "The Income Tax IS Constitutional," Tennesseans for Fair Taxation Web site, YourTax.org.
8. Tim Chavez, "So You Thought Bredesen and the Bunch on the Hill Were Keeping Spending Down," *Tennessean*, June 2, 2004.
9. Bonna de la Cruz, "Anti-Income Tax Pledges Challenged," *Tennessean*, August 14, 2001, p. 1A.

Chapter 10— The Final Showdown

1. Phil Williams, "Friends in High Places: Part 9—Memo: 'Relationships' Key to Business," WTVF-TV, October 10, 2002.
2. Duren Cheek and Bonna de la Cruz, "Opponents Wary of New Flat Rate Proposal," *Tennessean*, October 18, 2001, p. 1A.
3. Phil Williams, "Friends In High Places: Part 1—Governor Accepts Undisclosed Gifts," WTVF-TV, July 22, 2002.
4. Phil Williams, "Friends in High Places: Part 3—Was Parking Lot for Governor's Friend?" WTVF-TV, July 24, 2002.
5. Bonna de la Cruz, "Lawmakers Propose Charity, Not Taxes," *Tennessean*, December 19, 2001, p. 6B.
6. Martha Raffaele, "States Ask for 'Volunteer' Taxes," Associated Press, April 8, 2003.
7. Lois McComb, "Phil, Forgive Me," Equal Time, *Tennessean*, March 10, 2002, p. 18A.
8. Interview with Grover Norquist, president of ATR, June 1, 2004.
9. Duren Cheek, "Sales Tax Hike Lacks Votes in House," *Tennessean*, March 15, 2002, p. 1A.
10. Bonna de la Cruz, "Beavers To Fight Rochelle, Income Tax in Senate Run," *Tennessean*, March 23, 2002, p. 1B.
11. Interview with Mae Beavers, July 12, 2004.

12. Bonna de la Cruz, "Senate To Wait for House Income Tax Plan," *Tennessean*, April 10, 2002, p. 1B.

13. Duren Cheek, "House Leaders Offer Drastic Budget," *Tennessean*, February 22, 2002, p. 1A.

14. Duren Cheek, "Sundquist Praises Student, Derides Lawmakers," *Tennessean*, April 18, 2002, p. 4B.

15. Duren Cheek and Bonna de la Cruz, "Naifeh Seeks Votes in House for 4.5% Flat-Rate Income Tax," *Tennessean*, April 19, 2002, p. 1A.

16. Duren Cheek, "Naifeh Pitches Tax Plan to GOP Caucus," *Tennessean*, April 24, 2002, p. 1B.

17. Christian Bottorff and Bonna de la Cruz, "Protesters Return to Hill as Lawmakers Consider Tax," *Tennessean*, March 16, 2002, p. 2A.

18. Bonna de la Cruz, "Suspect Identified in Death Threat Directed at Naifeh," *Tennessean*, May 10, 2002, p. 2A.

19. Duren Cheek and Bonna de la Cruz, "Income Tax Proposal Is Down but Not Out," *Tennessean*, May 23, 2002, p. 1A.

20. Source: Tennessee Department of Revenue, fiscal year 1998-99 sales and use tax receipts: $4,317,430,739; fiscal year 2001-02 sales and use tax receipts: $4,646,336,755; increase: $328,906,016.

21. Taken from raw footage shot by WTVF-TV on May 22, 2002.

22. Taken from raw footage shot by WTVF-TV on May 22, 2002.

23. As reported by Phil Williams, WTVF-TV, May 22, 2002.

24. Tim Chavez, "Protesters at the Ready To Stand Up against Tax," *Tennessean*, May 23, 2002, p. 1B.

Chapter 11— Post Script

1. Emily Heffter, "Rochelle Says He's Suspending Reelection Bid," *Tennessean*, July 6, 2002, p. 1A.

2. Interview with Grover Norquist (president of ATR), June 1, 2004.

3. Phil Williams, "Friends In High Places: FBI/TBI Open Criminal Investigation," WTVF-TV, September 13, 2002.

4. "Grand Jury Issues First Indictment in 'Friends in High Places' Probe," WTVF-TV, March 11, 2004.

5. "Sundquist Official Ediger Found Guilty of Corruption Charges," WTVF-TV, May 26, 2004.

6. "Sundquist Friend Indicted by Federal Grand Jury," WSMV-TV, November 4, 2004.

7. Interview with Beth Fortune, November 8, 2004.

8. Bonna de la Cruz, "Tennesseans Paid Least Taxes in '02, Study Says," *Tennessean*, September 10, 2004, p. 1A.

INDEX

—A—

Adams, John, 36, 40-42, 94, 106, 108
Adams, Samuel, 96
Alexander, Rodney, 159
Alien and Sedition Acts, 41, 106-7
Amendment 23, 139
American Conservative Union, 6
Americans for Tax Reform, 31, 78, 186, 204, 229
Anderson, Betty, 122
Ankarlo, Darrell, 18, 69-70, 73, 78, 149, 174-75, 182
Anti-Federalists, 41-42, 106, 108
Arriola, John, 221
"Axis of Upheaval", 5, 13, 166, 234

—B—

"bake sale for higher education", 207-8
Baker, Raymond, 59
Bart, Teddy, 190, 192
Battle of Golden Hill, 92-93
Beaman, Lee, 66, 80
Beavers, Mae, 14, 22-24, 58, 74
    and 2002 tax protest, 202, 205-6, 212, 223, 227-28, 234

Beckel, Bob, 38
Bennefield, Jeremy, 56
Birtles, Beeb, 84
Black, Diane, 30, 74, 115-18
Blackburn, Marsha, 12-13, 22, 26, 119, 179, 202, 228-29
    and 2000 tax protest, 2, 51, 53, 57-58, 60, 65, 81
    and 2001 tax protest, 152-55, 164, 167
    and 2002 tax protest, 210
Bonnyman, Gordon, 103, 233
Boston Massacre, 93-94, 97
Boston Tea Party, xiv, 94-97
Bowdoin, James, 98-100
Bowers, Kathryn, 74
Bradford, David, 103-4
Bredesen, Phil, 7, 233
Briley, Rob, 221-22
Brown, Pat, 135
Browlow, William, 169-70
Bruce, Douglas, 138, 140
Bryson, Jim, 179, 229
Buchanan, Pat, 79
Buck, Frank, 24, 122, 206, 222, 224
Burchett, Tim, 20, 32, 162
Bush, George W., 38, 40, 81, 229
Butler, Judi, 154-55

—C—

California property tax revolt, 129-138
Chavez, Tim, 195, 226
Chumney, Carol, 159
Circo, Remo, 214-15
Civil War, 98, 108-13, 127, 169
Clark, J.R., 22
class warfare, xi, 19, 38, 63
Clement, Bob, 6
Clinton, Bill, xii, 15, 45, 203
Cole, Dave, 218
Conference Committee, 60, 65, 76, 78
Continuing Adequate Taxes and Services (CATS), 206-7
Cotton, Gene, 171, 173
Couch, Scott, 218
Cunningham, Ben, 155, 161, 163, 177, 185-86

Cuomo, Bill, 84

—D—

Davidson, Gene, 200
Davis, David, 58
Davis, Gray, 137, 230
DeBerry, Lois, 17, 219-20, 224
de Talleyrand, Charles Maurice, 41, 106
de Tocqueville, Alexis, 37
Dixon, Roscoe, 150
Downsizing Ongoing Government Services (DOGS), 206
Dunn, Bill, 22, 51-52, 57-58, 216-17, 220

—E—

Eckles, Mary Ann, 178-79
Ediger, Joanna, 231-32
Education Networks of America (ENA), 200
Elsea, Gene, 197
excise tax, 10, 102, 105, 141-42
external taxes, 36, 91, 98
Eyman, Tim, 142-44

—F—

Fardon, Zach, 232
FBI, 118, 231
Federalists, 40, 44, 108, 112
Ferguson, John, 10
Ferrell, Brian, 115-16, 118
Fisher, Sherry, 228
Ford, John, 29-30
Fortune, Beth, 10, 16, 26, 118, 232
Fowler, David, 17-18, 22, 28, 153, 166-67, 208, 210-12
Franklin, Ben, 91, 97
Fries, John (Fries Rebellion), 41-42, 106-8
Furr, Pamela, 155

—G—

Gage, Thomas, 90
Ganier, Al, 200, 232
Gann, Paul, 133, 137-39
Garr, Tony, 193
gas tax, 48

Gaspee Affair, 94-95
General Assembly, xii, 8, 227, 230-32
    and 1999, 14, 22-24, 27, 29, 33, 172, 180
    and 2000, 4, 53, 62, 65, 69, 75, 78-79, 81
    and 2001, 151, 158, 162, 165-68, 197, 201-2, 206, 209, 213
    and corruption, 122-23, 193
    and Tennessee State Constitution, 216
George III, King, 91-92
Gibbons, Sam, 19-20
Gill, Steve, 7, 18, 24-25, 31, 195, 203
    and 2000 tax protest, 54-56, 58-60, 62-63, 66-69, 72, 76, 78
    and 2001 tax protest, 155, 173
    and 2002 tax protest, 209, 211-13, 216, 222
    and encounter with "Homeless Jim", 125
    and horn honking, 173-76, 178
    and Keith Westmoreland, 190-92
    and move to WTN, 149-151
Gore, Al, xii-xii, 15, 81, 83, 228
Greene, Mike, 156
Grover, Thomas, 99

—H—

Hall, Ben, 221-22, 225
Hamilton, Alexander, 36, 40-44, 101-6, 108, 122)
Hancock, John, 92, 100
Harwell, Beth, 17, 28
"Hawkeye", 4, 51-52, 71
Head, Tommy, 16, 18, 150, 221, 231
Hedgecock, Roger, 230
Hennessy, Patrick, 55-56
Henry, Douglas, 28, 65
Henry, Patrick, 89
"Hillbilly Mafia, The", 82
Hobbs, Bill, 21, 23, 195
"Homeless Jim" ("Homey"), 124-25
Hooker, John J., 9, 26
Hopkins, Terry, 68, 171
Hopper, Tommy, 119
horn honking
    and 1999 tax protest, 32-33, 173-79
    and 2000 tax protest, 54-55, 58-59, 61-62, 64-69, 71, 73-74, 76, 79
    and 2001 tax protest, 151, 154-56, 164-65

    and 2002 tax protest, 204, 209, 214-15, 218-29, 222, 225-26
    and intimidation, 119
    and Lebanon, Tennessee, 125
"Hot Lips", 68
Huckabee, Mike, 202
Hutchinson, Tom, 96

—I—

income tax
    and first, 110-11
    and progressive income tax, 45-46, 48
    and Tennessee in 1999, 16-33
    and Tennessee in 2000, 1-5, 51-85
    and Tennessee in 2001, 149-168
    and Tennessee in 2002, 199-230
Initiative 695, 141-43
internal taxes, 36, 40, 42, 91, 98
Intolerable Acts, 97

—J—

Jackson, Andrew, 110
Jackson, Doug, 206
Jackson, Tom, 157
Jarvis, Howard, 129-33, 135-38, 143, 185
Jeffers, Kathy, 218-19
Jefferson, Thomas, 35, 42, 45-46, 49, 105-8, 112
Jeffersonian Republicans, 41, 105, 107
Johnny B, 4, 51, 71, 124, 151-52, 154, 231, 234
Johnson, Phillip, 179
Jones, Ulysses, 65

—K—

Kaufman, Keith, 56
Kennedy, John F., x, 40
Kerry, John, 38, 232
Kisber, Matt, 21, 205-6, 216-17, 224
Krasinski, Ron, 84
Kyle, Jim, 13, 208

—L—

L.A. Times, 203
Lenker, Lydia, 60-61, 64, 66, 71, 76, 194

Lennox, David, 103-4

"Lexus Brigade", 61, 64, 66-67, 71, 76, 194

Light, Paul C., 45

Limited Liability Corporations (LLCs), 11, 180

Lincoln, Abraham, 109-10

Lincoln, Benjamin, 100

lobbyists, 3, 11, 18, 115, 119-22, 156, 161, 179, 201

Londo, "Big Wally", 174

Lopez, Tony, 231

Lynn, Susan, 179

—M—

Madison, James, 42

Marshall, John, 35

McDaniel, Steve, 206, 220, 223

McFarlane, James, 104

McGovern, George, 83

McKinney, Richard, 22

Meyers, Rick, 219

Miller, Jeff, 16, 22, 27-28, 202, 206

Miller, Kate, 70, 76

Miller, Larry, 154

Miller, Oliver, 104

Miller, William, 103-4

Molasses Act of 1733, 88

Moore, Dan, ix

Motor Vehicle Excise Tax (MVET), 141-42

—N—

Naifeh, Jimmy, 17, 24, 72, 82, 121-22, 124, 151, 231, 234
    and 2000 tax protest, 5, 63, 73-74, 78
    and 2002 tax protest, 206, 208-13, 216-17, 219-26

Nashville City Paper, 192, 196

"Neanderthal Caucus", 25-26

Neville, John, 101, 103-4

New, Michael J., 136

Newton, Chris, 190

Niswonger, Scott, 201

Nixon, Richard, 31, 131, 192-93

Norquist, Grover, 31, 78, 204, 229-30

—O/P/Q—

Odom, Gary, 221
O'Donnell, Lawrence, 38
Open Meetings Law, 72
Person, Curtis, 74
Pinion, Phillip, 64
police and protests, 60, 156-58, 160-65, 167, 215, 218-19, 221-23, 225
property tax, 43, 131-34, 136-39, 185, 230, 233
Proposition 4, 137-38
Proposition 11, 137
Proposition 13, 129-39, 230
Quartering Act, 89-91, 97

—R—

Ramsey, Dave, 18, 70, 78, 174, 216
Reagan, Ronald, x, xi, 6, 40, 135
Reiner, Rob, 39
Revere, Paul, xiv, 96
Rhinehart, Shelby, 220-21, 229
Richardson, Randall, xii
Rinks, Randy, 71
Rochelle, Bob, 17-18, 21, 28-33, 82, 124-25, 227-28, 233-34
    and 2000 tax protest, 2-5, 51-54, 57, 60, 63, 65, 68, 70, 73
    and 2001 tax protest, 150-54, 164, 167
    and 2002 tax protest, 206-8, 212-13
rock throwing incident, 160-62, 194-95
Rogers, Steve, 158-59
Romer, Roy, 138-39
Rowland, Donna, 152, 178-79, 205, 212

—S—

sales tax, 10-11, 22-23, 28, 46-48, 137, 203-5, 208, 217-19, 228, 230, 233-34
Saltzman, Bruce, 201
Seibert, Rusty, 66
Senate Finance Committee, 17, 28-29, 31-32, 55, 175
Shanklin, Paul, 61
Sharp, Jack, 217
Shays, Daniel, 99-100
Shays Rebellion, 97-110, 113
Shears, Billy, 54-55
Sons of Liberty, 89-90, 92-94, 96-97
Stamp Act, 88–91

Stamps, John, 200
states' rights, 112-13
Stratton, Bob, 156
Strickland, William, 169
Sugar Act, 88-9
"sum sufficient", 23
Sundquist, Don
    and 1999 tax proposal, 16-29, 196
    and 2000 tax proposal, 5, 52-53, 60, 65, 72-73, 78-79, 145
    and 2001 tax protest, 160-62, 166-67
    and 2002 tax proposals, 201-2, 209-10, 218
    and business tax, 10-12, 14, 18, 180
    and Diane Black, 115-18
    and education bake sale, 207
    and Education Networks of America, 200
    and education spending, 199
    and his political change, xii, 5-9, 79-82, 231
    and "Neanderthals", 25, 181
    and Republican party, 6, 229
    and Tax Structure Study Commission, 234
    and TBI investigation, 231-32
    and TDOT, 172
    and TennCare, 15
Sundquist, Martha, 8, 80

—T—

Tax Structure Study Commission, 234
Taxpayers Bill of Rights (TABOR), 138-41
Taxpayers Network, 144-45
Taylor, Pat, ix
TennCare, 15, 66, 193, 233
Tennessean, 67-68, 70, 76, 122, 158-59, 164, 172, 190, 192, 195, 199, 204, 209, 226
Tennesseans for Fair Taxation (TFT), 143, 193-94, 197
Tennessee Bureau of Investigation (TBI), 156, 228, 231
Tennessee Department of Transportation (TDOT), 172
Tennessee State Constitution, 23, 27, 216, 226
Tennessee Tax Revolt, 143, 155, 161, 164, 176-77, 185-86, 193, 202, 233
Thompson, Tommy, 79
Townshend Acts, 91-95, 98
Townshend, Charles, 91-92, 94

—U/V—

U.S. Constitution, 35, 98, 100, 112
Valentine, Phil
 and 1999 budget, 9-32
 and 2000 tax protest, 1-5, 51-83
 and 2001 tax protest, 150-168, 176-78
 and 2002 tax protest, 199-226
 and education, 199-200, 207-8
 and Elvis impersonation, 203
 and e-mail, 182-84
 and first protest, 32-33, 171-76
 and Friends of Phil (FOP), 183, 213
 and his father, ix-x
 and his position on taxes, x-xi, 43-44, 46-48, 144-47
 and Homeless Jim, 124-25
 and landfill protest, 170-71
 and lobbyists, 119-22
 and media bias, 66-67, 76, 167, 194-96
 and the Valentine Doctrine, 43-44
 and "What's That Noise", 83-85
 and WLAC, 8, 18, 149, 174, 191-92, 213
 and WTN, 70, 125, 149
Valentine, Susan, 8, 155-56, 161-62, 167
Volunteer Tax Me More Fund, 202

—W/X/Y/Z—

Wade, Paula, 66, 195
Walker, Raymond, 74
Wallace, Larry, 156
War of 1812, 42, 49, 108
Warren, Earl, 130
Washington, George, 100, 104, 106
Weicker, Lowell, 21
Werbin, Ted, 59
Westmoreland, Keith ,187-93, 229
"What's That Noise", 83-85
Whiskey Rebellion, 100-8, 113
whiskey tax, 102-5
White, Joe, 196
Whitsell, Cheryl, 176
Whitson, Zane, 217

Wilder, John, 3, 31-33, 153-54, 231, 234
Willhite, Rachell, 215
Williams, Mike, 25, 75, 201
Williams, Phil, 200
Windle, John Mark, 160
WLAC, 7, 8, 18, 32, 69, 149, 174, 191-92, 213
Wright, Edith, 190-191
WSMV-TV, 187-88
WTN, 18, 69-70, 73, 125, 149-50, 155, 173-75, 213
WTVF, 61, 66, 218, 221
WVLT-TV (Knoxville), 158
XYZ Affair, 41, 106